Island Sojourn

Graywolf Memoir Series

1 9 9 1

Other books by Elizabeth Arthur

Bad Guys

Beyond the Mountain

Binding Spell

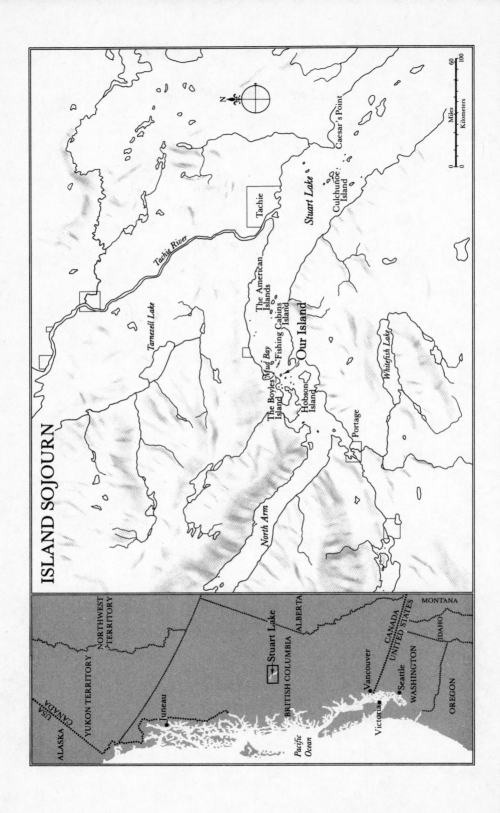

ISLAND SOJOURN

Tachie

Tachie River

Stuart Lake

Caesar's Point

Culchunoc Island

The American Islands

Fishing Cabins Island

Our Island

Mud Bay

The Boyles' Island

Hobson Island

Portage

Whitefish Lake

Tanzezell Lake

North Arm

Miles
Kilometers

ALASKA

CANADA
USA

YUKON TERRITORY

NORTHWEST TERRITORY

Juneau

Stuart Lake

BRITISH COLUMBIA

ALBERTA

MONTANA

CANADA
UNITED STATES

Vancouver

Victoria

Seattle

WASHINGTON

IDAHO

OREGON

Pacific Ocean

Island Sojourn

⋙⋙⋙⋘⋘⋘

ELIZABETH ARTHUR

Graywolf Press / Saint Paul

Portions of this work originally appeared in *Mariah/Outside* and *TWA Ambassador*.

The song quoted on page 126 comes from "The I Don't Know Where I'm Going but I'm Going Nowhere in a Hurry Blues." by Steve Goodman. Copyright © 1971 Kama Rippa Music, Inc. All rights administered by United Artists Music Company.

Publication of this volume is made possible in part by a grant provided by the Minnesota State Arts Board through an appropriation by the Minnesota State Legislature, and by a grant from the National Endowment for the Arts. Additional support has been provided by generous contributions from foundations, corporations, and individuals, and through a major grant from the Northwest Area Foundation. Graywolf Press is a member agency of United Arts, Saint Paul, and is the recipient of a McKnight Foundation award administered by the Minnesota State Arts Board.

Published by GRAYWOLF PRESS
2402 University Avenue, Saint Paul, Minnesota 55114.

9 8 7 6 5 4 3 2
First Printing, 1991

Library of Congress Cataloging-in-Publication Data
Arthur, Elizabeth, 1953-
    Island sojourn : a memoir / Elizabeth Arthur.
        p.   cm. — (Graywolf memoir series)
    Reprint. Originally published: New York : Harper & Row, 1980.
    ISBN 1-55597-149-0 : $9.95
        1. Arthur, Elizabeth, 1953- —Homes and haunts—British
Columbia—Stuart Lake Region. 2. Frontier and pioneer life—British
Columbia—Stuart Lake Region. 3. Stuart Lake Region (B.C.)—Social
life and customs. I. Title II. Series: Graywolf memoir.
F1089.S88A77   1991
971.1'82—dc20   90-28351
[B]

For Bob

Although this is a work of nonfiction, some of the names have been changed.

Contents

Acknowledgments

My thanks to David Godfrey, the noted Canadian writer whom I was lucky enough to have as my teacher at the University of Victoria. He understood what I was trying to do; he encouraged me; he gave me perceptive criticism. More of his energy went into this book than I could have hoped for.

My thanks to Corona Machemer, whom I was privileged to have as my editor.

Preface

The island lies in the western part of Stuart Lake. Although it is near the northern edge of the inhabited area of British Columbia, it is located close to the geographical center, three miles south of the famous longitudinal line 54°40'. North of the island lies a piece of roadless country which stretches to the Alaska Highway. West of it there are lakes and mountains almost to the sea. Forty miles to the east, on the end of the lake, is the small town of Fort St. James. Closer to the island are the Indian communities of Portage and Tachie. Portage is six miles to the west and Tachie ten miles to the east.

It was April 1974 when we first saw it. The lake was frozen, covered with smooth corn-snow, but the sudden movements of the little plane made the earth itself look unstable. As we approached the cluster of islands, the certainty with which the pilot pointed out the one for sale seemed ludicrous. With the islands moving and turning beneath us, I did not see how he could be sure which one it was.

As we descended and I got a clear view of it, I was even more doubtful. That lump of land could not be our island, the one which we had not yet bought but to which we had given our hopes. It was ragged, steep, and dark. A cliff of rock and scree plummeted to the water at the western end. Huge firs blew and twisted off the south side. Angular rocks and enormous misshapen trees had been dumped in a pile in the middle of an open bed of snow.

The pilot made a perfect landing along the northern shore, and we walked through knee-deep snow to what should have been the beach side of the island—the lower, eastern end. The bank there rose abruptly from the frozen lake, climbing toward a summit one hundred and fifty feet above the water. We climbed also, floundering without snowshoes.

The heavy moss which covered some of the visible boulders had a malignant look to it. There seemed no easy way to get onto or off of the island; the trees were dense with dead limbs which had never been touched or storm-felled. The snow was dirt-yellow in patches where moisture had dripped from the trees. After we had plowed from one end of the island to the other, we knew that it had no first-rate building site on it.

Below the top of the hill, though, there was an open field which was, if not level, at least only slightly sloping. The sun shone across it, and the view was open to the southwest. We sat in the snow and listened to the stillness. The absolute silence was comforting; if we were not welcomed, at least we were not rejected. As I looked across the lake to the uneven horizon set with jagged spruce, and to the hills beyond the trees, I realized that one segment of the wilderness is much the same as any other to a stranger's eye. If this was not yet the right island, it might become so in time.

We moved to the island in May, in a secondhand, leaky river boat filled with all our possessions, a good many tools, some lumber, two rifles, a dog, and a cat. The dog was happy, her front paws resting on the side of the boat, her nose wet in the wind. The cat hid in the bows. We perched among the supplies, amazed at their bulk. Before leaving the Fort, we had ordered all the basic materials we would need to build a house, and arranged to have them delivered to the island by barge. We expected them within the week.

It was sunny the day we moved out. The water was rising fast as the mountain snows melted; the beach was almost submerged. Bob cut the engine when we were thirty feet offshore, and we drifted in gradually through the waters likely to contain hidden rocks. A graceful row of poplar trees stood with their roots in the lake. One enormous boulder, dry though surrounded by water, extended the limits of the island beyond the bounds of the shore. There was a smell of wild roses as we pushed the river boat onto the land.

The island, bare of its snow covering, looked even more mountainous than I remembered it. Approached from the water, it rose like a big wart, or a bishop's mitre—higher than the land and islands which surrounded it. Even the eastern shore rose abruptly, at a forty-five-degree angle for the first six feet of the hill. We scrambled up the bank of water-weakened humus; and we were there.

When we moved to the island, we dreamed of making a permanent home in the wilderness, apart from the forces we thought were destroying and polluting the world. In the isolation of an island sanctuary we hoped to find a life of simplicity and peace.

This book is the story of what we found. It is partly the story of learning to cope with the practical requirements of a wilderness life—building, hunting, keeping warm. It is partly the story of learning to understand the origin of our needs and desires, and of coming to see our place in the natural world. It was when I went to live on a wilderness island that I learned what it means to be human: both inextricably linked with and forever isolated from the rhythms of nature and the tremendous energy of change.

1

CONTAINERS

⟫⟫ (1) ⟪⟪

We got to the island two days ago. When we first arrived, we pitched the big green and yellow wall tent on what is left of the beach, in the midst of piles of sticks and logs which have been pushed up by the water in past years. They are perfect for making fires with, since they are now as dry and porous as balsa wood. But the water has been rising at the rate of six inches a day, and this morning I scooped a cup of water out of the lake as I lay in bed.

So today we found a place in the woods on top of the island to set up a permanent camp. I cleared and levelled it with the ax and saw, while Bob built a small table out of logs and plywood, to put the stove on and to store food beneath. We also built a platform for our equipment in the trees, attaching its four corners to four young spruces. Tomorrow we will have to cut a path to the house site. The route is heavily overgrown with trees and bushes. Once we have a path, it will be easier to move.

Even without paths, we have managed to explore most of this tiny world. I am amazed that such a clot of land can contain so many different spaces.

The sloping space where we sat in the snow is a large grassy meadow where wild roses trace delicate patterns through the green. The meadow is a good place to lie in the sun and watch the wind blow. One tall old fir bows overhead with somber grace. The fir is the largest tree on the island; the two of us can just link arms around its base, corrugated with rivulets of heavy bark. It stands alone, swaying over the long-leafed grass, backed by a tangle of young firs and berry bushes. Its elegant domination of the meadow makes the island unique among its neighbors.

3

If you follow the tangle back to the north, the land slants up to a great moss-covered rock. Looking down from the top of the rock, you can see a steep, moss-covered chasm, with a huge tree lying on the bottom, rotting. It is charcoal-burned about the roots. I imagine that great tree when it was young and stood upright, soaking in the green sunlight. When it fell, it shook the rocks. In this crevice of the island, the oldest trees grow, hung with lichens, rusting in their roots; the crevice has steep, damp, and slippery sides. It is not a place to go into, but a place to look into, like the kingdoms inside of sugar eggs, a place that will always be yonder.

Backing down off the moss-covered rock and heading west, you pass into forest, the trees predominantly spruce, with some pines and a few firs. The ground is covered deep with spruce needles, and footsteps make no sound. There are no sticks to crackle underfoot, since the dead lower branches of the trees have never been knocked off by wind or snow. Much of each dead branch is covered with fine green lichen. The land here is flat and dry, but there will never be any buildings on it. The trees are discouragingly dense.

After several hundred yards, the land begins to sink toward the western end of the island. The western promontory, from which a sheer slope of scree falls to the water, looks out to sculptured bays and the higher hills which mark the progress of the mountains. The island feels very much a part of the land at that point, close pressed against it. It's a private spot, a place which is good to visit alone when the sun is setting over the hills, or when the stars are out.

An eagle used to live there. At the very top of the rocky cliff there is an old nest, a circular arrangement of large and small sticks, some as big around as a man's thumb. The sticks taper from a high, thick edge to a low and cozy center, the diameter of the whole more than four feet across. Though the structure is collapsed and grey now, it is not hard to reconstruct the time when the eagle also sat on the western end of the island, watching the sun set, or the stars on a moonless night. At one time, the eagle must have felt that the island itself was eyrie enough for him, the flowing lake an unconquerable moat. Now he and his mate have moved into the tallest spruce, in the middle of the dense woods on top of the island. In the early morning we hear their children shrieking.

To get from the west end to the southwest corner of the island is difficult, since a huge crack lies in the way, filled with moss and jagged rock. But if you retrace your steps through the dense woods and circle back, you come to it, an exposed place, rocky and unfriendly, the wide lake lying dark and bottomless below; a misstep is likely to be fatal.

The meadow is always the place to come back to, though, and I'm glad we'll build the house there. Just below the meadow to the south there is a rocky point, flat for an area of perhaps twenty square feet. The sun shines on it for most of the day, and the ants love the crumbly, pine-littered soil. It is a place to sit and smell the air. It is a place to absorb the substance of the island. It is a place to watch the lake below, rolling and capping in the wind, reflecting the sunlight.

I am sitting there now. The lake is bursting; I can see a storm blowing up from the west and feel the wind quickening with shocking speed. I think of the real-estate agent's last words before we signed the contract to buy the island, words brought on by who knows what promptings of his conscience:

"Stuart Lake isn't a kid's lake, you know. It's a man's lake."

He was looking at our youth, no doubt, and our air of intelligent earnestness, and he warned us as best he could. The lake is a man's lake. He meant simply that it has killed many men. It is not a man's lake or a woman's lake, but its own lake forever, and it is capable of killing those who trust it too much. It is a fierce lake, and the islands which live in it survive only by being equally fierce.

When the glaciers passed through northern British Columbia, shoving the earth carelessly before them, they left behind a few tough survivors, rocks from the core of the earth, which were easier to go around than to bulldoze away. The islands remained unchanged as the water rose and isolated them, and the soil grew deep, and the trees were twisted to the shape of the night wind. The community which the islands now inhabit is one of distances. Since we've come to live on one of these islands, I guess it is both the quality of their survival and the quality of their distances we hope to come to know. If we put enough space between ourselves and the rest of the world, then similar strengths may come to us.

But I do not delude myself into thinking we will ever know this island. It has many parts; morning parts and evening parts and parts that stay always in twilight. We have still not explored it all, nor ever will. It is 3.3 acres large and several millennia wide.

->>><<<-

It is raining. The morning dawns in mist, and the lake creeps up the beach before my eyes. I take the machete and the ax to clear a path up the hill, ripping out thorny bushes, chopping down tiny firs. The humus is wet and smells as rich as gardens newly turned in the spring. Pine needles lie inches deep, and I scrape them to the edge of the path. After clearing a wide swath from beach to hilltop, the slope seems steeper than before. Eventually, I think, we will need a set of steps and landings, like the sea steps which oceanside dwellers climb to view the world beyond the shore. I slip and slide on the humus; already, immovable rocks expose the tips of their noses to the wet air. At the very bottom of the path I can feel a huge boulder just beneath the surface.

We move to our new camp in the rain, hauling supplies—sleeping bags and packs, food and tools—up the hill in a furious struggle with slippery duff. I start to sweat, the moisture prickling on my face, mingling with the mist in the air, everything damp, even the cardboard boxes. We nail a large piece of plastic above the platform in the trees, and shove all the boxes underneath it. Bob stands for a moment in his sou'wester hat, a drop of water on the tip of his nose, looking at the already rusting tools. I wrap my French straw hat in a special piece of plastic and tuck it under the table.

After everything else is up, we go for the tent, pulling out the stakes while standing in an inch or two of lake water. Bob bundles the heavy canvas into his arms and takes it to the new campsite, where we peg it up again. Although we have tried to level the site, the tent stands at a slight and dispirited-looking angle. We toss in the pads and sleeping bags and crawl in after them, sitting and staring out the open door through the dark, streaked trees, at the quiet lake and the rain.

About noon it begins to clear. We lunch on peanut butter and jelly sandwiches while the sun starts to break through the clouds. The smell of the island begins to change. The rainy smell is cool, it does not sneak into your senses without assistance—it has to be inhaled. Humus and rotting wood and the sap running and dead leaves and cloud mist compose it. When it starts to dry, the heat strikes the nostrils with a physical impact. It smells like young leaves and green bark and pine needles steaming; since it requires no effort to absorb, it encourages laziness.

But there isn't time for laziness. Doug Hoy will be here in a few days with a bargeload of house materials, and we want to have the site ready and the pier holes dug by then. So we begin working in the meadow. The location of the back wall of the house is clearly dictated by a rock. A large boulder which could not be removed by anything less than dynamite stands right in the middle of the flattest stretch of meadow. It is just as well; we don't waste more than five minutes deciding on the position of the house. The boulder will cause us more work, though; the house will span such a downward slope that the front foundation piers may have to be almost seven feet tall.

Somehow when we were designing the building, before we ever came north, it didn't occur to us that it would stand on a real site, in a real place, with bumps and dips and peculiarities all its own. We thought only of the shapes and spaces that we wanted to create. By the merest chance, the front door is at the southeastern corner of the house, the only place it could reasonably be. The fireplace, however, is to stand just where the land begins to curve downwards; which means we will have the job of building four or five feet of concrete foundation before the base of the fireplace is level with the floor of the house. Since the house was largely designed around the fireplace, there is no way to change its location and still build the same house.

The northwestern stake is the first to be driven. The foundation at that corner will be at ground level. That pier will determine the level and location of all the rest. We measure forty feet off from the stake, using the new fifty-foot tape measure, an absurdly thin and wiggly piece of metal. We try to make the foundation run directly in line with the island itself, so that the front of the house will get the southern sun and view.

Once the two rear stakes are in place, it is a straightforward matter to draw two lines at ninety-degree angles, measure twenty-eight feet along each line and drive in two front stakes. Although straightforward, it takes forever. We pull the strings tight, and they sag. We pull the tape measure tight, and it sags also. We run back and forth, checking and measuring and making minute adjustments. Bob carefully squares the corners with string and board and measuring tape. At last we measure the distance between the two front stakes, and it seems, as close as we can tell, to be exactly forty feet. Tomorrow we'll check it all again.

The rectangle looks far too small to be the perimeter of what I know will be a fairly large house. Marking off the space reminds me of the children's game called House, in which lines are drawn in the dirt of an empty lot, and all the players move carefully within the lines, never exiting anywhere except through the imaginary doors.

One difference is that we have a tree growing in the middle of our rectangle. Before we can do any further work, the fir has to come down. Knocking it over will prove that we are ready to work changes on the island.

The chain saw is tucked beneath the plastic sheet. A logger's saw, it's a pretty orange machine with an enormous blade. Bob fills it with gas and oil. I think of the movies I have seen of great trees lurching over with elephantine grace, the sound of their branches like electric wires in the air. The chain saw starts with a burst of angry energy, and while I move back well out of the way, adrenaline pumping, Bob pushes the blade slowly into the tree, and slowly draws it out, until there is a wedge in the front of the tree the size of a piece of firewood. The saw goes into the back, and with sudden protest the tree starts to fall. For a moment it stays upright, then it tips over, the top branches whipping backwards as if in a great stormwind, while the whole trunk below them pulls them down. The cracking sounds like rifle shots. The bottom rips off the stump and into the air, shooting up toward the sky while the top comes down to meet it. Like a huge spear, the tree shoots forward through the wind that it creates, and falls so that it shakes the rocks.

The smell of the tree permeates the air. The moist, orange wood is opened to the sky; it shines like ripened pumpkins. Wood seems to me the friendliest and most agreeable of substances. From tiny twigs, warm and flexible, that droop like cats' paws in the sun, to great round poles of the straightest mien, wood will respond to shaping, by rock and water, beaver and man.

The tree lies straight across the house site, crushing the rose-littered grasses with a heavy mantle, its rivuleted bark a stage for the shadows thrown by other trees. Several of the upper branches have been driven like posts deep into the ground, and hundreds of twigs lie scattered around like confetti. We spend the rest of the afternoon segmenting the trunk. The chain saw is very heavy for me, so Bob does the cutting while I roll the great stumps down the hill and out of the way.

The sawdust will mix with the earth in a day or two. The roses will be trampled, and the fir will never again bend over the grass. We have taken the irrevocable step—we have no choice now but to build the house, here, on this island.

The sun stays in the sky very late now. In the evening we take a ride in the boat, listening to the loons and watching the eagles hunt.

$\rightarrow$$\gg$ (2) $\ll$$\leftarrow$

Bob. He is up early this morning, eager to get started, ready to focus his rather formidable energy on building a house. When I met him two years ago, he was teaching mountaineering, an apt expression of his character—he prefers concrete objectives, though not traditional goals. I am still amazed by his unwavering concentration when there is something specific he wants to accomplish. He works hard and steadily and rests hard and steadily: he finds it hard to compromise. One of his friends adroitly summarizes this aspect of his temperament with the comment that Bob has two speeds—Off and High. He further comments that what Gathercole needs is a little more perspective, a little more ability to draw back and take a wide view.

It is true that when things beyond his control go wrong, he is often devastated. Since worries and doubts are essentially foreign to his nature, they induce despair when he does experience them. But he's one of the most honest people I've known—a man who has never lost touch with his gut. Right now, he is in his element, intensely contented to have a large and clearly defined project before him.

He is whittling pegs with which to mark the locations of the pier holes. He sits on a large rock in the sunlight, carefully slicing wood off the end of the pegs with a hand ax, placing each peg to one side as he completes it, picking another one up from the pile until there are nine bright points to sink into the earth. Although he's just under six feet tall, the impression one gets is not of a tall man but of density, solidity. Muscular in a classically male though presently unfashionable way, he seems designed for trousers with tucks in them, thirties style, and loose V-necked sweaters.

Now, he is wearing a blue and white striped rugby shirt and a pair of denim shorts trailing strings of thread. In the pure sunlight the lines of his face are clear, the colors slightly dimmed by light. The green-brown of his eyes is not visible at this distance, but the curly jumble of his brown hair seems lighter in tint than his eyebrows. His large nose stops short of being too large, and is one of the strongest lines on his face.

I have my favorite parts of him. I like the indentation between the two halves of his chest. I like his hair and his eyes, and I particularly like his hands. The fingers are short and square, the palms wide and thick. Unusual hands, which I could pick with little uncertainty from a bunch of hands, so often have I watched them set to work: fastening a sleeping bag onto a pack, finding a good set for a piton in a rock crevice, rubbing my skin or his own, measuring a length of board. Driving the sharpened pegs into the soil now, they are powerful and he unconscious of my gaze. I feel a little lost, desiring some direction. I cannot believe that we have entirely arrived. An impulse to rush over and hug Bob, so intent on his measurement, propels me to my feet. But I only go in search of a shovel.

Soon we will begin to dig.

→≫ (3) ≪←

Digging these small holes is rather like digging to China. The chances of ever reaching a conclusion seem nonexistent. The earth smells cool and acrid, the soil is as rocky as it can be, and I completely abandon myself to scruffing around in the dirt. The piers should either stand on bedrock, or be sunk below the frost line; four feet in this area. Four feet is remarkably deep.

The problem is in the rocks. The earth is quite movable, though its fluidity is elusive and slightly stupid. But the rocks want to remain rooted where they are. Rocks which seem small at first, chunks the size of my fist, turn out to be only the warts on vast systems of bouldered ledges. They have been cracked by frost, and can be gradually worked apart with a pick and shovel, but there is much more rock than dirt in every cubic foot.

If the soil contained no rocks, it might be possible to send a hole almost straight down, with just a slight widening around the top. But every time I remove a rock, its absence causes the side of the hole to crumble and collapse inward. I feel like Gollum, eyes always downwards, investigating the roots of the mountain.

When I do manage to lift my head, the leaves are glistening in the sunlight, and the water is still. A woodpecker is intent on some bugs in the bark of a nearby tree, and every once in a while the eagle lets out a raucous shriek. The trees impress me with their slow sentience. Their roots have done a lot of my work for me, cracking the slabs of rock as they sought moisture far below. Their small and agile leaves, the color of light jade, give the roots the strength to crack the rock. A filmy web of light and color which blows above my head affects the earth below me in hidden channels.

I crumble the earth in my hands and smear it on my face and arms. I take off my shirt and pour it over my chest. I toss a shovelful above my head so that it showers into my hair. Cool and dry like powder, it is gritty like sand; it smells like dirt. I can't convince myself that this dirt belongs to me. We have only just met.

->>><<<-

Yesterday we finished the pier holes, nine of them, like craters blasted from the sky. There are piles of rock and earth everywhere, and the roses have all been crushed. We built a form to mix the cement in, and then finished straightening the path down to the beach. We took the afternoon off to bathe and lie in the sun. I say bathe, but the lake is so cold that that is all but impossible—I leapt in with a screech and out again with a scraped shin.

The barge came this morning. I could hear it for a long time before it arrived. Its sound is distinctive; once heard and identified, it could never be mistaken for anything else. Like a heartbeat, it is almost imperceptible at first, but you can feel with your body that something is throbbing somewhere. The barge goes about five miles an hour with a load; the time between the first intimation of its approach and its arrival on the beach was almost two hours.

Since we haven't got a dock built yet—probably the first job we should have done—there was no real indication for Doug of what might be the best route in to the beach. But he expertly maneuvered forward and backward until he found the one route which avoids all underwater rocks and ledges.

The deck of the long, wooden barge rides about three feet above the water. At the back is the cabin with the controls, little bunks, kitchen, and a shelf of books for the long trips from the Fort. In the front is a pointed metal scow, flat bottomed, which serves as a permanent gang-plank and space for extra cargo; it also acts as an armored surface for confronting rocks. Doug shoved the metal scow right up onto the beach.

Unloading took a while. We had ordered 90 joists, a lift of one-by-fours, 25 bales of insulation, 80 sheets of plywood, 150 studs, 8 rolls of 90-pound roofing, 11 windows, and 2 doors, already hung. Also 100 pounds of nails, 6 gallons of exterior stain, and 15 bags of cement.

Doug is a great pirate of a man, with a kind, drooping face and a hearing aid. He has a gurgly voice, low and soft but penetrating. He also has incredible strength. His current assistant is a spare, quiet man named Bob. The four of us unloaded the barge in three hours, piling everything onto the beach, as far up as we could go, but still only two feet above the present water line. We're going to have to move fast to get it restacked up the hill before the water hits it.

→»«←

I carried lumber again today. Bob carried plywood. The plywood is too wide for my armspan to handle. Bob can take two sheets at a time, over his head.

Studs are the easiest lumber to carry, since they are only eight feet long. I can slide five or six off the main pile, straighten them up, and slip a sling around them and over my shoulder. That way most of the weight is on my shoulders, and all I have to do with my arms is hold the studs together as a unit and balance them front and back. Even so, the hill is hard to get up. Each time I think, "Well, this trip is making me fitter." But each trip is just as hard as the one before. All morning and all afternoon, I carried lumber. We made a dent in the pile on the beach, but the water is still rising.

I am becoming acquainted with the stubborn indifferences of the inanimate world. It is perfectly content to stay where it is. When we decided to move to the island, and away from the life which is centered on the materialistic world, I never imagined I would gain here such an intimate knowledge of things. Piles of boards, stacks of insulation, boxes of nails, cans of wood stain—they demand attention, not shrilly, but patiently.

Sometimes I feel almost as if I am making an offering, an offering to a nonexistent house. But the object which makes me heave and puff and feel that I really am accomplishing something shrinks in size and importance once it arrives at the house site. The offering is rather pitiful after all.

And the worst of it is, when the whole pile is up there, when nothing is left on the beach, it will still only be the beginning. The material will still be there, still waiting to be used.

I can't imagine ever getting to like this stubborn persistence. But I suspect that if you don't like the material world, you can forget about escaping from it.

→>> (4) <<←

Well, having gotten all the stuff off the beach at last—some of it jammed between the trees right above the bank, some of it halfway up the hill, all of it dribbled all over the island—we are ready to start on the foundation. At last. But it is hard to see how that is going to be much easier; we have to haul up sand and gravel as well as water to mix it with. Water! We flee its encroachments, only to have to drag it up the hill. Even now we need almost five gallons a day, just for cleaning and cooking and drinking. We've been hauling water in two galvanized-steel buckets, but on our first trip to town I want to get some closed containers. We could probably grow rutabagas on the path, watered only by accidents.

Right now we are looking for sand for the concrete. There are graveled beaches all around us, but fine sand is hard to find in adequate amounts. Many bush cabins have wooden foundations because their builders never do find it.

Apparently the millions of tiny glistening pieces of rock are the best agent for maintaining the cohesive form of cement. Once rock, they take naturally to being rock again. Well-made concrete will not fall apart with the passing years. The remnants of fireplaces and foundations persist long after the building which surrounded them has crumbled back to soil. A house built on sand is the best kind of house to build.

Today's foray in the boat did not discover any sand beaches, though we found some lovely logging roads on the shore of the bay behind the island, and several old booming grounds. We also explored some cabins.

When we first flew out to the island, I had the impression that ours was one of many uninhabited rocks. None of the cabins is visible from the air. But there have been plenty of others here before us.

Due east of us there is an island which we have named The Fishing Cabins Island. Three buildings are on it, one large one and two small. The large one is twenty feet by twenty, the two small ones only ten feet by fifteen. All are in the middle stages of disrepair. One night last week when we were out in the boat for an evening of relaxation, we heard a terrible crashing from the island's point. A man was chopping the lock off the door of the big cabin with an ax. A cruiser was pulled up to the dock and three children played at the water's edge. They were pretty clearly not the owners of the island. I was shocked that a father should set such an example, particularly when the family was obviously not in need of shelter. But now I have explored the island thoroughly, and I think a place can help to prompt such action, a place that no longer has anyone who belongs to it. Old shutters hang askew. The boards of the porch floor are warped. The cabin sits in the darkest part of the pine woods and it is dark in color and surrounded by the litter of gasoline cans and washing. It looks like a commodity which has been used and discarded, and now takes its place among found objects. According to sea law, any vessel found deserted on the surface of the sea belongs to the person who salvages it. The same law seems to apply to Fishing Cabins Island. The island and the people who built the cabins have lost touch with one another.

All the cabins were open today. They are bare, save for a few broken utensils and shredding pieces of vinyl furniture. In one cabin there is a huge pile of thin mattresses, unprotected against mice.

We visited "the Boyles island" also. Centered at the entrance to what we call Mud Bay, it is a very flat island, and quite unique in that its trees are almost all aspens. The dock is on the sheltered northern side, and the house is situated just far enough inland so that no high water can touch it. It is a perfectly symmetrical cabin, surrounded on all sides by a porch, which is roofed as an extension of the house's own roof. The front and back doors lie opposite each other, and all the windows are in line. Screwed into the center of the back door is a little brass plaque, with "Mr. and Mrs. Roy Boyles" inscribed in delicate script.

The downstairs of the cabin is one huge room, with a huge table. One end is given over to kitchen cabinets, a sink and pump, and a cookstove; the other end is built around with bookcases and bunks. Up-stairs, there are thirteen bunks in a long attic dormitory. Nothing essential has been left out and nothing extraneous put in. It is clear that when the Boyleses come, there is not need for much furniture, because the cabin is bursting with people. Thirteen bunks.

On a birthday card in the bookshelf, addressed to "Dad," there are seven signatures. That accounts for nine of the bunks. The attention of many different imaginations is evident in the handiwork which decorates the walls. An Indian prayer for the house is inscribed on birch bark. A piece of driftwood has become a stork with the addition of grey twig legs. There are posters of mysterious intent. "The Past is One; the Future has Plurality." Next to one window is a collage of broken pieces of metal and wood, which is dark and densely lovely.

Without the people who should fill it, though, the house does not invite a long stay. A storm blew up in the time we were inside, and we fought our way back to our island through cross-waves and bursting spray.

❦

Since we have not yet checked out the lake to the west of the island, we are heading for the North Arm. The Arm is the deepest part of the lake, a large finger of water which points northward. Doug Hoy told us it's so deep that some winters it does not freeze until long after the rest of the lake. Sometimes one section will remain open almost until spring.

Just before the entrance, a cove opens out to the west. We nose into it, separating the long fronds of water grass with the snout of the boat. At the head of the bay there is an Indian village. The village is called Portage, because it is located at the point in the old trading trail where the water route crossed a five-mile neck of land. The fur trail crossed the Rocky Mountains to McLeod Lake, wound through the hills to Fort St. James, crossed Stuart Lake by water to Portage, and then picked up the water again at Babine Lake.

No traffic goes by Portage now. It has become a backwater, accessible only by water and air to those who want to go there. The old trail is used by the Portage Indians, who travel regularly to Babine Lake for fishing, hunting, and trapping.

We pull up as far as we can into the swampy cove, and then cut the engine and glide in over the grass and lilies, which sweep the sides of the boat with a gentle susurrence. At the head of the bay is a flat sand beach, almost covered at high water. The village starts so near the sand that it seems inevitable it will also be engulfed.

Several Indian men are working at caulking and painting a blue and red boat which is turned over on the beach. I know they must be Josephs; all the eighty Indians who live in Portage bear the same family name. We say hello and introduce ourselves. I admire their boat, and after a while we ask them if they know of any good sand beaches likely to survive high water for at least another week. They don't, and we push off into the grass and turn into the North Arm.

The Arm has been logged in parts, and young aspen and willow trees decorate the western slopes with startling color, so light in comparison with the black green of the predominant spruce that it looks painted on—a spring green from an artist's brush. The booming platform remains, huge logs spiked together with mammoth spikes. Chains and rusted steel cable twist and mesh with muddy earth. The weathered foundations of some huts are visible through the grass and deadfall. The logging here was done at least twenty-five years ago, but we find an almost perfect peavey in the earth.

Twenty-five years seems ruinously long, the booming grounds much older than the bays where there is no evidence of human occupation. But we are drawn to signs of visitation. Across the Arm from the booming grounds, I spot a very bright building on a large island. We gun the engine and move toward it. The building is white, and from a distance that makes it look trim, occupied. We move closer and see several buildings, which take shape as a shed, a log cabin, and a frame house. They are built on a grassy point, not too high above the water but just high enough to give them aristocratic remove from beach life. Since no dock is visible below the houses, we drive around the point to find a place to land.

The bay on the other side of the point is still, and the water is clear enough for us to see the bottom. A large dock, now high and dry on the beach, twists in the middle so abruptly that it has almost split in half. We pull the boat up in the general vicinity, and I jump out and tie the bowline in two half hitches around a rusty spike.

Another building is on this side of the point—a large boathouse, with shed doors standing permanently open and a set of iron locomotive rails leading down either side of a wooden ramp which ends in the shimmery distortions of the underwater world. The rails, once used for pulling a large boat into the boathouse and lowering it into the water again, are split, twisted, buckled, rusted, bent into strange spirals by the careless power of the winter ice. Such rails are often rendered useless within a winter, and these have been worked on by ten or twenty. They are the visible and definitive statement that the island we are about to explore has ceased to serve any will but the fantastic capriciousness of weather.

The boathouse contains an old rowboat and a thirty-foot river boat. One corner holds a pile of chains and a one-hundred-pound box of nails. I open the box and try to pull out a nail. It is impossible. They have been welded together by rust into a one-hundred-pound lump of brown iron.

The rest of the interior is scattered with tools, all made quite useless by cracks and rust. Two fifty-five-gallon drums rest on a set of sawhorses, and I inspect them, hoping they will be usable. Each one has holes in the bottom, openings surrounded by the delicate and paper-thin flowers of metal which has almost returned to dust.

The beach leads to a dirt path, a laughably short trail onto the plateau above, grassy and rose strewn. The first building we examine is the log cabin. It has been hand-notched by an expert. The main section of the cabin is so well fitted that it has not even been chinked. A shed attachment at the back was clearly built at a later date and by a lesser craftsman. The door to this is open and we walk into a kitchen.

The kitchen smells typically musty. But there is an additional smell, a smell of warmth, which should not be there, I think, until I look up and notice that there is a hole in the roof, a hole which lets in the sunshine, to dry and clean. The kitchen is unfurnished but has a kerosene refrigerator in one corner, and a sink which drains to the outside. The cupboards contain china—untouched by dust, not of a set, but great piles of English bone china, decorated with roses and lavender, lilac and thyme, sassafras. Some of it is gilt edged. There is also a china teapot, the spout a classic S-shape.

A tiny room off the kitchen contains a mirror, a window, and a drop-leaf table, finished once with oil, now dry and splitting. The other door leads into the cabin proper, a large room with a cathedral roof, six small windows, and a front door standing open to disclose the porch beyond. A well-constructed fireplace, built of round stone, is centered in one wall. The floor is of three-inch hardwood, filthy and with widening gaps that reveal the earth below. A green wool carpet, ten by fifteen, covers much of the floor. Its edges are darkened with what was once a pattern worked in blue wool. There are five spring-box beds and a pile of mattresses. The sunlight streams through the cracks in the roof.

We walk onto the porch; the slant in the floor which was noticeable in the main room becomes so pronounced that it is difficult to keep our footing on the slippery wood. Chairs which are wooden frames seated and backed with straw stand askew and trail their bottoms on the floor.

Jumping off the porch to look underneath the house, we learn why the floor slants, why the porch droops, why the living-room ceiling of poles has split apart to let in the sunlight. The cabin has been built on log ends set into the ground. With the passing years they have settled, shifted to get more comfortable with the frost-changes in the ground. A few more years, and they will settle once again, and the house will collapse in a graceful faint, burying the wool carpet, the lavender bone china, and the drop-leaf table beneath its heavy bulk.

We walk over to the other house, a frame construction of more recent vintage, the white paint on it peeling but still covering its exterior. This house has a porch all the way around it, a porch enclosed by copper screening. One large room holds beds, chairs, and a large cedar chest, which, when opened, reveals the rags and scraps of quilts and pillows, and a large piece of red satin—a petticoat. Gingham window curtains are still bright in the chest, though the mice have explored the taste of the stylized flowers which decorate them.

On the porch again; a robin has followed us in through the open screen door. Now he beats frantically against the screen, trying to find a way out. His only chance for escape lies through the door by which he entered, but he has gotten so turned around by panic that he is at the opposite end of the porch. He claws the screen, beating his wings, throwing himself at the wire; when we stand behind him, his efforts increase. He is killing himself trying to escape.

A small bird who gets trapped inside a house is as panic-stricken as this robin. But the bulk of the robin, the sheer size of the wings and the heartbeat, pump panic into the air which a small bird can never produce. As I watch, I feel it; my throat too is tight, I too am desperate to escape the confines of this structure. I move to the screen, and grasp the robin in my hands. He is warm and smooth as Indian beadwork. His heart beats, but I hold his wings down to his sides. His eyes close in resignation to captivity just as I open my hands outside the porch. He plummets a foot toward the ground, extends his wings, and flies into the woods.

It is good to shake off the houses and walk in the grass again. We have only been here twenty minutes, but I have crossed back to the years when these houses were new, and though it has been as effortless as falling asleep, I am eager to forget remembering. We walk into the woods, thinking to explore the island further, seeking not relics but simply the roots of trees. Not far from the clearing, however, I glimpse a pile of grey. It is a roofless log cabin, old, far older than any of the other buildings we have seen. The walls are only six feet high, the roof lies on the floor, a floor which was never more than pounded earth. A window one foot square is cut into one wall, and framed, but there is no sign that it ever contained glass. The cabin is no larger than a store-room. Since the island is quite far from any of the old settlements, it is not too far-fetched to surmise that it was a place where a trapper wintered. There is no sign of a stove, but a square cut in some of the roof logs is the right size for a stovepipe.

This cabin pleases me. It is a remnant ancient enough to have lost the pain of disrepair, and retains only the grace of storybook death, like an odor of sanctity.

Circling around the island brings us to dense woods, and we turn aside and walk to the beach again, following its line back to where the boat is tied. Since the beach is small, I slip off my shoes and walk barefoot; only when I feel the piles of rough grit beneath my feet do I notice that the beach is a sand beach, a wide beach of the most perfect fine white sand. I think of the house which sags only twenty feet away, and the china which was fired in the kilns of England and will outlast the house for no reason other than that the makers had the knowledge to build it right.

The island is too far from our island for its sands to be of much use to us. We climb into the boat, Bob starts the engine, and we head for home. We will have to find our sand another day.

⇛ (5) ⇚

The morning light came through the green and yellow tent with a characteristically feverish tint this morning, but it was darker than usual; the rain lightly struck the canvas above our heads. Two puddles were just inside the door, and the air was both hot and damp. My back was stiff from a night on an incline, and Bob had slipped down and was scrunched into one moist corner. He half-emerged from his bag with a sudden thrust and wriggled back up the hill.

"Lucky no one can see this," he said, smiling sleepily, his face sticky and flushed from overnight immersion in his bag. "The mighty woodsmen." He stretched his arms behind his head, poking one finger at the sagging tent wall.

"Woodsman?" I asked, accusing, coming wide awake at the suggestion of male chauvinism.

"Woods*men,*" he said. "*Men.* In other words, people." He cringed in mock fear, inviting a fight, which I was too lazy to give him. I negotiated some rocks and curled myself lethargically around him.

"Why not say woodspersons, then?"

He gagged. "Woodnymphs?" he suggested.

"How about just plain blockheads?"

"A good compromise." He nodded, playing the professor.

"I just hope the house doesn't turn out this way," I said.

"Green and yellow?"

"Very funny. Sagging, slanted. Maybe we should level it or something, for luck. So the house will turn out O.K., you know? Stay upright for a while?"

"My lifetime's long enough for me," said Bob. "Who cares what happens after?"

He does, of course. So do I. So I said:

"No building for eternity?" What a strange idea it sounded.

"Jesus, Arthur, let's take one day at a time, what do you say?"

"Ha."

"What do you mean 'ha'?"

"I mean *you're* the one who's always being gloomy about what it'll be like in twenty years."

"What what'll be like?"

"Everything. You always think either in terms of the job at hand or the deterioration of the world."

"Well," he said. "I just face facts, that's all. Undoubtedly *you* have no trouble ignoring the fact that in twenty years Hobson Island will be subdivided. There'll be thirty little cabins on it and a ferry at this end of the lake. Or maybe a bridge to the mainland, who knows?" Bob enjoys the role of doomsayer.

"God, you're impossible. Solid nothingness for forty miles and you talk about a bridge to the mainland." I rolled my eyes and started to tickle him. He is very ticklish but also, unfortunately, strong. Quickly he had pinned my arms.

"Look at history," he said portentously. "Look at history." He let me go, cupped his hands together, and peered through a small crack in them, gasping in amazement. "You want to see history?" Proffering his hands. "Or you already know all about it?"

I laughed. "I don't want to know all about it. If you want to know what I think, I think the lake is going to stay the way it is now forever. Pooh to history." We wrestled for a little while before getting up to work.

Afterwards I wondered if I really thought that at all. Forever. Even here and now I often find it hard to grasp the fact of our surroundings. I stand and look toward Hobson Island, trying to absorb the scene—either with or without thirty cabins. I breathe deeply, as if that might help. A familiar sensation of disappointment overtakes me; the air reaches the bottom of my lungs and can go no further, stopped by the limits of the wall which contains it. I shake myself and turn away, impelled to seek activity—building, fashioning, searching for sand.

$$\text{->>>}(6)\text{<<<-}$$

We found the sand at last, only a mile away, on the north shore to the east. Now the piers build toward the sky slowly, foot by foot, their growth controlled by the speed of the moisture's evaporation; each layer has to dry before another can be laid on top of it.

We rise early and start the stove and put the coffee on. While it is heating, we walk to the house site to see if the concrete we laid yesterday has hardened. Bob knocks off the square wooden forms with a hammer and feels the concrete. The demountable sides of the forms are still working well, and he is pleased. The concrete is dry enough to work on.

We read at breakfast, lingering over coffee and toast with jam. The toast is fried in a pan bubbling with butter; fried toast is coming to mean the island to me.

After a time, we set up the forms on the piers again, eight or ten inches higher than yesterday. The sides slide together and are tied with a rope twisted like a tourniquet. While Bob checks to make sure the form is level, I start to mix the first slow batch of concrete, pouring one bag of cement into the wooden box and adding four parts of sand and gravel from the large piles on the sheet of plastic on the ground. Already the day is like yesterday, and tomorrow. As the sand and gravel and cement are mixed together, shoved back and forth with a hoe, picked up and dropped with a shovel, and scraped from side to side with the hoe again, Bob goes by with the buckets.

On the trip back up the hill some of the water spills over the sides, particularly when he tries to get too quickly over the rocks, but he is pretty good at carrying water, and most of it makes it to the cement-mixing box. He takes over, and pours one bucket of water into a hollow at the center of the pile of mixed materials. The other bucket is set carefully on level ground. With the hoe, the water is integrated into the mix; with the shovel, the damp masses picked up and dropped. After a few minutes, the other bucket of water is poured onto the drier patches and mixed also. But there is still not enough moisture in the concrete, and I start down the hill with the buckets to get more.

One batch of concrete takes over twenty minutes to mix. The muscles ache from the rhythmic repetitions—but it is satisfying nonetheless to watch all the different materials, with different forms and different flow rates, coming together to create a satiny, grainy, grey solid-liquid, viscous, glistening like mercury.

The concrete is shoveled into buckets and carried to the growing piers. Its weight stretches the arm muscles like a rack, so we find it easiest to carry two buckets at once and set up an equilibrium. Bob pours the liquid rock into the wooden form, adding some solid rocks to take up space, and also some iron cables we picked up at the booming grounds, which give the pier a continuous core.

Several repetitions of the process bring us to the end of the sand. It is afternoon. Bob takes off his leather gloves, which are damp and wearing through in many places from the concrete abrasion. My hands, ungloved, feel as if the skin itself is wearing through. I race down the hill, whooping, and our dog Bundy, who has been lying, bored, under a tree, races down too, her four paws kicking up the dust behind. She reaches the beach, turns around, and races back up the hill again, passing me on the way without a glance. After locating the figure of Bob heading down, she turns once more and plummets to the boat.

The empty garbage can is already in the back of the boat, so we just toss in the buckets and shovels and start the engine. The dock, quickly knocked together, is showing its weaknesses, bloomping down at the end when two people step on it.

The lake is only slightly rough, but it is a pleasure to cut the engine and drift in to the sandy beach. I hop out of the boat while it is still far from the shore, just to feel the water-covered sand rubbing my bare feet.

We each take a shovel and a bucket and start digging. Each day it is a little harder to find good sand. We poke around for good patches, filling the buckets and dumping them into the can. When the can is full, the beach looks empty, but tomorrow the sand will be back.

Bundy loves the trips to shore. She has taken off—her black and white fur vanished immediately into the woods—and it takes some time to call her back. When she appears at last, tongue lolling happily, we load up and shove off, watching the clear white bottom of the lake until it falls steeply away to darkness.

-->>)«<-

The eagle is teaching the eaglets to fly. They crash and waver through the air, bumping into trees, catching their wings on obtrusive branches. The smallest, brownest one is particularly awkward; he punctuates his shaky flights with yelps and screams of frustration. Our days are distinguished by the eaglets' progress and by the slow rising of the piers. At last there are nine. The front one is seven and a half feet high—and we are out of cement.

We don't want to go to town for more cement. But we're also sick of piers and concrete. This afternoon we made one last run for gravel from the mainland behind the island. Each smooth, dark-grey pebble has been rounded by the water's long touch, and the gravel slides into the bucket like a waterfall, glittering with the clear polish of the waves.

Evening brings peace. Rocks and sand and lime fade with the prospect of sleep, a prospect which roundly fills the evening hours, as the light grows more ethereal and the lake blows up.

-->>)«<-

We left for the Fort very early in the morning, and got to town before the stores had even opened. The morning sun threw a golden light down the house fronts, the streets were silent, and the dust not yet stirred up. All was quiet and motionless except the straight columns of smoke rising from many chimneys.

Blocks away from the cafe, I could smell the grease in the morning air. Frozen and stiff as we were, it smelled delicious, and we followed it to its source, where we feasted on greasy pan fries, greasy eggs, greasy toast, and muddy coffee. Being in town made me giddy, and I talked nonstop while shoveling in mouthfuls of food and looking over the pile of mail. While we were mopping the plates with toast, and thinking of ordering another breakfast, trucks started to shoot by on their way to the sawmill, and men began to filter into the cafe to have their thermoses filled and to order huge stacks of pancakes with bacon and eggs. They glanced at us incuriously and looked away.

After breakfast we picked up our truck and drove it to the dock to get the garbage from the boat. The black bags of garbage, packaged on the island, carried to the beach, loaded into the boat, and now transferred once again, entirely filled the back of the truck. It strikes Bob as ridiculous to lug our garbage all the way to the town dump, but I don't want to fill the island or the lake-shore woods with junk. Most people who live in the bush take a certain amount of litter for granted, and even in the Fort, the litter of living is to be found all over. On our way to the dump, we passed a good many front yards which looked like dumps themselves. One contained several rusty propane tanks, some old car batteries, a pile of metal parts, a broken freezer, a mound of grey boards from a shed which had been torn down, a drying rack with a moose hide stretched across it, and a steel washtub with legs. Everything is either presently in use, waiting to be used, or saved on the off chance that it will someday come in handy.

In a way, the Fort itself seems like a miscellaneous collection of found objects. A perfectly preserved log cabin of the most expert craftsmanship is used for a shed by a family who live in a boxlike, purple development house with stylish adornments pasted on like decals. Machines fill their grass lawn: two pickup trucks, three snowmobiles, an outboard engine, and a chain saw.

One section of the Fort has houses so similar they look as if they have been stamped out on a die press. In another section, the uprooted trees and stumps are still burning in a waste of mud, while a cabin lingers in the middle of the clearing, plastic stapled to window holes and smoke rising from a single tin smokestack. A few houses are well designed and set in plots of grass carefully fenced with little white picket fences.

After we dumped the garbage, the stores were still just opening, so we went to the hotel to call the lumber mill and put in an order for some rough-cut two-by-eights with which to fix the dock. The only public phones in town are located in the laundromat and the hotel lobby. It's a toss-up which place is less pleasant, but the hotel is usually quieter. The lobby reeked of stale beer, and I walked across the carpet trying not to imagine what the various dark stains might be. When I approached the phone, an Indian man was leaning against a nearby wall, and just as I stepped in front of him, he slid to the floor with a thump, and stayed there.

The lumber would be ready by early afternoon. In the interval we completed our other chores—among which the purchase of adequate containers had high priority. We bought a green plastic garbage can to use as a barrel for storing water, two closed five-gallon jugs to haul it from the lake in, a five-gallon steel tub to heat it in, a bright-orange two-gallon bucket for convenient handling, and an enameled dipper.

So we'll be able to haul the water up in one container, pour it into another, scoop it out with a third, drink it from a fourth, and heat it in a fifth. Water, following the path of least resistance, accepts such endless transfers without retaining the form of any of its containers, which makes it useful, annoying, and somewhat mysterious. No matter how much I resist, I will always be affected by the form of my surroundings, and I rarely follow the path of least resistance. Instead I make a stand against Fort St. James and try (with Bob) to fashion an island. Jugs and tubs loaded into the back of the truck, we drove to the lumber mill early, eager to get away, eager to get back home.

After transferring the lumber from the truck to the boat, Bob went up the lake by water while I drove out to the village of Tachie, there to meet Bob, in the hope that we could find a place to dock the boat and park the truck in the village. The Fort is too far away to be a useful land base, but Tachie is only ten miles from the island by the most direct route.

The road to Tachie isn't paved. Washboarded and winding, it crosses the railroad tracks about ten times in the first ten miles. The country it passes through is monotonous beyond belief—there is not one field or house for thirty miles. Lodgepole pines are the predominant growth in the forest, and since they have shallow roots and are easily storm-felled, the woods are crisscrossed with long, straight pieces of deadwood. Power poles run alongside the road, looking like lodgepoles which have been strung with wire.

The village is divided into two parts, separated by a neck of land surrounded by lake and swamp. The older section is on the east bank of the Tachie River, although it is believed the original settlement was actually on the west bank. There's no bridge over the river, and no road on the other side, but there are two log buildings built by the Hudson's Bay Company for a trading post and to house the trader, probably in the twenties.

Tachie is dominated by a little white Catholic church with a tall wooden spire. Close up it is shabby, with rotten doorsills, cracked windows, and peeling paint. Next to it is a small cemetery; the graves are marked by white wooden crosses, and the fence surrounding them is in the Russian Orthodox style one sees in other parts of British Columbia. Curvaceous and delicate, it is topped with circles and crescents.

That fence is almost the only fence, either real or imaginary, in the entire village. The houses are scattered about in a random fashion. No lot division or zoning has ever dictated house placement, and the builders have put their houses up wherever they wished. All the land in the village is communally owned. There is no way to judge where the perimeter of one house lot begins and another ends. The land between houses is dirt, rutted where people feel like driving, and grassy where wild grass grows.

Most of the houses in Tachie are inexpensive, boxlike development houses. They come in all colors—bright yellow, purple, aqua blue, and green. But there are at least three log buildings in Tachie which are still used as family houses. These, and the numerous weathered sheds, boathouses, and docks, seem to belong to the landscape of lake, river, and grassy point.

We went first to the chief's house to ask his permission to park the truck in Tachie and his advice on who would be a good person to look after it. Surprisingly, it was simple to reach an agreement. We can park the truck behind his house for five dollars a month, and he will try to keep an eye on it and see that the children do not play on it too much, or throw rocks at it. He advised us to leave the boat at August Matisse's dock, or rather, at the big wharf in front of August Matisse's house.

The pace in Tachie is slow. No one there has pressing business, so although it is a village, it feels more like the bush after the excitement of Fort St. James. We wandered down to the big wharf, looking at the brightly colored river boats pulled up at the many docks. Some children gathered behind us as we walked, talking together in low tones and staring in a friendly way. The eldest girl had a face as calm as a soapstone sculpture.

The big wharf is on the shore of the lake itself, just down the hill from the church. Tremendous, solid, it is plenty high enough even in high water. The house behind the wharf is brick red, and we knocked on the door softly. It was opened immediately by a short, broad man in a white T-shirt and blue jeans. He was barefoot, and his rather large stomach was girdled by a belt with a beadwork buckle. Although he looked to be in his early sixties, his hair was still dark. He had a broad nose and a heavily creased, leathery face, which broke into a smile when he saw us. We introduced ourselves and asked him if he was August Matisse.

"Yes, that is me. And you must be the new millionaires!"

"Well, my name's Liz and this is Bob, and we live on an island up the lake. But we aren't millionaires. Really, we don't have much money at all," I said.

August smiled. "That is what they all say. It is O.K. with me, though. I like you anyway."

When he invited us in, we went into his kitchen. August's wife sat uncomprehendingly in a chair near the sink. I said hello to her, but August waved my greeting away.

"She is drunk. Now, what can I do for you?"

We explained that we were looking for a place to leave our boat when we go to town. August told us that he would be happy to look after it if we left it at his wharf. He was upset: some kids had recently broken his kitchen window. He said he had many children and grand-children of his own—who were "better than some"—and that he liked young people, except when they were just plain bad. He gesticulated and chuckled. We got the impression he would watch our boat like a hawk. He also offered to sell us gas, an oil mix for two-cycle engines.

We went out into the late sunlight toward the shed to buy a token two gallons, all we could fit into the tank. In the light August squinted a bit and rubbed his eyes with his left hand. I looked at them closely, and could see that they were red and rheumy, with the white glaze of cataract. August noticed me looking at them, and said, "Pooh, they want me to have operation on them. What good would that do? Anyway, I can still see pretty girl like you!"

We had quite an audience while we loaded the boat. A number of children played on the beach, and August came out and shouted good advice. When we started the engine at last, the lake was for once quite calm, and we moved through the water easily, evenly.

I was full of the excitement which fills you when you return to a place you know you should never have left. I had unfinished business walking and carrying, smelling and seeing. During the crossing to the American Islands, which lie between Tachie and the south shore, the lake roughened slightly and we slowed down. That was fine with me. It gave me more time to anticipate our arrival home.

I stood beside Bob and scanned the horizon, looking for the island long before I could distinguish it from the mass of land around it. The waves rolled under us, dark and smooth, and I could see no sign of human visitation anywhere upon the lake. My hands resting on the edge of the cabin roof, I searched the lake and the hills and the sky. No cabins, no boats, no signposts. Although I knew the woods were filled with evidence of passage, I could not find them. The years lay calmly on the shore, and it seemed that nothing had changed on Stuart Lake since the days when many gods had ruled the world, before even the Indians came out of Asia. Stuart Lake still broke and rolled, and the granite wore away as slowly now as it had then. The wind whipped my hair straight back around my head, and I felt suspended in a long and timeless moment—all that had happened between departure and return to the island was compressed and gone. I had returned to the same moment I had stepped out of, no time before.

The lure of the wilderness is mostly this timeless quality it grants to life. There are many ways to induce a familiar and therefore time-transcending state of mind, but going back to the wilderness has always been the simplest and finest for me—when I leave behind the world of man once more, all time draws together into the present. If I come upon a man-made object in the mountains, I am disturbed—not because it is ugly, but because of the ghostly hand I can see throwing it down. The convolutions of human history are contained in that one object, carelessly tossed aside. Now, with the boat pushing us onwards and only woods and lake in sight, I strained ahead waiting, suspended.

When at last I saw the island, as a darker lump against the shore, and felt the kind of release I have felt before only on the first day in the mountains, I was amazed. My ritual has become the place that I call home. My own creation and the wilderness have come together like the two faces of a sphere, and I can ride to them together and climb inside.

The dock was awash at one end, since a log had broken off and floated down the beach while we were gone. After we tied the boat up and splashed through the dock to the shore, we walked up the hill right away, leaving the unloading for later. I couldn't wait to see the house site.

When I saw the foundation, the product of such long labor, its simplicity awed me. The piers looked like the careful excavation of some great Stonehenge buried centuries before. They punctuated the air like statements to the stars. The land sloping away below them gave the impression that they pierced the air randomly, each pursuing some ancient path of its own devising. The sides, perfectly smooth and neat, did not disturb the impression—it is the task of certain ruins to make you breathless with their perfect preservation. And the top of each pier was not completely smoothed—a jumble of sand and rock had not yet been brushed away. The shifting clouds reflected strange lights upon the piers, all the shades of timeless grey.

There was nothing more. Just the stone shafts littering a clearing on an island in the middle of the wilderness. Delphi could not have touched me more. The process of time was revealed; backward or forward it moves the same. We are always living in ruins which have not yet crumbled, or in buildings which have not yet been built.

→≫ (7) ≪←

After two days of the most depressing rain, the sun was shining in a clear blue sky this morning. Since we got back from town we have been working on the fireplace foundation, trying to get it to the point where we can sink the floor beams into the concrete. It has been the most endless labor. Almost a week went into it—more than sixty hours for each of us. The base is seven feet long and five feet wide, sinks four feet beneath the surface of the ground and rises four feet above it. A monolith. Two hundred and ten cubic feet of masonry.

At last the thing is done. We can't pour the final smooth slab until the floor is in, because the joists have to be secured by the last layer of concrete. Some builders think it unwise to tie the house into the fireplace at all, in case the foundation settles; but if the fireplace settles, all the piers will settle too, since we've built them all the same way. And if the piers settle, the whole house will collapse—so why worry about the fireplace?

Today we put in the floor beams. With eighteen feet between some of the piers, we need very strong beams, ten inches by twelve. Since it is impossible to buy a piece of lumber like that, and we could never get it in place if we had it, the beams are constructed, in place, of five rough-cut two-by-twelves nailed together sideways with huge spikes.

I can't quite believe that the beams are going to be strong enough to hold up a whole house. After all, a house weighs tons and tons, and what if the beams start to sag in the middle, and then splinter, and break? Once they were all in place, though, I heaved myself up onto one beam, legs dangling to either side, and bounced up and down. It seemed strong enough.

→≫)《←

I stand at one end of the house and squint sideways along the beams. It looks as if they are sagging. That seems unlikely, since there is not yet any weight on top of them, and I call Bob over, asking him if he thinks this is an optical illusion. He squints too, and groans. In a way it is an optical illusion, and in a way it is not. The beams seem to be sagging because the central pier is an inch or so higher than the two end piers. There is going to be a hump in the floor.

Bob is in a state of reckless self-accusation, and I am trying futilely to explain that a lump in the floor never hurt anything. We should probably take down the beams and adjust the piers, but winter comes early, and we have to have the roof on by September. We grimly decide to go ahead with the floor.

I start to carry the joists up from the middle of the hill where they are piled. They are long and awkward. It is all I can do to carry two at a time. I huff and pant as if each trip up the hill is my first. As quickly as the floor joists arrive, Bob puts them in place. He nails on the sills first, flat on top of the beams, and then nails another piece upright along the outer edge. All the floor joists will be nailed to that piece, the header. The floor joists jump into place, bang bang bang. After all the weeks of carrying and digging, and mixing cement, suddenly everything is going fast. The floor joists line up symmetrically, spaced like a lesson in perspective, golden and smooth.

-⟫⟩⟨⟨-

While Bob measures and cuts the plywood and puts it in place on top of the floor joists, I nail it down. After three pieces are nailed, we suddenly remember the insulation, and I drag great bales onto the joists. Each bale is jammed into a plastic bag, and when I rip one end of the bag open, the insulation expands and fans out to twice the compact size. Peeling one bat off the pile and sticking it between two joists doesn't seem to offer much opportunity for getting covered with fiberglass, but soon my entire body itches.

When enough insulation is in, Bob starts to lay plywood again, and I nail it down. The suddenness with which each nail finds its way through the cells of the wood surprises me. At first, when I took the hammer in my hand and brought the head down on the nail it was with the conviction that it would miss or bend the nail sideways or feebly push at its surface. At first the hammer did all those things. But now I have developed a rhythm, and the nails sink out of sight with resigned grace.

The secret is not to concentrate so much upon one particular nail as to feel the rhythm of a whole series of nails. By the time I actually sink a nail, I am already mentally halfway to the next one. And if the nail at hand is already behind me, then clearly it must have been sunk.

I nail a great many nails. When the floor is finished, plywood nailed from end to end, it is an unbroken plane of golden wood, a platform beneath the sky—a finished product, uniform and clean. I lie flat upon it, reveling in the perfection of the level surface, a surface made to defy the swirling, changing, curving growth which surrounds it. It is utterly alien to the rocky island. I love the floor like this, just plain, open to the sun. I am amazed at how easy it is to walk across it. Our cat Boots leaps and whirls upon the floor, jumping in astonishment at imaginary enemies, stalking bugs, and batting nails from paw to paw.

-⟫⟩⟨⟨-

We are starting to put up the walls. I never realized that walls are so easy to build. The studs are laid upon the floor, spaced, measured, and nailed to the headers and sills. Walls pop into shape, blowing up like inflatable rubber rafts.

The studs are all piled at the back of the house, to be shoved onto the platform as they are needed. We take a number of them to the front of the platform and lay the two-by-fours neatly side by side, placing them sixteen inches apart on center. Other two-by-fours are laid across the top and bottom. We nail the pile of pieces together. The big picture window will go here; we frame the six-by-seven-foot window space in the center of the wall.

After the entire living-room wall is nailed together, we lift it into place and pin it there with a few nails fastened to some temporary diagonal supports. We stand back and examine it critically, peering at it sideways and up and down, to make sure that it looks right. Bob goes below to look up at it, and I stand back ten feet to admire its lines. As I watch, it seems to me that the wall is moving forward. I know it cannot be doing that, so I stay where I am. As I watch, the wall sways, tips, and, gathering momentum, crashes off the edge of the floor into the seven feet of empty space below. I croak a feeble warning to Bob, who dives under the floor before the wall hits the ground, splintering and shaking the earth.

The wall isn't irrevocably wrecked. In fact, only a few of the studs are unusable. But it is a depressing lesson in the difference between building a pretend house and a real one. In a real one, you either put things together, or you don't.

→>>> (8) <<<←

It is evening. After dinner, when I want to be alone, I climb down to the western edge of the island where the last rays of the setting sun throw their light over the rocks. I lie back upon the rocks and pine needles and reach out my right hand to the pile of sticks beside me. Idly, I break some twigs in half and sprinkle them over my stomach. The pile of sticks are the old eagle's nest, I realize suddenly. I must be tired, not to have noticed that. I brush the twigs carefully off my stomach back onto the nest, laughing at myself as I do so. Several little pieces remain imbedded in the wool of my sweater—I can feel them when I run my hand over the fuzzy yarn.

I close my eyes, and drift. Suddenly, it is colder, and a rock has grown beneath my left shoulder blade. Sleepily, I make my way back through the dense woods to the tent. Bob is already asleep there. The dark, level platform of the house floor is framed against the light, northern-summer sky, like a stage after the lights have faded. I drag my sleeping bag and pad from the tent, and crawl up to sleep on the floor, beneath the sky. I try to imagine what it would be like with a house around me.

$\Rightarrow\!\Rightarrow\!\Rightarrow (9) \Leftarrow\!\Leftarrow\!\Leftarrow$

The exterior walls are all framed and sheathed. It is strange to stand inside the house, like sitting in a shoebox from which the lid has long been lost. I feel like an object stored away. The unsheathed walls were playful; a barred prison from which it was easy to escape at any time. The sheathed walls are not playful, but fully serious in intent and accomplishment.

I cannot any more just jump out of the house onto the ground whenever I decide I want to be outside. I have to walk around and find the back-door opening, crossing what seem to be vast expanses. The sun no longer shines in everywhere and at all times. The early morning sun enters only the window openings, and it is not until midafternoon that the floor is again carpeted in sunlight. I can't just sit down anywhere and watch the lake—the boats going by and the moving water. The covered wall studs are cut by powerful openings, but in many directions there is nothing to be seen but plywood. The sky is framed and limited by angular walls. Nothing is immediate now except the box itself, not an interior but a fence, a ruin—this time recent and uncleansed. It is as if a bomb had swept away the roof. The plywood is now stained and gritty, surrounded.

The rain starts to fall just before dinner time. The cat and dog climb underneath the floor and curl up together in a pile of dirt. Boots licks industriously at an invisible smudge on Bundy's forehead. Bob goes to the tent to read, on the theory that the rain will stop before we get too hungry. I climb back up onto the floor, and linger there, wet and wondering.

It seems to be taking so long to get this house built. The scraps of unused lumber clutter the floor, and shreds of the insulation protrude from around the fireplace base. While the house goes up, so slowly, it also ages. The rain drips down the walls, leaving large, long patches of darker wood behind it, and sometimes dragging brown stains out of the nails toward the floor. I stand in front of the large opening where the picture window will go, and watch the rain pressing on the lake, until it seems to force from it a smoky mist—as if, squeezed between the fingers of the rain, the lake pushes up again to the sky. Everything is getting greyer with the coming of evening. It is very cold for July, and my slightly damp feet begin to turn numb. Still I stand and watch.

I've always wanted to build a house with my own hands, I suppose because I thought it would be a way of controlling my life. People are always given meaning by the structures they build and the value of any life is shaped by the walls around it. Nothing exists without a form to contain it; no life exists without a shape to define it. But I was stupid to hope that if I built my own roof, it would protect me. When— and if—we finish it, it will keep the rain outside. No more. The house will stand on the earth like a fist beneath the sky, a shrine to the power that drove it here. Slowly, it will fade and vanish.

The plywood on the floor bubbles and warps, and the piers are streaked with patches of darker grey. I sit on the edge of the window hole and pick up an empty can from the floor. It is rusting and the lid has been lost. The sticky remains of marine varnish coat the sides and bottom. I scrape a bit onto my finger tip and lift it to my nose. It smells dusty and sharp, like something that should be washed. After a time I turn and throw the can out of the window into the woods below.

It is easy tonight to toss all things up as but containers.

→>>‹‹‹←

After a night of rain, the sun is hot through the canvas tent. It is transmuted into a green light as rich as the sea. I stretch and pull Bundy toward me. She licks me frantically, trying to make up for a whole night of abstinence. Bob is already outside. The stove's metal pump whoomps in and out, in and out, until at last there is a rush of ignited gas. The eaglets are squawking. Already a boat engine buzzes in the distance. The smell of coffee drifts through the door while I think about today's jobs. The interior walls have to be finished, and a set of stairs built up to the front door.

I know, as surely as I have ever felt the opposite, that we will build our house, and it will be beautiful.

2

BUILDING

(1)

I cleaned the house this morning, and went through the boxes of clothing and books, untouched since we arrived, to see if I could find the whisk broom—it's hard to get the dirt between the cracks in the plywood with the big one. The whisk has vanished without a trace, but I found a lot of other things I had forgotten we owned. My French straw hat, carefully wrapped in plastic and still quite dry, now has seven or eight holes neatly chewed in its crown. The Christmas-tree lights are still unbroken; I cannot imagine why we brought them with us. I found a fish scale—who could care how much a fish weighs, as long as it's big enough to make a meal of? After putting away the scale and the lights, I put the hat on my head and finished sweeping the floor.

It amazes me to think how much we have accomplished in two and a half months. Accomplished in leaving behind—I feel so far away from French hats and Christmas-tree lights and fish scales—and accomplished in building up. When I look around at the house, interior walls completed, stairs up to the front porch, fireplace slab dry and symmetrical, I have some difficulty even in connecting it to my own efforts. It would be easier to appreciate if someone else had built it. In much the same way that one's own hand seems sometimes like a strange five-limbed animal (while another person's hand looks merely like a hand), so the house right now seems odd and distant. Fascinating, lovely, strange. I run my hand down one wall stud, feeling all the little inconsistencies in the wood, the knotholes and the splinters. I have never noticed any of them before, and yet I put this stud in place. There is a slight reddish tint to one side of it, as if it had been sunburned. I hadn't noticed that before either.

37

Right down the center of the floor, forty feet in length, lies the recently constructed roofbeam. Made of three joists fastened together with plywood plates, it sags horribly when we pick it up. I cannot imagine how we are going to fasten it into the air seven feet above the place where the walls end. I stand looking at it helplessly while Bob unearths from our now neatly organized goods his old climbing rope and cuts it into three equal pieces, sawing through the many little fibers of the core. I am shocked, not so much at the cutting of the rope—the only one we have on the island—as at the expression on Bob's face, a placid acceptance of what I see as a symbolically charged event. Bob is usually more sensible than I am; he points out that the rope was ready to be retired in any case.

We tie the ropes around the beam—in the middle and at the two ends—and nail them securely. Leaving the beam for a while, we get three eighteen-foot joists and nail them into upright positions in the center of the house and at the side walls. Before putting up each joist, Bob nails a sling at the top and clips a snap link through it, and a section of the rope tied to the beam through the snap link. With this primitive pulley system, we haul the beam off the ground and into the air. Since there are only two of us, and three ropes to be pulled simultaneously, there is a good deal of excitement and recrimination before we fasten on the idea of hauling each rope only a few feet at a time, tying it off, and moving down the line until the beam is even. Then we pull the whole thing a few more feet.

The remarkable thing is that it works. The board sags and dances and seems about to break at several points during its ascent. Once one of my tie-offs slips, letting the east end of the beam drop three feet before the half-hitch miraculously tightens again. But at last the beam is up, straight and level for the length of the house, seven feet above where the walls end. We tie all the ropes securely, and Bob climbs up onto the two side walls to fasten the beam securely to the uprights. He looks very high against the sky; when he jumps off the second wall, grinning, and hits the floor, the house shakes and the joists all sway. But we have a roofbeam. I wish there was someone here to congratulate us.

Suddenly, we have a visitor. The bald eagle, who never comes too near if he can avoid it, flies lazily, in a single sweep, for the length of the beam, only fifteen feet above it. It is hard to decide whether he eyes it with distaste or indifference, but the yawn he gives at the midpoint of his flight is prodigious. The pink inside of his mouth shows clearly behind the curved beak. I can see each talon and the feathers, smoothly layered. He comes to a fir tree and, with the extreme exertion characteristic of an eagle's landings, manages to stop by gripping a branch tightly with his feet as he beats his wings backwards.

He relaxes, cleaning a feather here and there and staring pointedly down. Fearless and calm, casually opening and closing his beak, he is framed against the tree, against the sun, against the beam—he is the moving part of a still life which includes my whole world. His tiny eyes, made for seeing clearly at a great distance, probably don't see our house at all. He is probably looking through us to the lake, hungry for the sight of fish. But we stand, staring, until he flies away. The beam looks even better now. Isolated and high above, its imperfections are erased by distance. The plywood plates are square and professional, the delicate dusting of nails a pattern of choice.

->>><<<-

It is not, unfortunately, always possible to maintain a reassuring distance from the products of our construction. We started today on the task of putting up the roof rafters, forty two-by-eights which have been piled for months in the rain and sun and have consequently warped dramatically. Wood continues to reveal itself as far more pliable than it at first appears. Some of the rafters are warped sideways, some are warped lengthwise, and some combine both tendencies. A few are still straight. They were all piled this morning at the back of the house, ready to be fitted snugly against the roofbeam.

The only complicated part of roofing is cutting the rafter. You have to cut the beam end of each rafter at the proper angle for it to meet the roofbeam flush, and you have to notch the lower end so that it will fit over the top of the wall. Both angles can be calculated with a T-square, and since they are uniform for the entire roof, one calculation should solve the problem. Working on that assumption, we measured and cut eight rafters and then tried to put them in.

In order to reach the roofbeam, we laid ceiling joists across the walls, loosely, as a kind of scaffolding. Plywood was shoved over it in the essential spots: just below the roofbeam, and right next to the walls.

Bob climbed onto the scaffolding with a hammer, some nails, and a measuring tape. I shoved the end of the first rafter onto the platform, and he pulled it up and lifted the end until it was flat against the roofbeam, slanting down to the wall. He toe-nailed it into place. Then he crawled back to the wall and pushed the bottom end of the rafter into place. The notch fit perfectly over the wall, and he drove the nails to secure it there. While he crawled back, I carried several more rafters over and shoved them onto the plywood. Then I started to cut some more, struggling to make sure the cuts were straight, but watching them emerge slightly slanted. The saw is getting dull.

You have to have quite a few consecutive examples of any tendency before you will admit a pattern to it. So when the third rafter Bob nailed didn't fit as well as the first, there was no cause for conclusion. When the fourth one fit even worse, there was still no alarm. But when the sixth and seventh rafters hung over the wall with their notches avoiding almost any contact with it, it was clear that something was wrong.

Bob climbed down to look at the roof. Observed from below, the rafters seemed to spread all over the place, slanting this way or that, bending in the middle. I cut some new ones with experimental measurements. When he tried those, which should have worked well, the gap between wall and notch was less evident but still noticeable. Bob ripped them off, tearing the nails out with incredible energy, and tossed them over the edge of the house onto the ground below.

"These goddamn boards!" Bob shouted. He glared down at me as if I were directly responsible for the growing catastrophe.

"Christ, Bob," I said, "everything's warped; that was plain before we ever started; what do you want to do, burn the place down?" I glared back.

"We might as well." He spoke with the conviction of a perfectionist in an imperfect world, and sat down on the plywood.

"Are you kidding?" I asked, more angrily. "They're not going to show when it's done. Nothing in the whole house is straight, anyway. Just nail them down."

"Oh, just nail them down, that makes a lot of sense. How long do you think the roof's going to last then? Ten minutes? Is that what you want?"

"What I want!" I stared up infuriated. Bob's position seven feet above my head gave him a distinct advantage. I searched for a logical basis for continued action. "Anyway, some construction methods don't even require notching, you know."

"Yes, I know," he said, vastly patient. "And then you have to put blocks between all the rafters. We don't have enough money. Anyway, that would be just as hard to get right. I'm ready to pack it in."

"Great. That's marvellous. I can hardly wait until it snows. If you want to go fishing or something, I'll take over the roof."

"Go right ahead. Just make sure you get those notches right."

"If I'm going to do the roof, I'll do it right. But it doesn't have to be perfect."

"I'm sure it won't be," Bob said, descending.

"Why do you have to be such a perfectionist? It just makes you miserable."

"A perfectionist! You'd think someone was a perfectionist if he wanted to build a set of stairs you could actually walk up!"

Bob went to the tent, grabbed the fishing pole and a sweater, and headed for the boat. I wish I had gone with him. We both need a few days off. And though I said I would do the roof, I have not been in any hurry to get started. Tomorrow will be soon enough.

➤➤➤❯❮❮❮❮

The sun is warm and encouraging on the plywood scaffolding. I pile about six of the cut rafters onto the platform, then climb up after them with a hammer, nails, and a measuring tape. Since the rafters are cut in variations, and the roofbeam calls for variations, I figure I will just try different ones out to find the best match of rafter to location. A good deal of shuffling gets one happily located. I hold it in place with one hand and the hammer with the other. I find I need three hands, one to hold the nail with. Laying the rafter down again, I nail the nail into the rafter a little way, then put the board back up. It is hard to hammer over my head; my forearm quickly becomes sore. One final thump sends the nail all the way through to the beam, and I drop my arm, letting the blood rush back.

Two more forays of arm and hammer sink two more nails, and I can leave the upper end of the rafter and crawl along the scaffolding toward the wall. It makes me uneasy to feel the boards bounce beneath my body, but I finally get to the other piece of plywood and adjust the rafter's position. It is even more awkward nailing this end in, since I have to drive the nail at an angle toward me. One nail emerges quickly from the side of the rafter. I smash it flat. The next one hits the first one. The third nail sinks into the wall, and the rafter is secure.

I fit another rafter, nail it, fit another one, nail it. When they are used up, Bob hands me more. He is still cutting them to the original pattern, so not all of them fit well, but at this point I don't care. Get them in. Bob works with his shirt off, using the window ledge in the front wall as one sawhorse and the worktable as the other. It occurs to me that I would be more comfortable with my shirt off also, so I take it off, amazed at the feeling of muscular freedom which results.

I work. I carry rafters and hoist them up and nail them in place. After a while there are long spans of time when sweat pours and muscles move and little else. I cease to perceive my surroundings: Then a small sight catches my eye—a bent nail lying on the plywood, or a knothole. I stare at it. There is me and the knothole, there is the knothole and me, there is only the knothole.

The number of finished rafters increases steadily. Bob climbs up to help me frame the chimney hole in the center of the roof. There is half a roof, naked and open. We move all the scaffolding over. More rafters are nailed in place. There is three-quarters of a roof, and the sun is sinking toward the northwest. I nail the last rafter in place. I climb down.

I lie on the floor and close my eyes, emptied. A plane flies in from the distance, and I open my eyes to look for it. When I look up, I see a roof. My own roof. I built it. The plane flies overhead, and I wave madly.

$$\Rightarrow\!\!\!\Rightarrow (2) \Leftarrow\!\!\!\Leftarrow$$

We are just back from a trip to town, and I am trying to get things organized. Considering the amount of material we have now got loaded onto the island, it is amazing we should have been in need of anything more, but we seem to have developed an obsession for little objects: screws, drill bits, utility knives, hinges. The long and crumpled list which I made up before we left for town has all the items checked off, except the heating stove and the Selkirk chimney for the fireplace and stoves. Two pounds of finishing nails. Two pounds of roofing nails. A large drill bit. A trowel. Six bags of masonry cement. Two ax handles (they break all the time). A sharpening steel for the chain saw. An Aladdin-lamp mantle. A wick. Ten gallons of kerosene. Spark plugs. String.

One of the aggravations of building a house is that you have to start cleaning it up long before it is finished, and you have to find places to "put things away" when there is nowhere to put things into. All the recently purchased material is strewn around on the floor, along with a lot of junk: shredded bats of insulation, torn plastic, spilled staples, bent nails, sawdust. I am sorting it out, the tools into one box, the garbage into another, the scraps of lumber into a third.

Stuff doesn't go away. You can change the shape of things with tools, but the substances persist. A piece of wood which you cut to an appropriate length for use as a joist or stud will pay the dividend of a short board and a pile of sawdust. You can use the sawdust to insulate an icebox, if you are ambitious enough, and the short end to light a fire in the cookstove, but the ashes have to be cleaned eventually from the stovebox, and their bulk is always surprising. In addition there is a trail of soot which falls on the floor and has to be transferred to a sponge and washed out in a sink, if you have one. The sink has then to be scrubbed. The wood's persistent.

The dream of my generation has been to get away from the clutter which is taking over the world, the infinite succession of packages which make a fortress around our lives. We have tried to escape from what at times appears to be an enormous wastebasket.

But I have never in my life felt more completely tied to objects: raw materials and the tools to shape them with, garbage and structure. Yet something has changed in our relationship. I put the wood in one box, to be burned, and organize the tools neatly in another. I realize I am losing my fear of the world of things.

A house used to contain any number of secrets in its walls. Why did the water gush from the taps, just so? How did the floor support my weight; what was really beneath its surface? At what point had the doorways appeared in the walls? When I walked into a house, a peculiar weakness beset me. Because I could not fathom the reasons behind the shapes of things, they had power over me.

Mostly, this manifested itself in a reluctance to work with tools, to try to change shapes. Even looking at a wrench, or a saw, or a screwdriver, gave me a feeling of uneasiness, my lack of comprehension of their functions going deep into the heart of perception. It is not that I was never given the chance to learn their functions or understand their nature; but when I was small and watched my father fixing the lawnmower, or my brother making purple clouds with his chemistry set, or electrical-lighting boards, or just building wooden boxes, it was always like being at a show, entertaining and magical, and interesting because I lacked comprehension, not because I desired comprehension.

Later I viewed the machines and the cities with distaste and fear.

There is an exchange of power between us and the things we use. Unless you understand the nature of those objects with which you constantly interact, you will always be at their mercy. Not because of what they can force you to do, but because of the way they can force you to see. I polish the sawdust off a planer and set it firmly into the box. The wrench goes in next. Just a few days ago I was tightening a bolt with the wrench and I hit myself in the eye with it. It was very exciting. Stars everywhere. It was like saying hello.

I don't have to accept the domination of objects which used to leer at me, saying, "You'd better learn to live inside yourself, because you're never going to get inside me." I can. I can get inside a floor, a wall, a wrench, a boat. I can say hello. And once I've learned to do that, I can get inside of rocks, islands, clouds, and northern lights. Starting with a hammer, a board, and a box of nails, I can move on past the garbage dumps and into the world.

Why are children and so many men and women such avid consumers? (Oh, let's get that, what a pretty thing, what a fascinating toy, what a marvelous device. How neat!) Because mysteries are exciting. There is always the hope also that by mere possession understanding will somehow result. (This is mine, mine!) Expecting the genie to appear out of the bottle, bowing. (I am yours, master.) But commanding something's surface does not bring knowledge of its soul. For that, you have to be involved in the building.

->>><<<-

In a way. When we went berry picking yesterday, we found a bench. The hot August air was stuffed with the smell of berries, but when we went looking for them, we found, instead, the remains of a logging camp, on a high point shining with berry bushes. Behind the bushes, under a stand of old firs, a fifteen-foot-long bench was standing upright, looking across the lake, waiting to be sat upon. No logging has been done in the area for at least twenty years. The bench isn't warped, though, or falling apart. The boards are grey with weathering, but the sides still hold the remains of two clear stripes of white paint.

It is possible that other berry pickers have righted the bench in recent years, but it isn't likely. The patch was inaccessible from the water except by way of a fairly difficult scramble, and most people who prefer to gather berries on the shore do it because they don't want to exert themselves too much. In any case, the bench is there no longer, since we brought it home with us.

The bench is cleverly designed. Three two-by-twelves form the three supports; they have each been cut out in a graceful curve to form a pair of legs with a roof. Laid on top are the three pieces of the seat. On each side a board has been nailed to create a strong resistance to cross motion.

Now that the bench is here, it is hard to imagine how I ever got along without it. In some inexplicable way it completes the rocky point below the house and is necessary for looking out from it. The bench and I took to each other as if we had known each other for years. To the extent that the bench is wearing out, I feel as sorry as if I had deserted it myself to the fury and persistence of the winter snows. After the day is over, when the long evening pours out before me, I sit on the bench. The lake is satin grey, the sky is filling with clouds, and the trees look dull and muted. I remember, here, that in the towns the stores are filled with shiny colors, packaged in many different ways: a glazed plate, a notecard of sunsets, crisp fresh breads in yellows and browns, books in irresistible profusion, still bright blue and green like stones under water. Here, as the rain starts to fall in a light mist, many tiny darker dots sprinkling the bench on either side of me, I remember that not many months ago I lived in a place where illusions watered the ground more thoroughly than rain, and I lived with a heavy growth of poems like cancer on the brain. Now I can dangle my legs over the smooth bench, and build my thoughts slowly; more slowly even than the house has risen.

→≫ (3) ≪←

The roof is sheathed; Bob did the sheathing. We both feel better now, with the major job completed. Bob brings me coffee in the mornings and tells stories to make me laugh, imperiling the coffee mug. In the evenings I read P. G. Wodehouse to him, while he continues to work as long as it is light, contented with the progress we have made, taking time out to chuckle only so that I will know that he is happy. I could not, of course, read to him while he was on the roof. When we had to talk, I'd shout up through one of the remaining gaps. Even the hammer blows were muffled by the half-inch plywood. When the last piece of the roof went on, the house fell suddenly silent and dark, almost enclosed. It is time to put in the windows.

The windows are elegant even sitting between two trees. Looking through glass at other glass at other glass, the windows behind one another eleven deep, I imagine that the entire world behind them is a muted, cloudy, reflecting sphere of bark. Glass is not a true solid, but a hard liquid, which over the course of the years will be slowly tugged by gravity and thicken slightly at the bottom while it thins at the top. If it is badly made, it will distort the world behind it—if it is only slightly second-grade, then you will not even realize the distortion. We did not want poor glass in our house, whatever else may be wrong with it. The windows are the best that can be found nearby.

But I have resisted putting them into the house. For two reasons. In the first place, I do not want to carry them anywhere. I have an irrational fear of dropping my end, or sticking it onto a branch, or smashing it through a rock. It is not the spectre of wasted money which frightens me, or even the thought of wasted time and energy. It is a superstitious feeling that the smashing of one of the eyes of the house before it is even born would cause permanent damage to its vision. Absurd. The second reason is that once the windows are in, we will have a completely enclosed house. An interior. We will be able to move in, and live inside. I don't want to close in the walls without first being very sure that nothing will be permanently trapped inside. Again, absurd. Isn't the whole point of a window to teach you to see differently, framing and isolating for examination a scene which might otherwise be lost in the whole. How many cats are hidden in this picture? Can you find them all? How many dreams are there behind this window? Can you name them all?

However, Bob's brother will be coming this weekend for a visit, and he can help us to put the windows in. Although we have not had help with anything else, it seems appropriate that we should have some help with this business of establishing views.

The windows were surprisingly easy to install—the entire unit, double glass in a heavy wood frame, slides into the convenient hole in the wall, where it is wedged and nailed in place.

Bob and Charlie put one of the smallest windows in first, a four by three. With just that one window in, the house went through a transformation as sudden as the shift of patterns in a kaleidoscope. If I found a window fastened to the air in the middle of the woods, I would walk round the window, and look behind it, and pass my hand around it, and see nothing through it but what was on the other side, but I would still be convinced there must be something more to the window's purpose than simply to show me a scene which I could see just as well without it. Dogs and cats who see themselves in mirrors will check behind the mirror for the creature responsible and, not being able to find him, will eventually give up in disgust, as if to say, "What a foolish illusion!" That is what I felt when the first window was in and the tree outside it became a tree behind glass. "What a foolish illusion. What's the point to it?"

The big picture window was the next to go in, and I watched Bob and Charlie carry it up the path, backing up before them with my fingers in my ears so as not to hear the crash when it came. But it didn't, and I helped Charlie hold the window in place while Bob ran inside to wedge it.

It is gorgeous. Where the little window just made me think, "What's the point?" the large one made me feel, "Whatever the point is, it's splendid." It is splendid—symmetrical and big enough so it doesn't really limit what can be seen through it.

We spent a lot of time this afternoon just walking around the house. We sat on the floor of the living room and had a conversation, to hear the sound of interior voices. We walked in the front door and out the back one, and vice versa, several times in quick succession. Each time we undoubtedly passed through a house.

→≫(4)≪←

It is September, and the air smells autumny. Today the leaves are skipping across the beach and flinging themselves into the water like children running to take a jump. It is getting colder, and although the geese have not yet all left, it cannot be long before the last cordon sweeps over the house and is gone. The first group went by four days ago. We sat on the porch and listened. The moon was almost full, and the geese filled the sky with the mournful sound of their passage. They did not stop, but pushed on south as fast as they could fly.

The loons are still here though. In the fall they congregate on the water in large groups. Today they drift in front of the island, a small flotilla, moving slowly toward us, then away. They seem uncertain of their destination, and I leap at them shouting "bang, bang!" In a body they veer away, gliding out of reach of what they clearly regard as a maniac. Perhaps, they seem to think, they are invading the wrong beach. They float off, dispersing, and re-form their convoy near the next island over. Will the attack ever begin?

Winter is certainly coming. This morning the water was frozen in its plastic bucket. The cookstove we got last month has been rigged up near the back wall, and a stovepipe runs horizontally from it to the outside, but it warms only the area directly around it. We don't have a good heating stove, and without insulated ceilings even a good heating stove wouldn't help much. But we can't build the ceilings until we get more lumber, and we are out of money.

Today, we talked about what we should do now. We are no more certain of our next move than the loons seem to be, floating around on the water, not fishing, just waiting for something to happen. The house is completely enclosed and able to resist the weather, but we cannot keep it warm, and we are almost out of food.

"I just can't believe it," I said to Bob, after reaching once again the conclusion that we are broke. "We came here with eighteen thousand dollars. Eighteen thousand! We were idiots to pay cash for the island. It's all gone. Unbelievable."

"Actually, it's amazing it went as far as it did." Bob was glumly shredding little bits of the plywood floor and tossing them rhythmically away. "Why did we ever suppose we could do this?"

"God knows. We were sucked in by all those books, I suppose." I lay back on the floor, playing with the cat.

"We should have built a tiny log cabin. With skins on the walls. And gun slits. I hate being in debt," said Bob. "I just hope we can get jobs."

"We might get back this winter."

"Yeah. They'll have to be pretty good jobs for that."

"Well, next winter we'll be here." I looked for the silver lining. "And half a house is more than some people ever get."

"And more useless than no house at all," said Bob at once, exasperated and amused; he doesn't believe in silver linings. He smiled and shrugged and squeezed my shoulder. His sweater smelled wooly—I noticed a little hole in the arm. If we have to leave, at least we'll be leaving together.

Having to leave does not make it easier to do. I sat for a while on the edge of the porch and watched the water moving under the shifting light. I felt the sudden rushing consciousness of loss, the echoing realization of my inability to control my own life or the world around me. I do the best I can with whatever comes along, and make the next move trailing a haze of questions. I fling myself into the future because the past has tossed me forward. Right now I am disconnected from my surroundings; they seem brittle, easily shattered by vibrations—glass flowers quivering in space.

Later, we went down to the beach and walked around the island on the shore. The water is low enough for that now, for the first time since we moved here; all the jagged, dark-grey rocks at the west are dry and passable. I found a large deepwater spoon with some weights on it, and Bob found a long hooked pole, used by the Indians to pull in nets. When we got back to the house, we moved all the insulation into the living room and piled all the extra lumber and plywood under the house. The black tar paper stapled to the walls and the roof is easily ripped by the wind, so I went over it all once more with the staple gun, trying to make it secure. We plan to leave tomorrow.

→≫ (5) ≪←

I got a job last week. We're living now in a tiny cabin at Ted Martin's marina, five miles from Fort St. James. Bob has been working at a sawmill for three weeks, and already he looks worn. Not that I see much of him anymore, since we're working different shifts. When we do get together, we don't have much to say. After eight or nine hours of machine noise, silence is the best thing we can give each other.

The cabin we're living in is so small that you have to move the kitchen chairs to get into the bathroom. The bed creaks and sags, and the oil heater in the basement crawl space fills the rooms with the smell of partially combusted petroleum, as well as dry heat which makes the hair and clothes crackle with static electricity. The rent is low though, very low, and that is important. The less we spend, the sooner we can leave for the island again.

It is hard, though, to remember that we are living like this so we can return to the island—hard to keep in mind that working in town is just as much a part of building our house as putting on its roof. I feel as trapped in dead-end, mindless work as someone who really is.

My job at the bank carries the impressive title "Machine Operator." The "Machine Operators" sit in a small, windowless cement block behind the bank proper, and enter all withdrawals, deposits, and checks onto the appropriate account cards. When the bank is computerized, the job will vanish without a ripple. It is a computer's job, and after punching figures into a machine for at least five hours every day, I find that my nights are the nights of a neurotic computer. When I try to fall asleep, lying in bed on my side with my legs curled to my chest, it is to the accompaniment of visions of hundreds and hundreds of checks—blue, green, tan, or yellow, Madame?—ruffling desperately on the edge of my eyelids. Figures come too, appearing small in the distance and growing larger and larger until they pop inside my brain. They are subtracted, added, multiplied, and divided, and they share the stage with names, neatly alphabetized. James, Johannes, Johnson, Jones. $1500 - 385 = 1115$; $234 + 16 = 250$. Then more checks—blue, green, tan, or yellow, Sir?—until at last they are all sorted and entered, and I can sleep. Bob tells me the same thing happens to him, except that his eyelids are a black conveyor belt, and their decoration is endless sheets of plywood, endlessly appearing at one side of his brain and disappearing at the other. Sometimes the plywood whips off the belt before it gets to the edge of his eyes. He has caught the flawed sheet before it got away.

At least Bob belongs to a union and gets paid decently for his work. Bank employees are not unionized, nor ever will be if the initiative displayed at my particular branch is any indication. Since I make exactly half of what Bob makes in any given hour, I ventured to ask Anne, my fellow machine operator, if there had ever to her knowledge been any move to unionize bank employees.

"Gee, I don't think so," said Anne. "I mean, the men all get paid well anyway, and most of the women who work here are married, so it doesn't matter if we earn less, does it?"

Today was a typical day at the bank. Every day is a typical day there. I got to work at 8:00 and started "posting" on the machine. I forced myself to take my watch off and put it in my pocket, so that to look at the time I had to stop punching figures and get it out again. That way I looked far less often, and the minute hand had moved appreciably each time I checked on its progress. At 10:00 the coffee break moved into the back room, which is also the coffee room, and I got a cup of coffee and turned my chair around to listen to the talk.

Susan came in first, with Janice. Susan was wearing tight black pants and a silky, cowled white sweater, the extreme slimness of her body accentuated by the plain colors.

"Boy, it was cold out this morning; I can hardly wait for my vacation. We're going to Hawaii in November and . . ."

"Hey, who's got my cup?" Janice interrupted. She found it as soon as she asked the question. "Oh, here it is. Hawaii? We went to Hawaii last year. It was pretty nice. Maui and all that. This year we're going to Disneyland though."

"Dick says Disneyland is a rip-off. He says that when he went there, it cost so much money they could have stayed an extra week somewhere else." Susan settled into the best easy chair.

"Oh, Dick. He's such a cheapskate. He always says things like that. What's money for?" Janice carefully set her cup on the table next to Irene and dragged a chair over.

Other women came in. The men had gone to the manager's office for coffee. Shurli had gotten a new haircut, and everyone commented on how nice it looked, including Anne, who had told me privately that she thought it looked terrible. Anne had bought the new issue of *Better Homes and Gardens*, and she flipped through the pages, talking with Shurli.

"Have you ever tried one of these self-cleaning ovens?"

"Oh, yes, my mother-in-law has one, and it works really nice. I always say to John that it's so hard to clean our oven that we might as well not have one. I think he might get me a self-cleaning oven over Christmas."

"I find it's pretty easy to clean our oven, if I do it once a week, so it doesn't build up. I just use Ajax."

"Ajax is good, isn't it? When I was first married, I tried every cleaner on the market. But after a while I just decided that it was easier to stick to Ajax." Shurli took a sip of coffee, made a face, and flipped through a few more pages of her magazine.

At 10:15 the accountant came in. "All right, girls, time to get back to work now. Liz, Mr. Stevenson wants to see you in his office."

I went to the front office and asked Mr. Stevenson, the bank manager, what he wanted. His small, beanlike eyes were focused on a wastebasket in the corner of the room, and he doodled on a pad with a red felt-tip pen and said, "I'm afraid I'll have to ask you not to wear denim pants to work anymore. We like our girls to look neat and respectable. I'm sure you understand."

"I'm sure I do," I said.

Back at the machine, I punched numbers. Disneyland, self-cleaning ovens, Hawaii, Ajax, and, for Christ's sake, "denim pants," went whizzing through my head to the rhythm of the clacking keys. I put my watch back on my wrist and left it there.

In the afternoon, I moved into the front of the bank to sort the piles of incoming checks and deposit slips for posting to accounts tomorrow morning. I had reached the stage of resorting the checks from their initial alphabetical arrangement to exact account arrangements, when an Indian came into the bank. He was about forty years old, quite slim, dressed in a homemade moose-hide jacket and heavy West Pac boots. He took off his bright woolen cap and held it before him in both hands, looking about in some puzzlement. Delighted to have something different to do, I left my checks and asked him if I could help.

"I would like a loan," he said.

"Just a minute, the loans officer will want to talk to you," I said, and told David Brown that someone wanted to speak to him. He told me to send him in.

Back at the counter, I smiled at the Indian man and said, "Go right in, please. Mr. Brown will talk with you."

The desk I was working at was right next to David Brown's cubbyhole, so I could hear and see the conversation which followed.

"Well now," said David Brown in a hearty voice. "I hear you want a loan. What is your name, please?"

"My name is John Prince."

"John Prince." Brown wrote something on a form. "Any relation to Howard Prince?"

"My brother."

"Oh. And you want a loan, do you?"

"Yes."

"Well now, you understand that I'll have to ask you a lot of questions to ascertain whether or not you are what we call a good risk? Whether or not you'll be able to pay us back?"

"I will pay you back."

"I'm sure you will. But I have to ask you all these questions anyway. Now, how much is your annual income?"

"I have a trap line."

"Well, how much do you make on it, every year?"

"Different money. I cannot know until the Bay buys the fur."

"Just give me an approximation, please."

"I don't know. Different money every year."

"We'll leave that for a minute. Do you live on a reserve? And do you get a government check?"

"I live at Tachie. I get a check every month."

"But you know, your government check isn't good for collateral. How much of a loan did you want?"

"Two hundred dollar. My son Louis come back again from the government school, and he has spent a lot of money, and we need to get food and get the car fixed. Just two hundred dollar. And I can give you this for you to keep till I pay the money back."

John Prince handed over a sheet of creased and heavily worn paper. David Brown examined it.

"This is a license for a trap line. It leases the land to you to use, to trap on. This isn't any good for collateral. It's not negotiable. Only you can use the land to trap on, and you can't sell it or lease it to anyone else. This simply isn't any good."

"It is good. It is mine. If I give it to you, then I cannot use my trap line till I pay you. It is good."

"No, I'm sorry, this isn't any good. We can't accept this. Do you have anything else you can give me for collateral? You said you had a car. What year is it? Have you paid it off?"

"It is my wife's car. It is, I think, 1958. A sedan. It works good, mostly. But here, take this, it is my trap line. I will pay you back. You keep this, and I will pay you back."

He tried to hand the paper back to David Brown, but Brown wouldn't take it.

"No, that is not good. And I'm afraid the car isn't either. We can't give you a loan. I'm sorry."

"I need a loan. Just two hundred dollar now. I will pay you back, next month. It is my son Louis. He is wild; he spent the money. We need a loan."

David Brown stood up. "I'm terribly sorry, but we can't give you one. I'll have to ask you to leave now. I have other things to do, and I can't help you."

"You will not give me a loan?" John Prince looked at David Brown in amazement, as if he finally understood what had been said.

"No, I'm sorry."

John Prince took his trapping license and folded it neatly, putting it into his wallet and slipping his wallet into his outside coat pocket. He took his wool cap in his hands again and walked to the door. Before he left, he looked around, puzzled, as puzzled as when he had first come in. At the door he said, as if to the air, "It is good. It is my trap line." He put his hat back on his head and pushed open the double doors. Across the bank, I could feel the swish of cold air as they came together once more.

It was three hours before I could follow him through the doors. Strangely, when I came out, I saw him. John Prince was leaving the liquor store, a brown paper bag under one arm. Slightly drunk already, he walked carefully down the street, the light from the street lamps catching the tassels on his jacket as he walked. A little uncertain, his walk was not yet undignified. He was heading for the hotel and the huge beer room commonly called "The Zoo."

→≫ (6) ≪←

For us, at least, things are looking up. Our bills are paid, and already we have $150 in the bank. I begin to hope that we will be able to return to the island this winter and pick up our life there again. The weather has been beautiful this month and, more important than anything else, we are finally making some friends. Like a calm after a wind, that suddenly makes it easier to walk forward.

The marina and cabin park at which we're living is a good place to meet people; there are a lot of people around. Ted Martin, who owns the place, is a slim, energetic man in his thirties, with a small, trimmed beard and a thin, fine-boned face. He's a good businessman and a hard worker, with experience in a variety of jobs that range from grading and leveling ground to fixing diesel engines. Right now a lot of his time is taken up with the construction of a new boat for his summer water-taxi business; various people drop in from time to time to watch him at work in the barn, and to ask or proffer advice. The water-taxi takes him all over the Stuart-Trembleur-Takla Lakes system in the summer and fall—he knows, at least slightly, most of the people who have cabins on the lakes. Having achieved a measure of security in his business, he is discovering the pleasures of a more low-key life. After observing us on cross-country skis, he is eager to take up the sport. And he has plans to build a sauna on the bank of the river.

In the apartment on the second floor of Ted's house lives John Calhoun, also a slim man. Younger and more casual than Ted, he has an easy friendliness and a California-style appeal, tempered by a British Columbia life. His curly, dark-blond hair grows long, and his blue jeans are often torn. He's working at Takla as a lumber grader now, trying to accumulate enough money to pay for the log cabin he intends to build next summer on his land on Trembleur Lake. He enjoys sharing food and ideas and accepts a wide variety of people with ease. Last night he came for dinner, and we talked about buying lumber and house designs.

From John we learned of a couple who are working this winter as the caretakers of Culchunoe Island, a large resort not far from Tachie. According to John, Wally Monkman and his wife, Joyce Webb, extended, in the early fall, an open invitation to visitors from town, assuming that in such isolation they would enjoy even unknown callers.

Bob and I have determined today to snowshoe out across the frozen lake to see them. We would like to get farther down the lake again, closer to our own island—as if that will bring closer the day when we can be there again. We will drive down the Tachie road to Caesar's Point, a bulge of land four miles from Sunnyside. The Culchunoe dock is located there, on the mainland closest to the island. A missionary couple have made their home on the point; we are counting, therefore, on the driveway being plowed.

➤➤➤❮❮❮

It is. When it opens out into a large yard, we circle and park. Two cabins stand at the back of the clearing. They are very handsome cabins, not large but well proportioned, with solid, sheltering porches, big front windows and attractive siding—thick, rough-cut, vertical boards. Under each porch is stored split stovewood, and between the two cabins there's a mountain of unsplit wood. An unusually large and solid outhouse has been built in the woods, and a shed-garage in much the same style as the house stands in the drive. There is a tractor with a plow, a new pickup truck, and a huge boat in drydock.

A man appears shortly after we park, from the lakeshore behind the boat. He has been chopping a hole in the ice in order to pump some water up to his holding tank. He introduces himself as Flay Walker. A serious-looking man, handsome and muscular, his earflaps pulled down over his ears, his boots neatly tied all the way to the top. No one to try and con. We explain that we are going over to see the caretakers of Culchunoe and ask if it will be all right to leave the truck in his yard for the afternoon.

"Certainly," he says. "Wally and Joyce will be glad of some company; they haven't been out in three weeks now, not since the lake froze, and Wally is such a gregarious man." He pauses and for the first time smiles, which transforms his face. "He likes to tell stories. He'll be glad of a new audience."

We get our snowshoes out of the back of the car and, putting them on, say goodbye to Flay, who goes directly back to his job of getting the pump going. He works on the metal with his bare hands, adjusting the carburetor, filling the gas tank.

The wind is blowing on the lake, whipping the top layers of snow into funnels and ragged sheets of white dust. I am glad that I am wearing my orange down parka, but despite it, the trip seems long and chilly. On a lake or a desert the distances are greater than they seem. You can see everything, which distorts your judgment; in the woods you never expect to see something a mile ahead of you.

Just when I am beginning to wish that we hadn't come, we hear the sound of a snowmobile—an old snowmobile by the rough sound of the engine—coming around the point. After traveling along the shore for a while it starts to circle, stopping suddenly as it comes to a position from which we are visible. Then it roars toward us, coughing and vibrating, and stops five feet away. A short, broad figure, bundled in a huge green parka and baggy pants, jumps off it and hurries over. He throws one arm around my shoulder, urging me toward the snowmobile.

"Well! It's really lucky that I turned around like that and saw you. I wasn't going to go this way at all, but then I decided that I might as well take a look at the ice; we haven't taken the snowmobile over since freeze-up; and then I saw you. I'm so glad. Come on, come on." He talks nonstop in a deep, vibrant voice. "You can sit behind me, and you can ride in the sleigh; I just finished the sleigh, for Joyce, but you can try it out. There's even a blanket, see, in that little box on the end. Well! How nice that you could come. We're just about to have lunch." I grab him around the waist, and we all rattle off to the island, tipping over sideways once or twice, righting the machine with much breathless excitement, and arriving at the shore in a state of high anticipation, since Wally has been shouting over his shoulder the whole way about what we will have for lunch. I keep racking my brains to think where I might have met him; he seems to know me so well, and I can't remember ever having seen him before.

As we tear up to the cabin—Wally with one arm around my shoulder but with equal concern for Bob—I get my first good look at his face. It is a heavy, swarthy face, full of pleasant wrinkles and thick, dark hair. Wally looks to be about fifty-five or sixty, but he is bursting with health, and his eyes dominate his face, wells of laughter and interest. He looks like a voyageur.

The island on which Culchunoe Lodge is located is large, spanning twenty acres or more. There are several buildings on it. A main lodge is sprinkled with obligatory skins and bear rugs and Indian artifacts made by the Haidas on the coast, but never dreamed of by the Carrier tribe who resided in this region. A huge game room with windows on three sides dominates the southern cliff, its bright-red deck extending over the rock into the open air. Eight motel-like cabins furnished with motel furniture run down the beach. Sheds, boathouses, machines, boats—including a converted landing boat (the whole bow a huge gangplank which drops onto the beach) for taking the lodge jeep over to the mainland to pick up moose for its clients—all of it makes the island look like a small community. But from October to May there is no one there except the caretaker or caretakers—this year Wally and Joyce. Their only duties are eating and sleeping on the island, in the small cabin built for the help.

We go into the cabin, stripping off coats and boots by the door. It is deliciously warm and smells of good cooking. When I sit down in the rocking chair, Wally feels my socks to be sure they are dry. He introduces us to Joyce, a tired-looking woman with a tense face and nervous hands, but intelligent eyes. She is Wally's opposite, as closed as he is open. A life with such a dynamo would be likely to have that effect, I think.

While Wally improves on the soup, adding spices, ketchup, and bouillon, preparing sandwiches and cutting carrots, mixing up "a little cake— I so rarely have a chance to bake for visitors now," with quick, deft hands, broad and powerful strokes, he talks. He has not yet bothered to ask who we are or why we are here, but we are friends on sight.

"It is so good that you could come," he says, as if we had accepted an invitation to lunch. "It is so boring here, with nothing to do. I told them to give me a list of repairs they wanted done, or cleaning jobs, split wood, whatever, but nothing, they said, nothing to do. So I have been making jobs for myself. I made . . ." he lifts his finger and grins mischievously, "I made a big wooden box and painted it blue, and then I filled it with little chocolate candies. Next summer in my cabin on McLeod Lake I want to get the little girls who live around to help me gather rocks for my terraces. I will give them—a candy for every rock! Here, come, I will show you."

We walk back into the bedroom, and he pulls out of the closet an enormous wooden box, which is filled to the brim with round chocolate balls, homemade. I hardly think he will need such inducements to get the little girls to help him, but taste one and decide they won't hurt.

Joyce lays the table for lunch and we sit around it. The soup is exquisite, delicate as oriental broth.

"I enjoy cooking," says Wally. "Ever since I was a camp cook in Manitoba, I love to see people eat what I cook. Here, have some more," passing me fresh rolls, which I have not even noticed him preparing.

"Oh, so you are a cook?" asks Bob.

"Good Lord, no, not any more than anything else. Although I do have this idea to start a restaurant. It would serve only food that the voyageurs ate at the trading posts in the 1700s. Sherry. Sherry would be the only drink! Madeira is what they always drank. And whiskey, of course. No cocktails. No piped music. Big hand-hewn plank tables; and the food would all be, oh, beaver tail and sweetmeats. Everyone who came would have to wear a costume of the period; they could put it on in an anteroom." He explains his idea in detail.

"But no, if I am anything, it is a shipbuilder by trade." Listening to his tales, I think that if anything, he is a storyteller by trade. In the thirties he worked for the Hudson's Bay Company, at a bush trading post in northern Manitoba. He traded with the Indians for the furs they brought in, living alone in a cabin in the woods, and trapping himself in his spare time.

"I earned twenty-five dollars a week doing that. Twenty-five dollars a week, and in the Depression! Whenever I did go into town, I would look around me at the poor devils who lived there, sweeping up the sawdust in saloons, for pennies, and I felt so damn lucky. Out in the bush with no one to answer to, the great world around me, fresh air, and one hundred dollars a month which I had nowhere to spend. What a job! Of course I had to deal with the Indians. It wasn't so hard in those days, since they weren't permitted to buy liquor. But still they always needed credit, and if you gave them credit once, they were your friend for life—which meant they felt that they could always get credit. Still, it was a hell of a time I had, and I made a lot of friends. Legalizing liquor for the Indians has been the ruin of them."

As we finish lunch, listening to Wally, Joyce gets up to put on the coffee and finds that the water barrel is almost empty. Wally springs to his feet, and taking up two buckets he goes onto the porch. There hangs a beautiful old-fashioned yoke, padded with green velvet.

"I made this last week," he chuckles. "I carved it with my penknife; it was all that I had. It works pretty well though," he calls over his shoulder as he hurries down to the water hole.

While we drink the coffee and eat the homemade maple cake, Wally talks some more. He was a demolitions expert during the war. He has built wooden sailboats from scratch, and is presently building a birch-bark canoe, his third, in the exact manner of the voyageurs, a huge north canoe that will carry twelve people or more. His first one was bought by a museum in Vancouver, which paid four thousand dollars for it. During the sixties he ran a canoe-tripping outfit on the Nahannie River. He likes to write about the explorers of British Columbia—David Thompson, Simon Fraser, Alexander MacKenzie—and knows as much about the early forts as any book. His grandfather fought with Riel, and there is a pass in the Rockies named after him, Monkman Pass.

In the course of the conversation, the dishes are washed, the floor swept, and the pet crow invited into the room and introduced. The crow's name is Charlie, and Wally found him, wounded, on the Tachie Road. Someone had shot him through the wing with a .22, and Wally nursed him back to health. He can fly now, but he likes to stay around and be fed and pampered. He will sit on Joyce's hand, but he dives at Bob and me with a malevolent glare in his eyes. He does not like visitors.

During a lull in the conversation, caused by Wally stoking the fire, I suggest that it is time we got back.

"Oh, no! It will be warm again soon. I bet you are cold, that's the trouble! Besides there is plenty of daylight left. And I will take you back on the snowmobile when you have to go. The ice is thick enough now. The ice is thick enough, Joyce," he repeats, turning to Joyce. "We can go into town tomorrow if you like.

"You know, when I am cold, I sweat like a pig. I simply pour sweat when I am chilled. This has been true ever since I can remember. I don't know why. I have to sleep with a twenty-pound down sleeping bag, or I sweat. I take the sleeping bag everywhere; even when I had to go to the hospital, I took it. At first nurses wouldn't let it in the door; they said they had plenty of blankets; but when they saw that every morning the sheets were soaking, and even the mattress was wet, they decided maybe I could have it after all." He chuckles.

When we finally do leave, Wally takes us back by snowmobile, bundled to the teeth. It is just getting dark, and the headlights wobble on the snow ahead. When we arrive at the shore, we hug him and unload our snowshoes from the sled; he turns the snowmobile around in a wide circle and bobs off into the dusk.

->>><<<-

Bob and I go up to the Walkers' house to thank them for letting us leave the truck in their yard, and to let them know we are back. The lights in the kitchen are on, and a woman in a rose-colored dressing gown comes to the door when we knock. She has a finely featured face, with high cheekbones and gentle eyes. Her skin is very white, her hair carefully combed and put up. It is difficult to guess her age. Fifty-five, perhaps?

"You must be Bob and Liz!" she says warmly. "Flay told me you had gone over to the island. I'm Nadine, by the way," she adds in a high, girlish voice. Her accent might be midwestern.

At Nadine's invitation, we sit down at the kitchen table. She pours two huge, steaming mugs of coffee and sets them on the table, with cream and sugar and a plate of lemon cake. She pours herself a smaller cup and sits down also, smiling.

"I drink so much coffee," she says. "I'm trying to cut down. When the Indian boys come over, I drink and drink. Have some cake," she urges Bob, who needs little encouragement. She pats the plate forward with a fine, delicate hand, the wedding ring and diamond slightly loose on her finger. Her eyes are merry, and the very way she moves her shoulders and her arms expresses welcome and interest, contentment in her life.

Bob and I both take cake and mumble praises of it, intently polite.

"I like that cake myself," says Nadine, nodding emphasis to the statement. "And it's so easy to make, really. You just add lemon pudding to the mix. Isn't that easy? Most people like this kind."

"You said 'when the Indian boys come over,' and Ted Martin told us you were missionaries. What exactly do you do?" I ask.

Nadine laughs a little, leaning forward. "Well, sometimes I wonder myself. Flay is a minister, you know. We had a parish in Washington, and Flay decided he wasn't doing all he could there. For years we'd been sending stuff up to the Indians here—clothing and bedding, mostly—through Outreach. Finally we decided to try and move up. And here we are."

"But I thought the Indians were Catholic."

"Oh yes, that's true, and we don't do what you might call regular missionary work. It's more like family help." Nadine emphasizes certain syllables in a long drawl, cuts other syllables short, speaks both high and low.

"We talk to Indians a lot, to help them give up liquor and take the pledge. We've had fair success so far; Flay has."

"How long have you been here, then?" Bob asks.

"Oh, almost three years now. We moved in the summer, and lived in a little trailer while Flay built the first cabin. We had some help that summer, from people in the parish, but most of the time we've been here alone." Nadine has good reason to be proud of the work they've done.

"You've got a beautiful place here," Bob says.

"I know," she agrees without affectation. "Flay just finished painting the kitchen cabinets. He finished them two years ago, but he just painted them last week. Isn't that funny? They're a pretty yellow now, though." They are—rich and creamy, without tinny tones.

The door opens and Flay comes in, his face touched with pink, not the bright pink of bitter cold but the rosiness of health. He kisses Nadine and greets us gravely, then, smiling asks how we liked Wally. He puts his arm around Nadine's shoulder while she leans against it. It is warming just to be in their presence while they touch each other. If Nadine speaks, Flay watches her protectively. When Flay speaks, Nadine tilts her head ever so slightly to one side.

Under Flay's careful questioning we explain about the island, our plans and problems. Unasked, he offers to let us park the truck at their house when we return to the island. Since in the winter an engine left unused for long will rarely start when you want it to, Flay will start the truck from time to time for us. Nadine adds that that way they can keep track of us, also. We accept the offer with pleasure.

Reluctantly we decide that it's time to leave. Bumping into each other by the door, Bob and I put on our boots once more. Flay and Nadine follow as far as the edge of the porch, where they stand next to a log post, arms linked behind each other's backs, both of them waving farewell.

→≫ (7) ≪←

It's a very cold morning. The truck broke down last week. It died, completely, and with little hope of salvation. Since we have had no vehicle, I have been skiing to work across the lake—only a mile and a half direct, though five miles by the road. Every morning I put on my woolen trousers and parka and overmitts and goggles, and wrap a scarf around my nose, and then set off on skis, with a pack containing the day's offering to the gods of respectability—a limp cotton dress still smelling of cigarette smoke from the day or week before. I arrive at the bank door with my hat and collar, eyebrows and nostrils rimmed with hoarfrost. Pulling off my goggles, I ring the bell, and the manager opens the door for me and backs away in something like trepidation as I walk in steaming from the fifty-below-zero weather. The morning ski is invigorating, but to no purpose. The evening ski is bliss. The lake booms, the snow crackles, and the stars are already flaring out overhead.

This morning we are late. I stuff toast into my mouth while I slice more bread for sandwiches, and the water almost runs over in the sink while I cut some nearly frozen cheese, breaking and splintering it across the table. The thermometer reads fifty below again and there is a heavy frozen mist above the lake. As I dash to turn the water off, knocking the bread and cheese to the floor, it suddenly strikes me that I cannot go to work today. One more day at the bank and I will be ready to blow it up.

I pick up the phone and dial the bank. The manager answers, smooth as linoleum.

"This is Elizabeth Arthur," I say, like a signature. "I'm sick."

"Oh?" he says, questioning. "You're sick?"

"Yes, I'll have to stay out today."

"Oh. Please pardon my asking, but I'm sure you understand that we have to find out just what you are sick . . . um . . . of, so to speak?"

I think: I'm sick of you, Mr. Stevenson, and your respectable bank. I say, improvising wildly:

"Well, I started out skiing this morning, and I got about two hundred yards out onto the lake, and suddenly I felt so weak I almost fell down— I had to jab my poles in to one side and lean on them, and then there was a kind of darkness for a second, so I did some breathing exercises, but the air was so cold that it hurt my lungs, and so I came back to the house and got into bed. I don't really know what it is. Better put down 'general malaise.' "

Sounding thoroughly confused, he thanks me and hangs up.

Bob comes in from the bedroom, and says, "That was terrific. I wish I could lie that well." He tosses his Takla helmet onto the couch and picks up a piece of bread.

"Try it. It's fun."

Bob shoves some cheese shreds out of the way and dials the mill.

"Hello," he says. "This is Robert Gathercole, veneer plant, and I'd like you to report to my foreman that I'm sick today." There is a pause, then he says, "Yes, today, and probably tomorrow too. I don't know, maybe well into next week. In fact, let's just say that I've quit. That's right. Right. Robert Gathercole. Quit. Thank you. Yes, you can send it out anytime. Goodbye."

There is a long silence, as Bob stares out the window. Finally I say, "That was some lie. Do you think she knew you were kidding?"

"Hell, I doubt it. I did it pretty well, didn't I?"

"Bob, you just quit." I feel amazingly calm.

"You're right."

"If you call back right away, she'll just think you're nuts, and you'll still have a job."

"I don't want a job. I feel better right this second than I have felt for months. I really didn't mean to quit, you know, it just popped out. I'm glad it did."

"Well, what are we going to do now? I mean, there may be nothing nicer than quitting that conveyor belt, but what precisely do you intend to do now?" I listen to my own voice, wondering at the question even as I ask it.

"We've got over nine hundred dollars saved. Let's go back to the island."

The island. Snow covered, quiet. Wood smoke rising into the still air with the smell of celebration. Looking at the trees three days after a thaw, when little blobs of snow still wrap themselves around the twigs like pieces of putty, or little hands. Watching the birds eating crumbs. Frying moose steaks. Making love under down quilts. Building.

"Let's go. You're right. Let's go. Let's go now."

→→>‹‹‹←

We didn't leave that day, but we began preparing for departure. Bob built cabinets, a table, and a bed; we gathered food and supplies, a stove, firebrick, cement. We even found someone to fix the truck. We arranged to have Bruce Russel, the owner of the only snowcat in town, transport the supplies across the frozen lake. Today we followed him when he took them as far as Tachie on his flat-bed truck. We unloaded the materials, Sheetrock and all, into the drifts of new snow on the lakeshore. It took up most of the afternoon. When we finished securing them with plastic, it was already growing dark.

On the way back to town Bob and I decided to stop by at the Walkers', so we let Bruce drive on ahead while we turned down the winding road to Caesar's Point. When we arrived, Flay and Nadine were starting an early dinner, which they invited us to share. They are generous people. Already I feel as if we've been long acquainted; I could come to feel toward them as toward a second set of parents. When we left the Walkers, Nadine renewed Flay's offer to let us leave the truck at their house for the winter.

We headed for the Fort again in the black darkness, the monotonous road passing like a reel of blackened film. When we reached the main road to the Fort, we stopped. A huge line of cars and trucks, twenty or thirty at least, was backed up the hill and made it clear there had been an accident ahead. Turning off the engine, we walked down the road to see what was up. A white sedan, crumpled, lay directly across the road, and there was shattered glass everywhere. The car had collided with Bruce Russel's truck. He was unhurt, and his flat-bed had only a dent in the left front fender. The driver of the sedan was dead. The body lay under a heavy woolen blanket, beside the road.

People around us were talking, new people constantly added to the crowd of bystanders, trying to find out what had happened and who the victim was.

"I heard it was John Prince," said an Indian in a low tone to a new arrival. "He was drunk, and driving on the wrong side of the road."

"John Prince? I thought he took the pledge."

"He did. Troubles lately, though."

"Anyone know where his wife is?"

"She was staying in town with her daughter for a while. Maybe she doesn't know."

She did know, however. While we stood there, a woman ran out of the darkness on the far side of the road, panting and gasping, apparently having run the distance from town, over a mile, when she heard the news. The R.C.M.P. pushed her roughly back and bundled her into a police car and continued to stretch strings across the road at various angles and shoot flash pictures of the scene.

I was glad that John Prince had been covered with a blanket, and that all I could see on the ground next to the wreck was the gentle suggestion of a man. That way, I could remember him as I had seen him, folding his trap line permit and putting it into his wallet, carefully holding his cap in both hands.

Bruce Russel had disappeared. When the police finally opened the road, we went back to the cabin to do the last packing and called him at his home. He was there. He said that he would meet us in Tachie in the morning.

-->>)<<(--

Today, yesterday's drifts have shifted and changed. The piles of lumber and furniture, Sheetrock and stovepipe, have been slightly obscured, although there is no new snow. The materials are piled in front of Martin Felix's shed; in twelve hours of snow drift they have acquired a resemblance to the old shed. They have the same air of sagging permanence.

It is ten degrees Fahrenheit, which seems warm, since the sun is shining and I am warmly bundled. I have on my long red cotton underwear, a pair of heavy woolen trousers and my nylon wind pants; two pairs of woolen socks, rubber boots with thick felt liners and gaiters; three sweaters of graduated bulk and a down parka; a woolen hat and down hood; two pairs of woolen mitts and nylon overmitts. Bruce arrived wearing a pair of blue jeans, leather boots, a light jacket, and leather gloves.

I have noticed that the Indians around here seem almost inured to cold. The children play on the lake in the coldest weather, gloveless and hatless, and their parents ride snowmobiles at fifty miles an hour with nothing but a pair of ear muffs on their heads. Many of the whites who have lived here for a long time imitate these habits of dress. Perhaps they are similarly inured. Or perhaps it is a defiant gesture, a macho thing. But Bruce looks cold in his sparse clothing.

The snowcat is bright orange and looks like something which has escaped from a ski slope—a mixture of a snowmobile and a tank, finished in Disney colors. It pulls a sled which is no wider than the tracks of the cat, since the sled has to follow the cat's trail through deep, unyielding powder snow, and possibly through slush, the bane of travelers on the lake in winter. The load of snow on the lake acts as a warm blanket for the ice; the ice melts on the top, and the water combines with the bottommost layer of snow to form slush. Bruce seems to have no doubts about his machine's ability to get through slush, though he's a bit worried about the thickness of the ice. The many snowmobile trails leading away from Tachie reassure him.

The sled is loaded with all the component parts of the kitchen table, the cabinets, and the bed. Four oak chairs are tied securely on, and the whole pile is crisscrossed with one-inch rope. The boxes of nails and food and the packs and bedding are stuffed into the cab of the cat, and Bob and Bruce climb in after them. I remain behind this trip, to lighten the load and increase the breathing space. The engine revs to a start; the machine jerks once and then moves effortlessly forward, following and widening the snowmobile trail over which the Portage Indians travel to and from their village in the winter.

I drive the truck to the Walkers', leave the key with Flay, and walk back to Tachie along the road. After what seems like an endless time, the snowcat appears in the distance, crawling slowly across the lake. I greet the men with great cheer when they hop down from the cab, but they have little to say. Yes, the island is still there. No, the slush isn't too bad.

It takes four trips to get all the materials out. The day passes slowly, the hours yielding with infinite reluctance to the passage of the sun. But the cold increases, and by the time the sled is loaded for the last trip, and I climb into the cab with Bundy and Boots—both of them disgruntled—it is almost dark. The deadly thin light of the winter dusk is all around us.

We do not sink into the snow as I had imagined we would. From the inside of the cab the cat seems to float upon the pure white surface like a boat. It gets harder and harder to see through the misted windows of the cab, and the vibration is numbing to the senses. I sit in the back, where no heat from the engine penetrates. Slowly I lose all feeling in my feet, and then my hands grow stiff.

As we bob along, I watch the back of Bruce's head. Every once in a while he lifts a flask to his mouth and drinks. The red cap swings upward, and then back down again. He looks small and thin, his hands veined and white gripping the heavy black steering wheel. I assume he has been drinking on and off all day, probably for the momentary rush of warmth the liquor brings. Although he still seems perfectly capable of running the machine, his judgment has become somewhat impaired; just off the American Islands the slush is bad, but a fine trail, triply packed, leads out of the strait in the direction of our island. For some reason Bruce now decides the trail is unsafe, and we veer abruptly to the left and head into the fresh powder snow of a long and wide side bay. Perhaps he feels safer sticking close to shore.

I breathe on the frosted glass and peer through the tiny opening. The treads of the machine are sinking into deep slush, and the sled is piling higher and higher with wet snow. We move forward more and more slowly until the treads are completely obscured. The machine is incredibly strong—it keeps moving forward despite the load. I lean forward and tell Bruce what is happening in the rear. With a little urging from Bob, Bruce decides to turn around. The sled is by this time firmly jammed. The short stop is long enough to freeze it into place. So we all jump off into the night and the slush to get it unwedged. It is much colder, and I am soaked to the knees.

Gradually, the cat gets turned around and heads for the packed trail.

I can no longer use my hands without great effort and shooting pains. They are useless for the difficult job of putting my mittens back on. I nod as we rock along, sleepy, waiting for an end.

We reach the island suddenly, the headlights catching a wide area of crisp, circular tracks. The snow seems particularly deep on the beach, and as I jump from the cab, I sink up to my waist. I blunder around, trying to help unload, but Bob and Bruce have got an efficient system by now, which leaves me standing looking on. At last the sled is clear. Bruce takes one more swig from his flask, urinates into the snow, and leaves, while Bob goes up to the house. I watch the snowcat move out of sight. The course it follows seems blundering and erratic. The headlights jerk and dangle, now visible, now gone. Finally the lights blink out for the last time, and I am left alone with the night full of stars and the island.

It doesn't seem important to get up to the house. It looks terribly far away, and once I start to walk through the waist-deep snow, it seems even farther. I sit down on a box to rest. The night is all there is, the heavy, dark silence and the cold. It has pinned me to its surface.

After a time, I look down on the box upon which I sit. It contains fresh vegetables, and the fact that if they freeze they will be ruined penetrates my shrouded mind. I pick the box up in my arms and head for the house, sliding backwards in the snow with every step. At the top of the first rise my left knee slips and jerks beneath me. It is badly sprained, wooden, but it doesn't hurt at all.

The snow is odorless, and the night extinguishes all sound. At last there is the back door, where the light from the lamps shines yellow into the night, and the wood smoke gives the air some substance. The door to the cookstove is open, revealing coals of red and flames of golden yellow. Bob is sticking insulation into the kitchen walls and stapling plastic across the ceiling. I sit down on the box of vegetables and lose the remaining pinpoint of awareness. Later my sleeping bag appears. In the morning all the vegetables have frozen on the floor.

→≫ (8) ≪←

The snow falls outside with gentle apology. Everything is silent save for the buzz of the chain saw on the west end of the island, where Bob is cutting down standing deadwood. From my perch on the newly completed bed I can look out through the dining-room window to the lake below, and watch the snow falling through the trees. We set up the bed this morning; it went together easily, each part fitting into place just as I had imagined it would. The four sides are made of furniture-grade plywood, and as I drop my hand over the edge, I can feel it, very smooth and straight. The end of the bed has built-in cupboard doors, so that it is possible to get at the storage space beneath. The mattress is a firm piece of foam. We screwed it all together, and then with great ceremony spread the blue Indian-print bedspread over the mattress and tossed on our pillows and quilts. Bob picked me up and tossed me on too. Setting up the bed was our real housewarming. I still feel warm, comforted, tucked in.

When Bob saw me naked, he said, "You look so much better here than you did in town. You look great."

"Are you sure it's me? And not just the fact that *you* feel better now?" I said. "We've only been here four days."

"No, no, it's not me. You really do look great—so much more relaxed and sexy. You look thinner too, and your skin has more color. I'm glad we decided to come back."

"Me too. You don't look bad yourself. It must be the house," I said.

"It is," said Bob.

The bed stands now in the corner where the dining-room table will eventually go, when we have a bedroom we can heat. Right now we have closed off this kitchen/dining-room area of the house with plastic, and it keeps the heat in well, though once in a while cold drafts whistle through from the living room. We'll start with finishing the walls and ceilings here, and work outward. The space is already cluttered with Sheetrock, lumber, food, and railroad ties brought up from the beach.

➤➤➤≪≪≪

Today, Bob is starting on the panelling of the walls. I am sitting on the bed, resting my sprained knee. While Bob saws and nails and measures, I read aloud. We're reading *The Complete Sherlock Holmes*, and have started on "The Sign of the Four." Pauses for the sawing only add to the suspense of the story. Whether the reading is in any way helpful to the work, like the chants of the Volga boatmen, I don't know—but the ship-lap panelling is going up quickly. We tried to get tongue-and-groove lumber for the panelling but were quickly forced to abandon that fantasy. "There's no demand for tongue-and-groove anymore," they said, looking at me in wonder. In fact, we cleaned Stuart Lake Lumber out of their last eight-inch ship-lap; they haven't run any off for eight months. "Why don't you get wallboard?" was the unspoken question when we put in our order.

The pine looks clean and elegant, not marred by its imperfections. Light and smooth, the boards go up quickly. The smell of the pine as it dries is quite unlike the smell of pine as it burns in the stove—but they share a similar warm essence.

It seems to me now as if this house has been here for a long time, invisible, hidden, just waiting to be helped into the world. It goes up rapidly around me, becoming what I have so often imagined it could be—what it has, in fact, been, in my mind. When I designed the house, I wanted it to be food for our life—a space which we could expand into, like bread dough in a stone bowl. Spaces affect us as much as we affect spaces. Like a series of Chinese boxes, spaces open and close around us—skin, clothing, house, island, sky—and change us from the outside in.

Seeing the walls take shape around me so smoothly now is like clothing my naked body in the morning—it marks the transition between night and day. It marks an end to a long journey through darkness and dreams, and a beginning to the sunlight. Wearing this house, I will be changed. When we get the ceilings up and painted white, the house will be full of light—no dark and rustic cabin in the pines, but shining with sun and reflections of the color on the hilltop. It will be the end of a journey, and the beginning of an island life.

When I was quite small, my family lived in a Victorian gingerbread house with great high ceilings and filled with heavy furniture and books. Right next door there was a library, equally old, with even higher ceilings and many more books. It had a cupola on top, a great arched roof, and huge windows with window seats. The entranceway was a little hall lined with brass coat hooks, and usually littered with a tremendous assortment of coats and sweaters and rubber boots.

The library was my special place. My family's house was for everyday wear, but going to the library was getting dressed up. I felt toward it the way I imagine early Christians felt about their churches—a personal solicitude, a happiness intermingled with awe. Awe at the space around them and what it represented, awe at themselves for being part of it. I didn't have to do anything when I went to the library—study, take out books, or even read. I went there to absorb the space and let it absorb me. I went there just to feel good, dressed for a party and waiting for the bell to ring.

That's how I feel now, with this smoky interior around me. I'm waiting for the bell to ring. I'm sitting on the threshold between past preparations and future events and savoring the expectation and completion which meet here. It's the best feeling of all, that meeting. When you feel that, you feel your life is contained in the present moment. You feel you're in the place where you belong.

The house isn't just its design and its materials now, not just ship-lap panelling and large windows. They are only the outward symbols of a long and complex process of building. The house is an outward sign of an inward reality, our power to create the world we live in. It's that which makes so fascinating the exploration of other cabins on the lake. Like ours, they are invested with the lives of the people who built them. Each one of them is a threshold. We fashion the world, and then it holds us. It's that which makes this house a warm place for me to sit in. Like a party dress or a window seat, it's a space which defines my present and keeps it from getting away.

Of course I know the party feeling will fade, the dress will eventually become everyday wear. But right now I can sit on this high bed, blue cotton and white pine, surrounded by down quilts and books, clothed also in wood-warmth and marriage, clasping the house which is being draped around me, and there is no need to go anywhere, or think of tomorrow.

The snow falls outside with gentle apology, the green firs are sprinkled with heavy white, the trunks darken with the moisture on their crinkling bark. The squirrels chatter when Bob walks through the woods. Between the trees, out the dining-room window, I can see the snow covering the lake, the rocks and rotting logs and moss being submerged by yet another winter. No moisture drips from the trees, and the island sits like a cupped hand upon the lake. I can feel the snow heavy on my roof, the ice forming on my eaves, the winds blowing against my walls. For now, I keep them outside, while I am in. I drink a cup of cocoa and carefully line my furnace with wood.

3

BURNING

→≫ (1) ≪←

The days go by in peaceful variations. This morning I woke to hear the wolves howl. Almost asleep, I noticed the howling in the distance; when I woke again, the dawn had faded, and the day was light. I pushed open the window beside the bed, and cold, smooth air entered the house like a guarantee of the purity of the snowfall. I felt expectant; on a Saturday we might have some visitors from town.

Bob had lit the fires and was outside getting wood. He came in shortly after I woke, warmly dressed, his face pink with the cold, his arms full of split firewood, his down parka leaking feathers as he brushed against the doorframe. The stovewood dropped onto the floor with a series of dull thumps, and the reverberation, or something else, caused the cookstove to send forth a stern burst of smoke through the cracks in the plates. When I smiled, Bob pulled off his West Pac boots and came over to the bed. He was cool to the touch, and his skin smelled as clean as the air itself.

In the morning Bob worked on the panelling while I baked bread. When the six new loaves were cooling, I started on a stew. Pots were strewn about the kitchen, onion skins and potato peelings had fallen onto the floor, and the stove fire had just somehow died, when I heard a snowmobile approaching the island—very close by the time the sound was audible. We went onto the porch and peered through the trees, but couldn't see much more than you can in summer: the trees are now covered with needles of frost instead of leaves. The snowmobile came to a stop; we heard great shouts and laughs of triumph and knew it must be Wally and Joyce.

75

Wally had managed to bear a chocolate cake on a china plate all the way from Culchunoe, through who knows how many tips and stops, and he came up the path with it in one hand. He was breathing slightly hard when he got to the top of the hill, and shoving the cake into my hands he said:

"I must be getting old. I start breathing hard on a little hill like that one. We passed your island in the boat one day last fall, and after we met you, I told Joyce this must be your house, and she didn't believe me; she said she couldn't see any way up to it even, much less how two people could build it." He turned around and shouted down to Joyce, who was following him at a more reasonable pace, "It *is* theirs, Joyce!" And she nodded and smiled and waved, dressed in high black rubber boots, a man's canvas-covered parka, and a droopy wool hat, with thin, grey wool gloves on her hands. We all trooped in the back door, and to the general disarray and smell of baking was added a bundle of coats and boots and mittens and the smell of steaming wet wool. Bob got the cookstove going again, and I put on pots of coffee and tea while we got settled at the kitchen table.

Joyce remarked on the beauty of the cookstove, pulling out an English cigarette from a pack. Her blond hair was full of static electricity from the dry cold outside and the quick removal of her blue wool cap; there was some color in her cheeks, which made her look younger and more relaxed than she had the last time we met. She said she had always wanted a nice old woodstove, but she did not elaborate on the remark— Wally was cutting the cake, eager to offer it around.

After Bob and I had eaten several pieces of cake and Wally and Joyce drunk several cups of tea, Wally hopped to his feet and insisted on being taken on a tour of the house. He looked at the beginnings of the cathedral ceiling in the living room and made lugubrious remarks about the difficulty of heating all that extra space. But when we showed them the fireplace foundation, Wally was pleased.

"Not that it will give much extra heat," he said. "But it makes a room *look* so much warmer."

Back in the kitchen again Bob stoked the stove, and we continued our discussion of heating units while we waited for the stew to cook.

"You need so much wood to warm a house," said Bob, restacking some by the door.

Wally waved his hand at the oil-drum stove. "That stove throws a lot of heat, of course; it's very good, but you should have a thermostat on it; then you would have a really *efficient* system. The best heater is an Ashley. It damps itself down—Joyce and I enjoy it very much." He nodded toward Joyce for agreement, which she gave him. The tiniest of smiles tugged at her mouth.

"It is good," she agreed. "We stay warm all night long." She stubbed out her cigarette and tossed it in the fire. "Your stove is ingenious, though." She turned to Bob politely, giving him credit for the idea.

"We found that plan for an oil-drum stove in one of the Angier books," Bob said. "On building in the woods. You know them? Sometimes they're not much help, but they've got good ideas if you look for them."

"The Angiers!" said Wally. "Of course we know about them. Hudson Hope, where they lived, isn't far from McLeod Lake. But they don't live there anymore, you know. No, they moved to California years and years ago; I think they lived in B.C. for seven years. They revise all their books on the woods from a house on the Pacific Ocean." He laughed hugely. "Yes," he said, "yes, that's true," and laughed some more.

"These poor young people," he said. "They all pour up to Hudson Hope, especially Americans, hoping to find the key to the universe, all the answers, from the Angiers. One time a few years ago I met a young couple—they stayed with us for a few days—who were on their way to see the Angiers in Hudson Hope. I told them the Angiers weren't there anymore, and they said, 'Oh. Well, maybe we'll go see them anyway. We came a long way.' I couldn't convince them."

"A few days later they were back. I asked them, 'Did you find the Angiers?' They said, 'No, you were right. The people in Hudson Hope all told us they had left years ago and hadn't been back since. And do you know what one of the postmen said to us?' (All the letters, you know!) 'If you find them, tell them if they ever do come back here, we'll hang them!'" We all laughed uproariously, even Joyce.

We reflected on the extraordinary boom in books telling people how to build cabins and then how to live in them—most of the books are both outdated and deceptive. Wally was particularly virulent about books which give the impression that it is still possible to homestead in B.C., or anywhere else. He also didn't see much value in books about survival in the bush.

"Space blankets!" he said, rolling his eyes. "Flares! Useless, perfectly useless. Heads, that's what people need, brains! Once a government team hired me to organize their living arrangements for a trip to the edge of the barrens. They were studying caribou in winter. We were going to stay in some old trappers' cabins on the edge of the forest, and went in little planes which could only hold so much. When we got the planes down, it was fifty-five below; they all stood around, poking at their gear. 'First!' I told them, 'the propane tanks! Then the stoves!' We unloaded them, rushed them in, set them up, lit them. Ahhh! Then they could all function again. Surprise! Not flares, brains." He threw up his hands, then took a sip of tea, his face intent on recollection. Stories followed. Bear hunting in Alaska. Ice fishing on Lake Winnipeg, where he got caught in a blizzard with his partner and spent the night on the lake, chopping holes in the ice to keep from freezing. They chopped twenty-five holes before the blizzard stopped with the dawn. Canoeing on the Nahannie River—Wally ran commercial river trips there in years past. Many stories, and the day stretched toward evening.

It's staying light longer now, but it still gets dark too early. We gave Wally and Joyce several loaves of fresh bread when they had to leave, following them down to the beach—my first trip down since I sprained my knee. Wally bundled Joyce carefully, but the snowmobile tipped over twice before they finally got off, waving and shouting over the roar of the machine, which choked and gurgled and trailed great clouds of exhaust fumes. The splendid energy of the departure made me want to move myself—an infectious restlessness drifted behind with the smoke.

By four o'clock it is dark. I light the lamps while Bob piles the dishes into the sink. The Aladdin lamps are a little tricky to light, but once warmed up they throw a soft, strong glow. I put them on the end of the table in the kitchen, and we pull two chairs up next to them and next to the stove. Bob throws open the door of the heating stove and pushes in a few more pieces of stovewood. Completely warm, we prop our feet up on sticks of spruce, and read, from time to time adjusting the lamps, or watching the coals flaring and the flames wrapping themselves around the wood. Once I hold my hand over the iron plates, to feel the heat rising like a wall of warmth.

→≫ (2) ≪←

A good stove is like the sun. It pours life into the food it touches. A wood cookfire is the local branch of the universal explosion, its rays reaching the very center of the life it sustains, the bread it causes to rise. Our wood cookstove has given strength to my cooking which it has never had before. The food prepared on it has a richer texture, a more delicate flavor, a more nourishing effect. The most important difference between a wood cookstove and most other stoves is, I think, the care which it requires: care returns itself in care. A heat which is built slowly and patiently will burn more steadily than one which is ignited in an instant. Pushing a button or tossing a match onto gasoline is easy: the energy in gas and oil lies close to the surface. The wood, which has been a shorter time growing, clutches its growth more shyly. But once you touch that growth, it spends itself with radiance.

I like the stove because I can cook so well with it. I like it also because of its history, and I like it, finally, because it was so hard to get it here.

The stove was made in 1930. Somewhere in the intervening years it lost its water reservoir, but otherwise it is intact. The doors on the warming ovens and the main oven are enameled in white, and they do not lie flat, but curve outwards, delicately swelling. Grey bundles of wheat are etched into the white enamel, and the words HOME COMFORT are written in flowery letters across the oven door, surrounded by a wreath of wheat. The rest of the stove is enameled in salt-and-pepper grey. The cast-iron lids are pitted with oxidation, proof of their long years of use.

We were lucky to find the stove. In the north, wood cookstoves are not left outside to rust in fields or barns. Certainly the rising cost of energy is part of the reason, and some people just find woodstoves aesthetically pleasing, here as everywhere. But there are many cabins and houses which use woodstoves as their sole means of preparing food and heating simply because wood is available outside the door, while propane or gas would have to be transported for many inconvenient miles. Woodstoves make sense for remote locations.

So we were lucky to find such a special stove. On a trip to town in the summer, I looked over the classified ads in the *Caledonia Courier* and came across an advertisement for a diverse lot: several mattresses, a steel bathtub, baby clothes, and a woodstove. There was no phone number, just an address in Vanderhoof, forty miles south of the Fort.

Now "a woodstove" can mean almost anything. It can be an airtight heater which has warped and melted into near uselessness; it can be an oil drum which has been converted into a heating stove; it can be an Ashley thermostatic heater; or it can be a cookstove. Considering the other items advertised for sale, there was little chance that the woodstove would be what we wanted. But we needed something to cook on pretty badly, so we decided to go investigate.

The place was hard to find. We stopped for directions twice, and after a second trip down a heavily rutted dirt road east of Vanderhoof, we were ready to pack it in, when we emerged into a clearing which had been ripped out of the woods in a burst of furious energy. Stumps riddled the ground; ruts and hollows defined it. In the center stood a log building, which explained the stumps. It was the simplest log structure that can be made. In the side walls the logs were placed so that all the wide ends lay together in front and all the thin ends lay together at the back. This made the building about four feet higher in the front than in the back, and provided a natural slant upon which to construct a shed roof. The roof was made of unpeeled poles which jutted over both walls in broad, though leaky-looking, eaves.

The yard was filled with a miscellaneous collection of machines and animals. One old VW van had been placed on blocks, the four wheels still lying on the ground nearby. An ancient pickup truck was hitched to a grey wooden trailer, on which rested a white enamel sink and several lengths of iron pipe. A small, rusted cookstove leaned against a tree stump.

The moment we drove into the yard, it erupted with life. A large black retriever rushed up to the truck, barking fiercely. Five goats, most of them wearing bells, bleated and ran about in a frenzy of excitement, and three children emerged from the house to stare at us from a distance. A cat, after bleakly observing this confusion from his perch on top of the VW van, jumped off and departed for the woods.

When I got out of the truck, the dog sniffed at me once and then transferred his attention to Bundy, who was coming into heat, but the goats seemed unduly interested in me. Their heavy teats sagging with milk, they pushed against me and butted each other, making it impossible to move. Eventually the eldest child, a girl with straight brown hair and thick glasses, detached herself from her brothers and called the goats by name. They herded off toward her, and we were free to negotiate the set of boards which bridged the muddy puddles in the front yard. We arrived at the house as a few drops of rain started to fall, and asked the girl if her parents were at home.

Her face serious, intent on being polite to strangers, she responded in one long sentence. Her mother had gotten a ride to town and her dad was out hunting, but they would both be back soon and would we like to come inside and have some coffee? It is a rule of hospitality in this part of the world that you offer coffee to whoever comes to your door. So we went inside with the children, the girl directing operations, sending her two brothers off to chop some stovewood and get a bucket of water.

The inside of the house fulfilled the expectations aroused by the exterior. It was dark. The ceiling was low and sagged with black polyethylene, which had been stapled in to keep the insulation up against the roof poles. There was a table made of rough boards standing in front of the only window. Some wooden boxes turned on end served for chairs. A corner was hung with cloth that obviously concealed a sleeping area. Right in the center of the one large room, though, in the place of honor, was the HOME COMFORT, the door to the firebox open to reveal the glow of a deep bed of coals. When I told the girl what we had come for, she led me over to the stove and pointed out its excellent features. I asked her at one point how old she was, and she said "eleven" without interrupting the flow of her narrative. The door opened and the two brothers entered, the younger one, no more than seven, lugging a bucket of water, and the older one with an armload of wood. The girl sternly directed each of them to place his load down next to the stove, and then sent the wood carrier out for more wood.

While she stoked the stove, filled the kettle and set it on the stove, and took a cup of coffee out of a tin canister, the girl introduced herself as Alison, and her brothers as Joey and David. When the coffee had been tossed into the kettle, she offered to show us her rabbits.

I expected to go outside to a hutch somewhere, but Alison reached under the cookstove and pulled out a cardboard shoebox filled with cotton. Six tiny blobs of bare pink flesh nestled in it. Bob asked if he could hold one, and Alison scooped one gently out and put it in his palm.

"My dad thinks they are three days old," she said. "He killed the mother yesterday, and she was milky, so he looked for the nest and found all these rabbits. They don't have any hair on them yet, see, and their eyes aren't open." She pulled an eyedropper from the box and began to try and feed one of the tiny creatures, but most of the milk seemed to be running down its chest. I felt, though, that if anyone could keep them alive, Alison would do it.

While we were looking at the baby rabbits, Alison's father came back, with several grouse dangling from his belt. He greeted each of the children by name, and then said hello to us, while Alison explained that we had come to look at the stove. A slow-moving man, he leaned his shotgun against the iron bathtub next to the door and invited us to sit down.

"That's a beautiful stove you have there," said Bob. "Why are you selling it?"

Alison's father thought for a minute and then spoke. "We're moving on. We're going to the prairies. Didn't do so good here, with the land. We sold it for a good price; a man from town's going to put a house trailer here. The government in Alberta'll help us get started there."

As he spoke, his children sat by quietly, listening and looking at the rabbits. Once in a while the youngest boy, Joey, reached out to stroke one, carefully.

"So you're not going to take much with you?" asked Bob.

"Nope. Trying to sell everything, so's we can travel light. When we moved down here from Alaska, we brought a lot of things with us, and with the children, it made it hard. This time, we'll go light."

"It's too bad you've got to sell the stove, though," I said. "That's a really unusual stove."

"It is. A good stove. My wife'll be sorry to see it go."

"How much are you asking for it?" I said.

"Whatever we can get, I guess." He smiled. "We got some people looked at it already—the ones that run that secondhand shop in Vanderhoof—and they offered $150 for it. You pay more and it's yours."

I offered him $155 and he accepted. "Yes, that would be fine." He nodded once. I got the impression that he didn't want to sell it to a secondhand shop. The only problem with selling it to us was that he couldn't leave his wife without a stove for the week before they left for Alberta. It wouldn't be fair to ask her to cook over a fire, with the children. Could we come back for it next Sunday?

We said we couldn't, that we lived about seventy miles away on an island. He accepted that without comment, and then said he didn't like to leave it in the house until we could pick it up, because you never knew what might happen—someone might steal the lids, or even the whole stove, when there was no one there. He thought a little, and then said he would leave the stove at a friend's house in town. They could keep it in their garage until we got a chance to come for it.

I wrote out a check and thanked him. I said to please tell his wife I would take care of the stove. He nodded, and the whole family trooped out to see us off, the dog and the goats as well. We all negotiated the mud by way of the wooden boards—even the goats.

They stood in silence, watching us leave. Bob wished them luck in Alberta. Alison smiled then. Her father, his dark eyes fixed on Bob from a distance, answered that he thought they would do well there, with a lot of open country around them. Alison waved as we drove away.

No wonder I trust the stove. Not the Razzamatazz New Self-Cleaning Super-Plated Whiz Machine. The Home Comfort.

→≫ (3) ≪←

Tonight is lovely, so calm and still I can hear the snowmobiles as far away as Portage. As I take a fresh-baked cake out of the oven, the house feels warm as summer dust around me, but the night outside is warm too, laden with the expectation of new snow. Although it is February, winter seems to be receding. It is a time of quicksilver trees, and winds that are lean and smart, and blow from just around the corner, suddenly. I call Bundy, and we walk down to the lake together. I feel a special affinity with the night around me: rarefied—cool and thin, and a little taut, but with the expectation of change.

I consider the slowly falling dusk and the darkening sky, spreading the grey methodically over the world, tucking it in at the edges. I smooth out the wrinkles of the sky, privately, as I walk in silence out upon the crusty snow. I can see the lights of Tachie now, a brilliant white glow on the horizon. The village has only had electricity for the last seven years, but it seems to me the glow of light has washed away all the years of darkness. There is only light. Electric streetlamps have more power to change the deepest memories than any other shroud.

After reaching the midway point across the lake, I turn around and look at the house. I can see its shape quite well against the sky, but the yellow light which fills the picture window is the focus of my vision. Eyes meet eyes and cannot look away, drawn to light always. No matter where a light may show itself in the darkness, the mind tries to place it in perspective or to locate it in memory. So I compare the soft yellow light of the kerosene lamps in the picture window with the sterling white of the electric village. The electric light resembles the moon when it is full and just rising through the trees; the mantled kerosene resembles the sun when it throws its last long rays over the horizon on a clear autumn evening.

I do not want to go back to the house yet, and lie back, bundled in my parka, staring at the night sky. Time passes slowly; it gets no colder, but the night grows darker.

Hardly black. It is never black.

The dark night of myth is more than an absence of light. In the mind's lidded eye it seems not the lack of something but a being of its own; it has the power to drive forward and press against; it has the power to absorb. But that kind of darkness is rarely found outside the mind. When the sun has left for the day and the moon has not risen and the northern lights are rolling somewhere beyond the horizon, I can still see. Not well perhaps, but I can see. There is always starlight, even beyond the clouds.

Tonight there are no clouds. The Milky Way throws a soft and startling brightness upon the snow around me, so that it seems to glow with a radiance of its own. It is rare in winter to see such a plain sky—usually the northern lights move overhead. I can smell the woodstove from the house—so many nights I forget there is a sky here, so wrapped up am I in that drifting smoke.

Some philosophers theorize that all civilizations began with speculation about the heavens. I cannot even find the simplest constellations, though I can often make out a giant firedrake curled across the sky. It reminds me now that this galaxy is actually a great spiral of stars, a dribbling discus of energy thrown by an insouciant hand. The sun is located near the edge, and with the careless negligence of strength travels along the circuit at some incredible speed, but it takes two hundred million years to complete the circuit. How can anything that moves so fast take so long to get where it is going—which is back to where it began? And how is it that the same intelligence which has calculated the speed of the sun also invented "black night"?

My feet tingle with cold; it is time to go home. I get up, dragging my feet, walking slowly, listening to the snow crunch.

When I get to the beach, there is a turning. I smell the quick flashing wind that ripples the cold treetops, and suddenly I am bombarded with many other times and places of wind-driven trees. I stop, to breathe

the woodsmoke from the house—the wind takes it weaving over the snow, blowing to me the feeling of my other life, the life inside, the life where I am set apart. I near the steps of the darkened porch and take one last deep breath. When I open the door, the yellow lamplight is dim. I can see Bob sitting in the chair, reading, his brown curls touched with firelight. The door closes behind me, and the house burns away my coolness in a fire all its own.

-->>)<<--

We skied today, and Bob is still out on the lake. It is cold in the house; the fires have all died.

I am damp already, tired, numb. I consider the possibility of heat, but although I can summon tastes and smells, I cannot summon the feeling of heat. The wood lies by the stoves, ready to hand, but it has only a tenuous connection with the idea of fire.

The sticks are grey and lifeless. Like a poor magician, who does not believe in his ability to mystify and delight, I go through the motions of breaking tinder, and shaping it into a pile, and propping it up so that the oxygen can blow beneath it, and lighting a match to the finest twigs. For a moment the tinder does not catch. Then one short flame reaches upward, wrapping itself around a tiny twig, until the smallest match flame has become a candle flame, sucking the air. The candle burns into a torch, and the torch into a fire, the moment of each transition as imperceptible as the progress of a friendship. The growth of the heat is similarly untraceable: First there was cold, and now there is heat, shoving persistently at my hands and face like a calf nuzzling its mother for milk. For a moment I feel protected, loved, embraced. Then I notice that my back is still quite cold.

It is always a half-love when I sit before a fire. My front is warm, but my back is exposed. Like making love in a cold place, it makes me aware of my essential separateness; it reminds me that I am vulnerable—front and back, back and front—to cold, and to heat as well.

Finally the heat begins to fill the room. I take off my parka and relax in the growing warmth. My socks steam. Bob comes in the back door, knocking the snow off his boots, leaning his skis against the inside wall to melt the ice off them. "Ah, warmth," he says.

It's nothing to take for granted. Not the stove, not the wood, not the sun which made it. We have trapped the heat inside, but its natural impulse is to travel away, always away. I wonder how long it will stay, this time.

➤➤(4)≪≪

Bob works this morning on the fireplace. He has finished laying the bottom of the box; the concrete between the bricks dried yesterday. The remainder of the bricks are piled nearby on a sheet of heavy plastic, and Bob is pouring masonry cement into a tub, then adding water to it. The water contains shards of ice; the water hole was frozen solid when he went to haul the water for this batch. When it is mixed, he sets it aside, pulls a book toward him, and studies the diagram for a firebox once more. He has been convinced, like most people, that it is extremely hard to build a fireplace correctly; it cannot be as easy as it now appears.

While he studies the diagram, I watch his face and imagine I know what he is thinking. Though part of his mind is on the fireplace, part of it returns to a perusal of adventures, to past and future trips.

Maybe a river in South America? With a side trip to the Andes—and Patagonia? But who with? Greg's out for at least another four years. Incredible to think of him in the Navy, although it's true he can get along with almost anyone—even me—like on the McKinley climb, where he was thoroughly agreeable. Unlike me. At the top, though, when we knew there was more mountain to climb, it seemed as if we were entering a conspiracy of silence, all together; let's act as if this is the top, all right, fine with me, the first thing I ever agreed with all of them about in the whole two months. Everything falling away below us, nothing but the sky and the light above, and I thought we were just kidding ourselves about being on the summit. The effects of altitude. Strange.

Well, if not Greg, then maybe Tom? He speaks Spanish, doesn't he? But then South America's pretty far, expensive. We could try the Thelon River; we'd have to fly into the headwaters and then out from Baker Lake. There are still musk ox there and caribou—and white wolves. I bet Tom would want to go, if it wasn't for too long. Last time after four weeks he began moping for Sue. He's got such a long face anyway—when he started tripping over his own lower jaw, I knew it was time to get back. Bob smiles.

Or Nepal. Liz really wants to get there; how could we work it? Not much chance soon. Maybe we should've saved some money for travelling. No, I'm glad we're here now. But the Thelon is a possibility—and there'd be less people there, probably, especially since we'd have to fly in. Except for the flight, it'd be cheap. Beans and mac and a lot of flour for baking.

The first row done, Bob taps each brick firmly into place, beginning on the second row, slow and steadily. He wipes up some spilled concrete with a damp cloth, rinsing it in a bucket of grey water. I can tell he likes the way the fireplace begins to look, stepping back to view it from a distance. He finds it admirable, imagines the fire someday burning brightly within it. He sees another fire, a large campfire burning on the shores of the Thelon River, green and rich and rolling country all about, a moose floundering in the water nearby. After a minute, he finishes the second row, tapping each brick firmly into place.

After the fourth row is done, he begins to feel hungry. He rinses his hands, dries them on a towel, and hugs me in the kitchen, sniffing stew.

"You know a shark?" he says. "A shark has very little brain. He has only one thought, in fact, but he thinks it a lot."

"What thought is that?" I humor him.

Bob bares his teeth. "Food," he says. We eat. Bob pulls out an old *National Geographic*, rereads the article on Patagonia, looking at each picture with appreciation, studying the mountains, spooning up the stew.

Aconcagua might be nice. Uuummm.

"We better get some more wood up today," I interrupt him. "It seems to be getting colder out."

He pushes the magazine away. "Pest." He smiles. "Get your own wood."

→»«←

The winter is cold again, as cold as December, and the sun is far away. It's becoming a problem to supply ourselves with enough wood to keep the house warm—there's a lot of air to heat. We finished the interior panelling and the ceilings; last week we moved the stove into the living room and the bed into the bedroom. Just after we finished, the temperature dropped to thirty-five below. Now we scramble to find wood.

I don't think we are being wasteful of the fuel, but the stoves are not as efficient as they could be. At night we stuff both stoves with as much as they will stand for and damp the draft down as much as possible. The cookstove burns for an hour or two at the most, the heating stove until four or five in the morning. But unless one of us has the energy or fortune to get up then and stoke it, by morning the ashes are cold.

It is often in the high forties in the house when I wake up, and Bob gets up. If it were up to me to start the morning fires, it would be afternoon before it happened. A temperature in the high forties is not unpleasant when you are camping out—on the contrary, it is refreshing and stimulating once you manage to lunge out of your sleeping bag. But the cold which permeates the house in winter is a different kind of cold. When I look out and see the snow, and know that outside the house walls it is twenty below zero, the fact that it is forty-eight degrees inside seems ominous, chilling. It is the advance guard of death. The objects which reside in a house are not like the objects which reside in a tent. Tent-objects expect to be cold. House-objects do not. A cold chair is far colder than a cold flashlight. A cold kitchen counter has a sullen expression and a floor which is painful to walk on barefoot is outraged and vengeful.

Bob starts the fires while I lie under the down quilt. I love the way the tip of my nose feels then, like an ice cube to the touch, a tiny counterpoint to the mass of warm flesh beneath the down. Then, when I hear the wood start to crackle, I leap out of bed in my long underwear and socks, and pulling the bedroom door shut behind me, I rush into the living room, dragging my quilt on the floor. I dive into the chair which sits beside the stove, ousting the cat from his favorite perch, and huddle there, feeling the heat blowing over my face, the only part of me exposed. The stove pumps the heat out, but it takes at least an hour before the warmth begins to permeate the air of the house. So much space must be filled; the cathedral ceiling of the living room has to be stuffed with heat first. Then there are all the other ceilings, and the corners, and the cupboards, and the spaces between the walls. It is a long time before any randomly chosen cubic foot of air is seventy degrees, so I sit in the chair by the stove, where I can be sure the heat will at least go by me in its journey elsewhere.

After a time, the day begins.

A roaring fills the sky. It is late afternoon, and the wind blows from the east, faster and faster, desperately trying to re-establish the equilibrium of the earth's air—an endless, hopeless journey. I sit in the front room, listening to it blow.

The trees in front of the house bend over, straining to escape the power of the air, bending to let the wind pour over them, not wanting to be taken along on its journey. The sides of the house shiver with the impact of millions of particles of air colliding, jerking, and moving on. Like the trees, the house seems uncertain whether or not it is going to be forced to accompany the wind. Pushed from below, it shudders as if afraid that it too could be lifted and carried off by a force strong enough to tear away the trees, the soil, and the rolling water's moisture.

Suddenly, a ton of thunder slides down on all sides, and then a cloud of red lightning appears and is gone. The grey of the snow is now indistinguishable from the grey of the sky; the sieve above is shaken, and millions of round pellets drop in a bundle to the ground. For a time they dance furiously about, collapsing finally into weary little piles of white. Meanwhile, darkness presents itself, and the wind dies. Then there is only the sound of little planets falling onto the roof, setting seriously to the task of moving from the sky to the earth.

→→→《←←←

The wind blows again today. Now, though, it is a spring wind, and from the southwest, bringing warmth. It is far too early in March for spring to be here, but something has blown the cold and the storm away, and brought fresh smells and melting. I go to the water hole to fill the jugs. Rivulets of water run and crinkle in the lake's hard crust. Large blobs of snow on the trees slip and loosen their grasp and slide to the ground. There are the smells of green and water and even earth, though that is buried ten feet deep. It is invigorating to know something other than cold and smoke, if only for a day.

The wind brings me renewed evidence of my physical existence. It reminds me of the persistent solidity of my body. I stand on the beach looking west, and the wind blows around me. It is displaced entirely from the spot of earth on which I stand.

As it blows past me, it touches me all over, not like a lover but like a blind person. It probes the contours of my face and chest, acquainting me with them anew as it acquaints itself. Yes, that is my nose, and those my hands. The shape of the earth itself would be different if I were not here, and I am glad.

I load my pack with the jugs of water and head for the house. As I turn, a stronger gust hits me, catching the pack and pushing me sideways for an instant.

The wind blows hard here. Not as hard as it can blow, but hard enough. From east and west, rarely from north or south, it blows on and off, and sometimes furiously. It seems as if this is the place where the winds begin—and there are few such points of origin, places with sharp edges, places where no shadows distort the forms.

Yet the wind frightens me sometimes. I cannot forget the day I first learned the strength of it, the endless, careless power of the wind. I was trying to cross a mountain pass, far to the south of here, and I was full of the kind of strength which comes after weeks of walking in the mountains, an exhilarating ability to sweat and breathe. The wind had been puffing in gusts as I walked up the gentle valley which led to the pass. I was halfway up into the steep bowl of the pass itself when the wind started to blow. I could hear a high-pitched roar coming toward me over the top, and then the wind hit me with the force of a falling mountain. It knocked me down once, and I slid through the wet gravelly scree on my stomach, glad that the earth was there to catch me when I fell. It would have been too easy to have started whirling out forever. The wind stopped, and I got to my feet again and stuck my ice ax into the ground, and braced myself for the wind's returning. We fought for a long minute, and I stayed upright. When it went past, I rushed up the pass five feet, then stopped and braced myself again.

At the top of the pass the wind was even stronger. It was impossible to walk upright into the solid wall of air. When it knocked me over again, I took my pack off. It started to blow away. I hooked it with my arm and, dragging it behind, crawled across the pass until I found a boulder I could hide behind.

I was fearful of the wind. I wanted to turn around and come another day, forgetting the wind and how it blew. I couldn't bear to know that the wind was stronger than I. Yet it always is, even when it blows a summer breeze. It rips away my warmth and tosses it to the sky; the moving air keeps spinning past, not only cooling my body but riveting my mind. Air in motion has always the power to remind me that I exist—and how precariously.

→≫(5)≪←

Yesterday we saw people again.

After our long isolation together on the island, it is disturbing to touch the outside world now, even for a day. Although we may receive welcome and acceptance, there is still a sense of emptiness, a sense that we are touching only the tip of an enormous iceberg called humanity. Is it longing or distaste we feel? Alienation or a painfully sharp understanding? I don't know. But we had to go to town for fuel for the lamps and the chain saw; so yesterday we skied to Caesar's Point and drove the truck to Fort St. James.

The morning was a fine one. Cumulus clouds drifted by like the heralds of August, west to east. We followed the same route, skiing down the Portage-Tachie trail, and it took less than three hours to get in. At the river mouth a boy was running a snowmobile, dragging a great load of firewood on the sled behind him. All the houses in the village were piled deep with snow; a cat was curled on a porch in the sun. The air was still, and the smoke rose from many chimneys in a lethargic forward march to the sky.

Since the Walkers were not home, we reached Fort St. James in the early afternoon. After the first moments of excitement, the town seemed uneasy, frenzied. We had been too long away to adjust easily to the speed of life there, stimulating as a drug. Colors were overbright. Shop windows glared. We did our errands quickly, buying fuel and firebrick, insulated chimney and cement. We were back in Tachie by three o'clock, looking for snowmobiles with which to drag the supplies out to the island.

We went first to August Matisse's house. In the afternoon sun its brick-red color was startling. We hoped that August would be able to advise us about snowmobiles, and knocked on his door firmly, certain at least that he would try. But a teenage boy answered the knock, a boy with an unusually handsome face, his eyes set wide apart, his large, strong nose classically Indian. His long, dark hair was combed into two braids, tied with red cloth at the ends. He wore a beaded wristband, blue jeans, and a woolen shirt, grey and blue. When he opened the door, he stared at us questioningly but said nothing.

I asked for August. He had gone to town, the boy said. He introduced himself as Joseph, one of August's grandsons, living with his grandparents for the winter. He spoke shyly, slowly, but without embarrassment or mistrust. When we told him our names, his neutrality changed to friendliness; his grandfather had mentioned us. Bob explained we were looking for snowmobiles to rent, and after thinking for a long, quiet moment Joseph suggested his cousin, Maurice Joseph, who was living in Sunnyside for a time, and who owned two machines, twin TNTs. The directions to his house were confusing; after another moment Joseph offered to take us there. He put on his boots and coat, checked the wood in the stove, then damped it down and followed us out. We walked in silence across the lake and up the hill to Sunnyside, stopping in front of one of the oldest houses there, a sturdy log cabin, grey and quiet. One of the windows was cracked and had been carefully covered with heavy plastic.

An older man, sixty or more, answered the knock on the door. His face was small, as was his stature; his expression reflected the gentleness that sometimes comes from a lifetime of trial. At the sight of Joseph he smiled and stepped back, inviting us all in. Bob and Joseph went ahead, pulling off their boots in the entrance. In the doorway I stood for a moment unmoving. The room was full of people—I couldn't manage to grasp their numbers or their nature at first. I glanced one way and saw three children playing underneath a broad plank table, glanced another way and saw two teenage girls sitting quietly side by side on a couch with their knees pulled up to their chests. In the far corner there was an old man, wrapped in a blanket and coughing, coughing. From time to time he spat into a pan a bright-red spurt of blood. At the stove, a woman was putting on a pot of water, and then bent to stick several pieces of stovewood into the firebox, her great rump spreading genially behind her.

We were introduced to the man and the woman, Maurice and Doreen Joseph, cousins to Joseph Matisse in some complex and confusing manner. Doreen invited us to sit down, which we did on a long, high couch covered with an enormous crocheted spread. On the wall behind us hung a machine-made tapestry in gaudy colors. It portrayed a bull moose feeding on aspen twigs near a beaver pond. He was surrounded by a fancy green border of stylized leaves. The linoleum floor was grey and red, the walls painted aqua blue. Doreen filled three cups with tea and ladled sugar into them before passing them around. Joseph explained our mission to Maurice, while Bob and I sat and sipped tea, overwhelmed by the sense of community presence in the room, the silent curiosity.

"Up the lake," Joseph was saying. "I think that tall island with the lights."

"Oh, yes, I know. High up. Yes, that would be all right." Maurice nodded at us, accepting. "It's a long way out there, to walk," he said. "You don't come to town very often?"

"No." We spoke in unison, self-consciously attentive.

"In a way that is better." He nodded. "Sometimes craziness in town."

"Yes." A long pause followed while we carefully sipped our tea.

"You have children?" Doreen asked.

"No," said Bob, smiling and shaking his head.

"Ahh." Doreen thought. "Just married?"

"Well, a few years," he answered, stretching a point, or shrinking it.

"Ahh." She gestured encouragingly. "Sometimes it is that way."

"Yes. It must be nice for you to have such a large family," I said. She smiled slowly. "It is better. We have eight."

"And many cousins, too, I guess?" I said.

"Oho! Many many." She nodded and fell silent.

After we worked out the details of the rental, we set our tea cups in the sink and went out into the cold once more, nodding and smiling our goodbyes. Maurice prepared the snowmobiles while Bob and Joseph and I unloaded the truck and tied the supplies to the long wooden sleds. As he leaned over to set down a five-gallon tin of kerosene, Joseph's long braids brushed my hand.

"Thanks so much for helping us like this," I said to him, grateful and awkward, part of a couple, not a band.

"It is nothing." He smiled, less serious for an instant. He seemed to be smiling at the sound of the phrase coming from his own mouth. "My grandfather mentioned you."

When the sleds were loaded, Maurice showed us how to run the snowmobiles. We revved our engines quickly and moved away, eager to get the loads dumped, aware that the day was passing and our house was growing cold.

When we returned the snowmobiles, just at dusk, the Josephs invited us in once more; this time we refused their hospitality. Despite their efforts and our own, there was a gap between us which could never be bridged. Words between us seemed to fall into a vat of oil and sink. With our strong awareness of our physical surroundings, how could we ever understand their apparent lack of concern for theirs? With their strong sense of family and tribe, how could they ever understand our desire to be alone, or the need for privacy? We skied the long track home in the growing darkness, while the moon rose above us and threw shadows on the ground, long shadows, thin and purple.

It was good to get home again. The house was still warm.

→≫≫ (6) ≪≪←

The fireplace is beautiful, the stones set gently together. The fire burns in its new frame, the light moving happily over an area of stone hearth and cotton rug. Now that the fireplace is finished, I can't remember what it was like before we had it. The dusk is closing in, and the fire is reflected in the picture window, burning again in the outside air. We haven't lit the lamps tonight. We want to watch the fire until it's time for sleep.

At times it seems we paid a steep price for this pleasure: I find it difficult to forget the months we worked in Fort St. James, even now, so far away and so quiet. There is one memory of the time we spent in town that comes to me often—I think because I do not know whether it is a bad memory or a good one.

Bob was working the evening shift at the mill, a shift which began at four thirty in the afternoon and ended at twelve thirty at night. By a complex system of hitchhiking and handing over the truck keys we both had the use of the truck at least one way to or from work. Some nights I drove out to the mill to pick him up, in the absolute cold of the unheated truck moving through the heart of a winter night. The air was still, and the road, curve after black curve of it, remote in space and time. As I got near to the mill, I could hear the pounding, crashing rhythms of the machines, absurd and maniacal in the still night. A glow lit the black sky from all the yard lights, and finally, when I emerged into the mill clearing, I could see the steam. A great, solid, moving mass of white loomed over the yard, solidified moisture which was the white of unblemished snow or the finest cumulus cloud. Surrounded by the clanking of the machines, the cloud of steam had an impervious dignity. The startling glow of electricity did not seem to touch it. Nearby, a great conical burner threw a cloud of golden sparks in furious motion into the sky. Golden sparks that burned with brilliance and were gone, white steam that rode the sky, and the roar of ridiculous and febrile sound which could not be ignored. Finally there was the smell—a smell of burning wood, and sawdust and growing trees. I drove into the yard and lost the wonder of it, sitting numbly in the truck until the shift let out and one hard-hatted, booted, and bundled figure with a lunch box detached itself from the mass of figures and became Bob, and sat beside me in the truck.

One of these nights I did not make it to the mill. A wooden bridge which spanned the Stuart River was part of the road from the cabin to Takla. It was a narrow bridge, but old, and handsome as old bridges are. One night I got there and it was burning. Fire trucks were coming in from town, and cars were parked for some little distance along the road. The smell was awful—the pilings below, which had been doused with kerosene, were heavily creosoted. The fire crackled and flared; large yellow sheets licked the sides of the bridge; and I stood on the frosty road and watched, and wondered how Bob would get home, and watched it burn some more. As I walked back and forth and looked overhead, the northern lights crystallized into motion. Elongated beams of luminescent light swayed, darted, and crawled across the sky.

Around me people talked. Why would anyone burn a bridge? Some thought the Indians had done it as a protest. I heard one man jokingly suggest that the railroad was trying to increase its business by cutting off the main road into town. I didn't wonder. Arson lies close to everyone's heart, and to burn a bridge is a statement of final rejection.

The fire mumbles into coals. Bob pulls his sweater about his head and drops it into a chair. He stokes the stove and damps it down, and we crawl beneath the bedquilt, to sleep.

→»)«(‹-

Sometimes it seems to me that I spend the nights here gathering messages. I dream with a vividness and clarity that I have never experienced anywhere else. The silence really is silence; only rarely do sounds permeate the night. Wolves, owls, coyotes, loons can all be heard in the darkness on occasion, but the sound is so noticeable that it has little to do with the pattern of our nights. Usually I sleep, and dream, until three in the morning. I wake then from the soundest sleep for no apparent reason, and things are often going on. Boots may be playing with a mouse. Or the wind may have died and the lake be quieting at last. The fire may be furiously at work in the stove on the last bits of wood, burning with a devilish rapacity. The moon may only just have risen.

Some nights stand out. One night last September the wind was blowing, blowing with the intensity that shakes the roots of the house, before I went to sleep, and while I slept. I woke at three, not expecting anything special, just waking. The night seemed unusually light, as if dawn had come early. But the glow of light was emanating not from the eastern sky, but from the south. I rolled over and looked to the southern hills.

The sky was red with a false dawn. Large columns of white smoke funneled toward the east, with the wind. I could see no flame, but it was clear that just beyond the hills a fire was spreading, and spreading fast. The sparks that filled the sky were as clearly visible as drops of water are in sunlight. They looked like the glitter that spews from the charcoal burner in a sawmill, but I knew no sawmill was there. Loggers had been working south of the lake though, and I guessed a slash fire had gotten out of control.

We were protected by the hills and by the lake itself, but I could not believe that there was no danger from something so beautiful and wild. I opened the window and thought that I could smell heat in the air, heat and dusty smoke. Whether or not I could smell it, the smell was there, and coupled with the glitter of sparks and the glow, it destroyed all possibility of sleep. I lay and watched the fire until the real dawn lit the sky and took away some of its intensity. I fell asleep again then, and dreamed that I was riding a houseboat in a lake of fire, paddling with my hands, which did not touch the fire, but stirred a wind behind them which pushed me forward, across the stretches of light. There was no heat, just color and the sensation of floating always above the depths. I never did get to shore.

Just before that night, sometime in August, I was asleep in the tent, and woke suddenly to see a brilliant light in the trees. It was a fire, blinding white and fast. Wild fantasies flashed through my mind. Invaders from outer space were spraying electrical fire, testing it on a patch of undesired wilderness. I gripped my sleeping bag in frozen wonder, whispering "Bob, Bob!" as loudly as I could, knowing there was nothing I could do to save the woods, the world, or me.

It was the moon. It topped the ridge, a sliver of solid matter, a light of low intensity. The rays which filled the woods withdrew, pulled in their edges, and faded. The moon was calm and slow and silently laughing. I felt a fool to have been so deceived into panic.

This winter I had the strangest wakening. I woke in bed and felt an eerie sense of presence. I was lying on my side, and I could just see some bits of snow out of the corner of my eye. The snow was blue. It was clearly and distinctly blue, and I turned very slowly, frightened, feeling that I was being watched. The fir outside the bedroom window and the snowy ground for twenty feet around it were lit with a weird, glowing light. The sky seemed utterly overcast, a conglomeration of cloud layers which no moon could penetrate. The snow and the tree looked as if they were lit up by the beam of a blue spotlight, a light directed from somewhere above my head.

I lay frozen, still—whatever was lighting the snow was not a pleasant force. But I did not want to shout for help. I didn't want to wake Bob and get him to help me figure out its origin. It was not a threat to the world at large—the only danger lay in letting the source of the light know that I had seen it. Give it reason to notice that even one mind had been puzzled by its nature, and it would wipe that mind out. I stayed on my side, scrunched into a ball, trying to give out sleep vibrations. I kept an eye on the light, and after perhaps ten minutes it brightened, and then faded rapidly and was gone.

What, after all, happened on those nights? Some trees were burning; the moon had risen; an opening in the clouds had produced a strange light. Simple phenomena, when I list them simply, but enough. It is always enough, if it is fire. When I wake after such a night of waking or sleeping dreams, I am happy to see the walls of the house and the clean white ceilings, untouched and enclosing, keeping both wind and fire outside.

→≫ (7) ≪←

The evening holds me tonight. It wraps itself around me, and I wrap myself around it as well. We are equally strong and equally eager for the night to come. Like the evening, I want to be everywhere tonight—in the house, on the island, down the lake, in the sky. I look out the window at the almost iridescent whiteness of the snow, spilling down from the boundaries of the rock and on and on, the expanding edge of the world.

I go outside, no farther than the front porch, then no farther than the bottom of the steps. The path curls sinuously before me, and there is a flicker of white beach below. On the lake, the flatness must be tested. Is it really just as flat, the next step, and the next? There is no sense in stopping here. I walk and walk. Steps bring me back to the beach at last, with the coming of darkness which erases visions. I have walked far, and gone no further than my front door. I have rolled myself around the world, and found that I have hardly moved.

But I have moved enough. Now the calm is too calm, the evening too still and broad. I long for a sound, a motion. I pull a branch of an aspen tree toward me, and it bends and bends, and finally cracks. I hit it over a rock and it thuds. Walking up the path again, I drag it behind me so that it swishes through the snow.

When I walk in the front door again, there is an expectation of warmth and wood smoke. The disarray which meets my eyes bears so little resemblance to the static calm I left behind, and took with me, that for a moment, fleetingly, I wonder if I have come to the wrong house. The room is covered with a fine layer of white dust; the smell is of chemicals and harsh cleaning. The stove seems to have been ripped from the wall, and the stovepipe is lying in sections on the rug. Bob stands in the middle of the room, his arms hanging at his sides, his face streaked with white dust. I ask him what has happened, my mind slow.

"A fire," he says.

Bob was sitting in front of the stove after I left, reading a book. The stove had just been stoked. Bob moved the chair back slightly as the heat accumulated on his legs. In doing so, he happened to glance upward. Where the stovepipe went through the roof, there were bright flames pulsing rhythmically.

Dragging his chair over, Bob pulled the insulation from around the stovepipe—flames poured out. One entire section of the roof was on fire, from the eaves to the roofbeam. It was already almost beyond control. There was only one right thing to do, and only one moment to do it in. The fear that he would not be able to do it was almost stifling. The flames roared.

He jumped down again and seized the fire extinguisher, pressed the button, and stuck it in the hole in the roof. When the extinguisher was empty, he tore down the stovepipe with his hands and ran to the water barrel. Opening the stove, he poured water on the fire, which was pumping blinding smoke into the room, until the house was full of steam and dustlike particles of ash, riding up on the rising air. Some embers were still burning in the roof, and with several buckets of water he put them out, shoving his body into the hole as far as it would go, and hurling the water upwards, splashing it over and over until the roof was dead, black, stinking wood. Bob's hands are still covered with the charcoal.

Even as I walked out the front door and down the steps, the fire was starting. When I was out on the lake, following its flatness, expanding the view, the fire was burning toward the roof. The house's skin is not my own, any more than Bob's is mine. It seems, after all, that the things that enclose me, the things that I love, are connected to me only by a tenuous knowledge. The house could burn to the ground, and I would never know of it. Maybe, I would dream it, if I was smoldering too.

We could have lost it all—the little back porch; the kitchen window that frames the hummingbird feeder, red against the winter white; the big bed and the bookshelves; the table and the four oak chairs; our winter stores; the fresh-baked cake; the curtains; my journal; Bob's climbing gear. We could have lost it all. Another five minutes and the fire would have eaten its way over the roofbeam and down the other wall. Had the wind been blowing, we would have lost the house. But the ache of its connection to us would never have disappeared.

➜≫✂≪←

This morning I was making lunch and baking some bread, and I noticed that the house seemed to be smokier than it should have been. Actually, it is never smoky at all except when the oil-drum stove puffs a great gust out through the air vent because there is not enough oxygen for it to be burning properly, or when I am just getting the cookstove or the fireplace lit, and the draft has not been fully established. For a while I thought that the stovepipe had come uncaulked somewhere, and that there was a little smoke leaking out in a steady stream. So I checked all the stovepipe, and caulked up all the spots that looked a little loose or dry, and then went back to cooking lunch. But it got steadily smokier inside the house.

Bob had been down on the beach chopping wood, but when he returned for lunch he noticed the smoke too. Of course the thought in both of our minds was that there was a fire starting somewhere, so Bob climbed up the ladder through the trap door into the attic to check the air there. It was perfectly clear. He climbed back down, folded the ladder up, and sat down to lunch with me.

It is hard to understand why we didn't do more. I suppose mostly we thought that because we had had one fire, we should try especially hard not to be nervous about fires. I told myself that unless I could accept a little smoke now without being terrified of the house burning down, I might as well forget about living in the bush.

Bob was sitting in such a way that he could see the living room. Suddenly he jumped to his feet and dashed from the kitchen. I turned around in time to see him tear the asbestos board away from its position on the wall behind the stove. As it came off, flame spread across the wall. The wood behind the asbestos had been smoldering; and when the air hit it freely, it burst into flame.

I had known the house was burning again, only had been too stubborn to admit it, too stupid to see it, too vain to believe it. I didn't want to know that it could happen again, could happen endlessly, and forever, the house always half alight, poised on the brink of ash. When the wall burst into flame, I felt I might as well let the fire have its head; it was determined to burn—there was no sense in fighting it any longer. I started immediately to plan on what to do. It was twenty below zero. We could make it over to the Boyles cabin, and although it would be hard to heat, we could manage till the cold spell broke. What to take? Some food, the sleeping bags—I wondered if the cabin was supplied with matches.

Bob shouted, "Get some water."

I moved toward the water bucket. Before I got there, I remembered it was dry. I had used up the last of the water making lemonade.

"It's all gone," I said. The fire spread toward the window.

"Well, for god's sake, go get some!"

Bob was wrenching the fire extinguisher off the wall as I grabbed the two red plastic jugs and started out the door. I didn't have any boots on, but there was no time to put them on. I didn't have a hat or gloves either, but managed to shrug into my parka as I ran.

The night before, there had been a snowfall. Powder snow covered the path down the hill, and in my socks I slid most of the way, and fell the rest. The dock was slick, and I plunged onto my knees as I came alongside the water hole. Normally when I get water out of the cold lake, I wear rubber gloves, or tip the jug so that the handle is just above the surface. This time I shoved both arms in up to the elbows, and watched the bubbles rise with agonizing slowness. My arms grew numb, but I kept my hands tightly clenched, so that when I did pull the jugs up, the hands would be properly attached to carry them.

Finally they were full and I moved up the hill. My lungs wouldn't stretch wide enough, my legs wouldn't move fast enough, and they slipped backward in the snow. The landscape around me shifted in jerky enlargements until the door filled my eyes.

When I got in, the fire was out. I set the jugs onto the floor with a thump, and we drained together in puddles on the rug. The water run had been for nothing.

Nor had the fire extinguisher worked. When Bob ripped off the seal and pushed the nozzle, all that emerged was a thin trickle of white liquid. (Later we read the instructions on the side of the can, and in the tiniest of letters it said, "Do Not Allow To Freeze.") After tossing the can across the room so hard that it dented the panelling, Bob had gotten the hammer and ripped the burning boards off the wall, carrying each one onto the porch and tossing it into the snow. The studs behind were burning too, but he managed to beat the flames out of them with his leather gloves. He got several buckets of snow to throw on the studs, and cooled them down enough so that they did not flame again. With the water we drenched them thoroughly. It was a dismal, smelly mess.

We have moved the stove a foot farther from the wall. We had already, after the first fire, replaced all the stovepipe with the Selkirk chimney. On the next trip to the Fort I am going to get the biggest fire extinguisher in town. I am determined also never to let the water barrel run dry again.

Practical measures, singularly inadequate. The fires have already burned. I will never feel quite safe again, quite sure the house will stand around me. Both my house and I are vulnerable, now and for all time. When I light a tiny fire, it is in imitation of the sun. When I scatter fire about, there is no telling where it will land.

Now uneasy, I wonder about our future here. This winter has been so good—every day a gift of warmth, and the chance for skiing, cooking, talking, loving. Now, the years look long ahead. It may be that the house will burn and we will leave, and all that will remain here will be rock and ash. We'll see. Why, though, did I ever imagine that a house—the lumber dried with fire, the metal forged in fire, the windows shaped by fire, the lights rooted in fire, the heat springing from fire—why did I ever imagine that a house could protect me from fire?

→≫≫(8)≪≪←

The woods are awaiting their first wildflower. It is that season of the year, early May. Winter recedes, and the lake is full.

The sunlight in spring is like the light in the high mountains; it is pale on the pines, bright but far away. The sensation which it gives is of passing splendor. Although it shines in a rich blue sky, I do not take the light for granted. It is thin, even in its noon, and the glow on the green shrubbery has some of the qualities of moonlight.

On the lake the sun spreads out, the motion of the water blending with the sun to draw the eye into its rhythm. On the land it is the mind which causes motion, chiding the leaves into a magic lantern show. But everywhere the light falls it has the seductive, soothing quality of waves, and the eye rests on its patterns more easily than on the solid forms behind.

Where the sun is thin and elusive, it is precious. In a town there is not so much emotion tied up with the sunlight. A kind of dull surety that the sun will return before anything major changes pervades the consciousness. But here, as in the mountains, moods can be made or broken by light. A break in the clouds means a return of hope.

When the sky is grey for days on end, I get a lot of work done, but it seems less and less worth doing. Then one morning I wake up, and the sky is clear as far as I can see, and the world is transformed. On many days when the sun is shining I wander aimlessly before deciding it is clearly time to go for a ski, or a walk, or a boat ride. In the spring there is no need even to wander first.

The lake broke up early this year, and yesterday we took a ride in the sunlight. The trees are webbed with filmy golden green. The ruffed grouse are thumping all through the woods. As we drifted along the north shore, again and again there came the sound of thumping, like a diesel engine slowly starting in the distance. The sound is so penetrating that the earth seemed to shake with the vibrations—and it's so pervasive that trying to locate a grouse by its thump is like a game of hide and seek run by a master illusionist.

It was very warm, the first warm day of the year. Bob suggested we go to the bay where last fall we found a deer skull. The skull was still antlered, so there is no doubt that it was a deer's. It was surprising, though, to find it—neither of us has ever seen a deer or any deer tracks or scat in this country. The woods are mostly fir and pine, with heavy deadfall, and the winters are very cold, the snow deep. It is not deer country.

The skull was gone, without a trace. The water had not yet reached the upper beach, so it could not have washed away. It had probably been consumed. Rodents eat bones for the calcium, which is why the woods are not littered with them.

The next bay we entered was carpeted with a heavy growth of water sedges, rich green like trees before a storm. On our approach a single mallard lifted his head of iridescent green, and took off straight into the air, toward the sun. After he had gone, a duckling emerged from the grasses, swimming madly forward, paddling furiously with both legs in the direction his father had taken, but unable to fly. His little stubby tail bobbed up and down like a fan. At last he stopped, and floated disconsolately back toward the thickest sedges.

→>>‹‹‹←

I knew for sure it was spring this morning by the way all the clothes and sheets and curtains suddenly looked. They looked filthy. My long white robe had turned grey, the blue border on my parka almost brown. The sheets were stiff with dirt and sweat. It was like coming out of the mountains after a month in the same clothes, and stepping into a shiny white bathroom. Suddenly you see things as they really are—caked and streaked, stained and dusty, smelling of sweat, urine, and wood smoke. The smell is not a bad one at all; it is pleasantly warm and ripe, but it is strong.

So this morning. Same nose, same eyes. The change has taken place in the world.

When we came out here in January, I knew there would be no washing till spring. I am sure that if I were a proper pioneer woman, I would have relished the idea of melting snow in the five-gallon steel tub, going outside about ten times to gather more snow as it melted, until the pot was full of water. Then I would have stoked the stove until the water was hot and filled it with about one tenth of the clothes that required washing, stirred them about with a stick until they were clean, and so on, all day long, until everything was washed and rinsed. I would have strung lines all over the kitchen and hung the clothes on them, doing the cooking surrounded by the litter of drying clothes, and picking them all up again after they fell down when the line bounced. I did several times get as far as heating the water, but only, in the end, to take a bath in, my arms and legs and body from the waist up protruding absurdly from the tub. I even washed a few clothes after the baths were finished. But the major omission of almost everything was not fixed until today.

It was a glorious sunny day. I took all the clothes and curtains and sheets in four garbage bags down to the beach, and gathered dry driftwood and lit a fire. It was appalling how few clothes fit into five gallons of hot water. No doubt that was all to the good, however, since each item got some of the attention it deserved. The water the clothes travelled through was black as coffee is black, and almost as thick as coffee. One sweater went through eight washings, the last three all by itself, and it still ran smoky dirt.

We strung the long polyethylene line between two trees, and after each item was washed until the water came fairly clean, Bob and I together wrung it out and hung it on the line. The line was full, and I was beginning on pile number ten of clothes, while Bob chopped some driftwood up and Boots stalked mice, when an Indian boat pulled into sight around The Fishing Cabins Island. It was trolling and approached slowly, the engine going put-put-put. I waved, and the boat turned toward the dock, its occupants attracted, I thought, by the circustent appearance of the beach. I was wrong, though. They had been planning to stop in before I waved and before they saw the clothes. It was August Matisse and his wife, with Joseph and two smaller children, out for spring fishing and hunting, stopping to check on how our winter had been.

August's boat was newly painted, bright blue with a lighter blue inside. The seams were neatly caulked, and the benches had new cushions on them. When the boat pulled up to the dock, Joseph tossed the rope to Bob, and he secured it to the tie-on while Joseph hopped out and tied the other end.

"Hello," said Bob.

Joseph nodded. "Hello." In the boat still, August called out, "We thought we'd stop by and see how you are. Everything good this winter?"

"Great," I said. "I'm so glad we were here. The winter went so fast, I can hardly believe it's spring already."

August clambered slowly off the boat and onto the dock. At that, the two young children hopped out, and after glancing shyly at Bob and me, they ran down the dock to the beach and took off up the hill toward the house. August's wife smiled and nodded her head up and down slowly. She said nothing, and did not leave the boat, but sat peacefully, her hands in her lap.

"How's the fishing?" Bob asked August.

"Oh, not so good. We been hunting for a few days, and got good luck, though. Look at this." Proudly, August lifted a tarp on the bottom of the boat. He had three beaver skins, four neatly trimmed moose quarters, a moose hide, seven huge salmon, and a bear skin. The bear skin was beautiful, perfect from the tips of the legs to the end of the nose. The face itself looked exactly like a Halloween bear mask—soft and rubbery, with a hard black nose. Most hunters will let an expert skin the face, but August was clearly an expert himself.

"That's beautiful," I said. "Where did you learn to skin like that?"

"Oh, I skinned many bears in my life. It is getting harder now. I don't see so good. I try to teach Joseph here how to hunt. He's O.K. too."

August glanced toward Joseph, expectant; August's wife sat silent in the boat, listening. When no one else spoke, August kept talking.

"Yes, he's pretty good hunter already. But young men think they already know everything. Pah. So, you have a good winter?" he asked us again. "Your boat still O.K.?"

"Well, it leaks," said Bob. "It always did leak, but now it leaks worse. We couldn't get it all the way out of the water for the winter, so some water froze in it."

"That is bad," said August. "You should get it all out of the water. My boat, Joseph helped me paint it—he painted most. It is working really well now, no leak at all. We tarred it, with that tar you burn in. You should get some of that."

"We're going to try," said Bob. "Maybe we'll just have to get a new boat."

"That would be good too. Boats get old, they are not worth fixing up."

"Will you come up to the house and have some tea, or coffee?" I asked. "I guess the children are up there already."

"No, no," August said. "You are doing washing. We just stop in to say hello. And my wife, she would have trouble climbing that hill. Phew! Some hill, that is. We all think you are crazy, when we hear you are building a house there. But it looks like a nice house, now."

The children appeared, sliding and tearing down the hill. They came to a stop at the end of the dock, and eyed Joseph questioningly.

"We are going now," he said. "Get into the boat." As they went by, he nudged them with his knee. August climbed in next and then Joseph, and Bob untied the lines and tossed them in while Joseph jumped for the rear, next to the engine. We smiled and he started the engine. Slowly, the boat pulled away, trailing a fishing line behind it.

We finished the washing and, shortly after, a warm breeze blew up, ruffling the lake, and stirring the clothes on the line with questing fingers. I feel expectant, and restless. A new year is beginning. The lake is liquid once again.

4

WAVES

➤➤➤ (1) ◀◀◀

August's visit in his newly painted, newly caulked, and leakless river boat has inspired us to take a good look at ours—leaky when we bought it and leaky still, always sinking, though ever so slowly. A mist floats above the water this morning, and the boat floats in it like a nightmare vision of a deranged boatmaker. It looks so heavy on the water, as if it is longing to be encompassed by the lake. No doubt it will sooner or later sink beneath us, confirming our constant conviction that it is quite capable of doing so.

Even when we bought it, it looked a little odd to my eyes, something like an elongated box with bulging sides. It's a river boat, so it was fairly long—twenty-five feet—and had a flat bottom. Rather than beginning in a smooth and water-shearing point, the bow was cut off halfway up and presented the water with a square, flat wall against which to break. A little cap of a cabin was perched on top. We thought about the prospective purchase for a full day, weighing the pros and cons with absurd care. It was the only boat for sale in town.

With great ceremony and some trepidation we rolled it into the water and installed our prize possession on its tail, a brand-new 40-hp Mercury outboard with manual start. It takes a lot of quick strength and conviction to get the starting cord out on such an engine, and we had not been afloat ten minutes before I was convinced that I possessed neither the strength nor the conviction necessary. Although Bob's conviction left something to be desired, his strength sufficed, and we shortly got moving down the lake.

Even in virtually dead-calm water, the boat pounded. Every time it

109

hit a wrinkle on the glassy surface of the lake it would lift and then drop with a bone-jarring thud. Whatever water the bow confronted would smash against the entire length of its flat surface, shooting into the air and over the cabin roof. In addition, of course, the boat leaked— through the bow, through the stern, and through all the seams. It has been leaking ever since.

So I have a kind of steady job keeping the boat afloat. During the night it leaks and leaks, until in the morning there is anywhere from ten to eighteen inches of water inside. The first working hour of every day, I bail. I have claimed the job because it is mindless and meditative, and because every day it has a conclusion. I feel as if the boat is a kind of demon god for whose maintenance I am responsible.

A galvanized bucket is my bailer. I take off my shoes and roll my pants above the knees. Then I grab the bucket and climb into the icy water, knowing that my legs will be numb within seconds, bright pink beneath the water.

The bilge water is surprisingly pure. At first there was often oil or some bits of paper or dirt in it. Now it is just water. We probably have the cleanest boat on the lake. I take the bucket and scoop it full, dumping it over the thwart in a steady rhythm.

Whether it is sunny or raining or cloudy, I bail. I always take between two and three hundred gallons out. The last ten gallons require the other bailer, a Clorox bottle with a scoop cut out. We long ago took all the nails out of the deck so that the boards can be lifted, and the water scooped down to the bottom. When I lay the boards back in, I do it quickly, because I can already see the glistening which marks the lake returning.

We didn't travel much last summer, we were so busy on the island. This year, we'll have more time to explore. It's too bad we'll have to do it in this particular boat. I stand on the beach and look past it to the lake, dark grey and moving gently.

→≫≫≪≪←

We made our first trip of the spring to town the other day, to buy lumber for the house siding with our last remaining money. The boat was heavily loaded on the return trip, and a storm blew up when we were halfway home. When we left the Walkers, the lake was glassy, but the sky was clouded, and there was an oppressive moistness in the air. The boat moved steadily at about eight miles an hour, the drone of the engine soothing on the still lake.

I sat on the lumber, facing the stern, and watched the eastern sky. Slowly, it filled with darker clouds that towered above the horizon, moving up and out faster than we were moving away. When I turned to face the bow for a moment, I saw that the western sky was growing murky too. Although it was just midafternoon, it was suddenly as dark as early dusk; a strange purplish light suffused the air. We kept on moving.

Quite suddenly, the lake ruffled. The entire width of the lake was hit by a gust of wind which caught up with us, and then went on ahead, dragging behind it the uneven choppiness which is the first step toward waves. The wind was moving with us, so I did not feel its passage, but I could see that it was gusting powerfully. The water was stirred every few minutes by a gigantic sweep like the slap of a hand.

The wind strengthened steadily behind us, and the water was rising. The ruffles turned into rolls, and the rolls into bigger rolls topped by waves—all in the space of five minutes. The waves were two feet high and rising, and the boat bounded up and down with shuddering reverberations. I still couldn't feel the full force of the wind, since we were running with it. Heading into the waves would have been even harder on the boat—which felt in any case as if it were being shaken apart.

We kept moving. The waves were now running so fast that their speed was faster than the maximum speed of the boat. Each wave, instead of staying behind us, rolled under us. The engine would slip into a trough as if it were slipping backwards. Intermittently, water began to pour over it, and its roar was muffled. At any moment, I thought, it might be thoroughly drenched and die, leaving us adrift in our unwieldy wooden box. Each time, however, it climbed laboriously out of the trough and plowed on, only to be overtaken by the next wave. The boat bucked forwards and backwards, and we shipped water over both the bow and the stern.

The wind whipped my hair around my head, so that I could hardly see. The plastic sheet was torn off the lumber and hung for a moment in the air current before it ripped away. I found the bailing can floating at my feet and started to bail. The wind caught each load of water as I poured it over the side; half of it blew back into my face, soaking my hair and parka. At the wheel Bob stood soaking wet, his hair plastered to his head, turning the boat as the wind shifted, trying to keep it always exactly perpendicular to the waves.

The two life jackets were stuffed beneath the bow, well out of our way, inaccessible if we should swamp. Tossed back and forth, I crawled up and got them, pulling one over my head and handing the other to Bob. He took it and put it down beside him, smiling slightly. The waves caught the boat again; his face tensed, and he gripped the steering wheel more tightly. It was clear that he was far more worried about losing the boat than he was about losing his life, or mine. We were only a hundred feet offshore. Had the boat swamped, even Bundy could have swum to safety, but in the bounding wooden crate, it didn't feel that way to me.

We would have to get in to land, and soon. As we turned, I was exposed to the force of the wind, which shoved itself into my lungs without any help from me. For a moment I thought I would choke on the bulky air.

Twenty feet offshore I climbed up onto the roof of the cabin and slipped toward the bow rope. The shore wave shoved the boat in to the beach with venomous strength. Bob cut the engine and ran back to lift it out of the water. I jumped up to my knees in the lake and ran with the rope. I was just in time; as I wrapped the rope around a huge cottonwood, the next wave caught the stern of the boat and smashed it sideways, so that the bow now faced into the storm and the stern pounded against the sand.

Bob climbed out, and together we heaved to try and get the boat up the beach a little. Each time we hauled it in a few inches, the water came and tore it easily out again.

Finally, it started to rain. Huge sheets of water lashed the surface of the lake. We huddled under the cottonwood, watching the waves slamming the boat against the shore. I could almost see the sand being driven into the seams and stretching them apart so that more water and more sand could get in and stretch them yet further. The storm would finish the boat.

Bob thought so too. We'd have to chance the lake. We untied the line and straightened the boat out bow forward. Jumping in, we were immediately driven back against the shore.

By pushing off with two-by-fours we managed to get offshore far enough to lower the engine. Bob pulled the starting cord. It produced the familiar sound—whirring, catching—dying. The eighth time it caught, as the propeller ground against a rock. We moved out once more into the waves.

Finally, we turned into Whitefish Bay. It was like entering a house out of a blizzard—so quiet that my ears could not at first adjust. The bay is perfectly sheltered from an eastern wind, and the water there was dead calm as soon as we got a hundred yards past the mouth. I could look down and see the placid white sand of the bottom, four or five feet below. But I tensely probed the water all the way in with a two-by-four, and when I had climbed out over the bow and felt the land beneath my feet, I started trembling so hard that I had to sit down.

We decided to stay in the bay until the lake was quite calm, and spend the night if necessary. Bob went to find dry wood while I sat and shook. There were some hotdogs in the food box, which we roasted while building up a huge bonfire to dry our clothes. By eight o'clock the lake had not yet calmed. We set about unloading the lumber that filled the cabin, so we could stretch the sleeping bags out there. Although I rigged a piece of plastic over the entrance of the cabin, the roof leaked, and for the hour before I fell asleep I watched the drops of water gather on the wet wood, swelling and swelling until they were too heavy to support, and then dropping into a wet patch on my chest. They fell like punctual reminders of my helplessness.

There was water beneath me and water above me and water around me, in wet patches here and there, water which knew no boundaries. Each heavy, spherical, and sagging drop as it fell transcended its own shape and limitations, and became merely water, unified and penetrating. It was not the boat which was the culprit. It was the lake. Would a different boat have calmed the storm or kept the lake outside? At last I turned onto my side. The wind had died. An owl sounded in the woods, once, and once again. The lapping of the water was magnified in my ears to a rhythmic roar of waves, crashing, crashing, crashing. I longed for stillness; but no boat is strong enough to resist the power of the lake around it, and the water shoved me gently, all night long.

→⟫ (2) ⟪←

Drip. Drip. Drip. Spring rain falls from the branches of the trees onto the path below, bringing the sky down to the earth again. I am perched on the path halfway down the hill, hunched beneath my yellow girl-scout poncho. Bob runs up and down the great boulder, dressed in a ridiculous rubber raincoat with a hood, making notes on a small piece of cardboard. We are building sea steps to the beach, to celebrate the new year.

Castles in the air. The books never mentioned that you had to build steps up to them. Thoreau said something about putting foundations under them—but sometimes foundations are not enough. I wonder if anything will be enough, when you live on an island.

"Hey, Bob," I call down, "why didn't we build these steps first of all, anyway?"

"Just a second," he calls back, writing something down on a shred of cardboard, chewing his lip. "What did you say?"

"I said, why didn't we build these steps right off the bat, a year ago, and save ourselves a lot of frustration?"

"God knows," he answers. "Well, the water was rising, and we had to get the stuff off the beach before it drowned. We were probably just too impatient to get started on the house, but we can blame the lake, as usual."

"Yeah. We can blame the lake. Goddamn lake. Also, I suppose you think that having negotiated all those miles of water to get to an island, once you are on the island you must have arrived. What's left has got to be your destination. Which it isn't at all, but it takes a while to notice that. I mean . . ."

"Listen, will you shut up for a minute? I have to figure out this other angle."

"Oh, all right," I say. Which it isn't at all, I think. It's like what you do when you get to the top of a mountain. You keep right on climbing—down. So once you get to the beach—once the waves deposit you on the shore—you keep right on floating. You're still so full of the motion of the boat that you hardly notice what your feet are doing, for quite a while, until you realize that you're out of breath and exhausted, and the humus is wearing away. So you decide to build some steps, a year later, to make it easier to live on the island. Which it never will be, steps or no steps. The commerce between the house and the beach is only the beginning. What's left is the lake.

I can't believe the lake is so calm and self-contained right now. It wasn't this morning, when we woke up and wanted to go to the Walkers' for the rest of the siding. We wanted very much to go, for no good reason except that we had planned on it. After a whole winter during which it never seemed vital to go anywhere at a specific time, or to do anything in particular, suddenly it has started to seem important to do things when and as we plan to do them. In the summer, time speeds up. The restless water which surrounds the island imparts its restlessness to me. The lake again begins to be the focus of life, and the root of decisions. Always it is in my mind and body—calm or violent, it affects me. And the same waves which make me restless prevent me from moving freely.

When we went to sleep last night, we were ready for the trip today. The boxes of dirty clothes were packed to be washed. The bags of garbage were piled on the beach, each one neatly closed with a double twist tie. The letters were all stamped for mailing, and the list of three or four forgotten items was written out, carefully numbered. I looked forward to the trip to the Walkers'. I anticipated getting the mail in town.

When I woke this morning, it was to the sound of roaring wind and crashing waves—turmoil and fury. When I woke, it was to the realization that there would be no trip to town today. As I stared from the bedroom window down onto the lake, the driving energy of the moving air was tearing the roots of the water apart and crushing them back together, leaving no space at all for us to travel in. We build and build, and we are still helpless. Is this why all those cabins stand empty?

Life here is controlled by the wind and the waves it brings. The island is both hard to get to and hard to get away from. I would not mind so much if it were bigger, big enough to take a walk on, big enough so I could get away from the sound and the smell of the waves. It is small, though, and there is no place on it where I can escape the presence of the lake below. It is so small that I can never forget that it's an island, isolated from the main mass of the earth by a tissue of moving water.

Perhaps it is because we saw the island first in winter, when it was like a green gumdrop stuck into smooth white icing, that I can't quite believe the water should be there. The knowledge that I have been forced to stay here today makes me feel trapped upon a rock, calling for help, waiting for a sail. I take my pleasures now as a prisoner does—savoring their taste, but damning their limitations. I am furious at the deprivation of possibility—that powerful and tantalizing If Only.

Of course I know that a calm morning will come again. But the chances are that it will be unexpected and unplanned for. When a day—maybe tomorrow—dawns quietly and the green-leafed trees glisten in their shells, we will feel that we should go to town and do all the things we planned to do today. We will rush through the chores, and rush back again to the boat, hoping to find the lake calm still. The chances are fair that a storm will have broken once again, and the mail and the siding must keep us company because there is no safe way to get back home.

It is hard to accept the motion of the lake. I can do nothing to predict it and nothing to curb it. There are certain times of the day, of course, when it is often calm. Very early morning usually brings a lull. Often late at night the winds give the lake a few hours peace. Not always though. I would not mind travelling at night, or in the early morning, always. There is no such thing.

I stare balefully at the lake, calm now, but still furry from the rain, unnecessarily vast. Bob calls up, "What are you glaring at me for?"

"Oh, nothing, nothing," I say. "The only thing I can't figure out is why an island has to be in the middle of a blasted lake."

"They're just made that way," he says.

⇥≫ (3) ≪⇤

Summer moves in. The geese and ducks are heading north. Hot pine and earth smells call us outside. The eagle is building his nest on another island now.

I am in the final stages of staining the exterior siding—vertical and overlapping two-by-tens. The house is almost finished and the trees are almost fully leafed. There are roses growing again in front of the house, and long-stemmed grasses thrust their tips up everywhere around us. The day is calm and the lake is placid as the sky. The sun is hot on my face; when I lift my hand to my nose, I can smell my skin, warm and heady. The windows of the house are all open and summer blows through them. The curtains billow in the shifting air. I am barefoot and the porch is warm beneath my feet. Today, I am happy to stay on the island because I am free to leave it.

A boat sounds in the distance. There are many boats around now, like old friends. I listen to it approach, running the brush up and down the siding, squishing the bristles into the rough-grained wood, watching it darken and glisten, then dipping the brush back into the can once more. The boat gets nearer as I stand on tiptoe to reach a patch of wood far above my head. I put the brush down to go and find the stepladder, and the boat, suddenly enormous-sounding, pulls into our dock.

Bob has been working on the porch steps. He pokes his head around the corner at me, inquisitive, and together we walk down to the beach to see what is up. I am less sleepy suddenly, excited at the prospect of visitors. A large green river boat has been tied to the dock; three young Indian men are emerging from it. I recognize Joseph Matisse but not his two companions. All three men are about the same age; all wear blue jeans and plaid cotton shirts. Only Joseph has long hair.

Bob and I greet them, eager to be hospitable, happy at the sight of new faces. Joseph introduces his friends. John Felix, relaxed and humorous in disposition, and Louis Prince, wiry and dark and angry, suspicious of our island and its inhabitants. He nods reluctantly at both of us. John and Joseph take turns explaining that their engine has been acting up ever since they left Tachie; they have pulled in to change the spark plugs and check the carburetor.

We invite them up for coffee before they begin work. John and Joseph agree readily. Louis follows at a distance, compelled by the motion of his friends to make his way up the path and settle himself on the front porch. Once there, he mutters in a low tone to Joseph while I go to put some coffee on.

When I return, Bob is asking for news from town or Tachie. The three think for a moment; then John Felix speaks.

"You know about the blockade?"

"Blockade?"

"The rail blockade?"

"No. Where is it?" Bob leans forward, as if rooting for an answer.

"On the reserve where the railroad tracks cross."

"Ahh," says Bob. "You've set up a blockade?"

"Yes." John gestures with his right hand. A Seiko watch gleams on his wrist; he describes a square in the air.

"Five acres of track is on Indian land. A corner of the reserve. The government never got title to it. So we blockade it." He smiles genially. "If they try to break through, maybe we take care of it with guns." He chuckles, quietly exuberant.

"But what do you want?" I ask.

"Land," says Joseph. "Money, too."

"Oh." What else could they want, after all?

"We wait," says John. "They fly all supplies up to Leo Creek—Takla Landing. But we wait; they have had to close Silvican Mill. That puts one hundred fifty men out of work. Soon they'll decide to talk." He smiles again.

"What terms are you asking?" says Bob.

"Land, at three acres for one; on fifty acres," says Joseph.

"And then seven million dollars," adds John. Louis Prince sits apart, staring across the lake.

Bob and I don't know whether to grin or nod. I suppose in the end we just look vaguely surprised, since John goes on to say:

"Once we get the money we won't need welfare handouts anymore. That's why we want seven million." When he finishes speaking, he glances around him and moves back so that he leans against the wall. The gesture reminds me of the possibility of movement, and I jump to my feet and go for the coffee.

I return with a tray just as John says:

"Every year the trains kill lots of moose. They leave them dead on the tracks. If we have money, we can protect our village better, our hunting rights and way of life."

"Yeah, I see what you mean," says Bob, helping to distribute coffee mugs. "How long has this blockade been up?"

"A few weeks now," says Joseph. "Since fishing started."

The men drink coffee and discuss the fishing while I ply them with cookies and drift off in thought, listening to the fishing report with only one ear. The rainbows are getting scarcer. Someone caught an enormous lake trout near Woods Island. Char are plentiful.

How many moose are actually killed each year by the trains? Probably not a lot. What a perfect metaphor that is, however, for the impact of white civilization on the Indians. Since the railroad came through, and the road before that—only six or seven years ago now—Tachie has suffered the traumas of accessibility. The more remote an Indian village, the better its chances of surviving as a community with Indian values. The more trains come through, the more moose die.

We all finish our coffee slowly, glad to sit in the summer sun. At last John suggests they get to work on the engine, and Joseph and Louis follow him to his feet, Joseph still shy of us, Louis still silent and aggrieved. Bob goes down with them to the beach, but I demur and wave goodbye. Moving down to the south point, I stretch out there on the sunwarmed pine needles, sleepy and bemused.

A plane passes overhead, its gay colors bright against the sky, its heavy pontoons slimmed by the distance. Supplying the northern settlements by air? On the beach the engine putters into life. I think of the Indians trying to set up their island against the world, and us on ours, and how unlikely we all are to succeed. They are young—our age—and they fight to prevent the further erosion of their culture. We are young—their age—and we fight to escape the destructiveness of ours. That seems like a difference between us, but it is only skin-deep. Because what are they hoping for, really? For the railroad to pay them for their land, so they can protect their hunting rights? No, for the railroad to go away. For all the crazy white men to disappear into the blue they came from. For the boundaries of their world to magically expand again, to give them room to breathe and hunt their moose in peace. But the planes fly by them; there are no boundaries in the sky.

I turn my head on the pine needles, looking down the lake; sunlight sparkles on its moving surface, which laps the island gently, then harder as the wake of the departing river boat hits the shore.

→⟫ (4) ⟪←

As summer days surround us and we prepare to leave the lake behind for a time, it becomes ever more significant to me, ever more powerful and demanding. Whether the water rolls gently, bringing visitors, or whether it rolls harshly and is resented, preventing movement, it rolls. Surrounded by such rolling, unable to escape it, I feel more and more helpless—at times, bewildered. How can I accustom myself to this lake? Perhaps if I could run the boat, get away from the island by myself, it would make a difference to my life upon it. I pursue the thought, desperate and hopeful. It hardly seems possible that I am not strong enough to start the engine. Undoubtedly it is conviction that I lack, conviction that I can do it too—negotiate my own way around these dangerous waters. I wonder.

It is evening, with the long light hours of June ahead. I ask Bob to come down to the dock with me. He starts the engine and puts it into neutral. Then he climbs from the boat, calmer than I, although if I fail to return tonight, he'll be stranded without a boat. I back the boat up, turn it, and head for the southern shore. It is a cloudy evening and the eagle is fishing. He crosses my path twice as I gradually increase the engine's speed. The controls present no problem; I have often run the boat before, once Bob got it in motion.

In a short time I nose into Duck Bay. I move the black control handle into neutral and cut the engine. As usual, the sudden silence shocks me into awareness of sound which has vanished.

I pull the boat up slightly onto the shore and tie two half hitches around a tree. I don't have to pull up the engine, since the bank here falls off steeply, but I climb back on board to shove Bundy up onto the roof of the cabin, where she slips and slides in an awkward and terrified fashion toward the bow, jumping ashore with great relief.

The walk is dull. Grass sticks up at odd angles, and the silence is grim. After only five minutes, I turn again to the lake. I push Bundy on the cabin roof again, untie the two half hitches, and climb in, then shove off with the pole, set the controls, and go back to the outboard. As I grasp the handle at the end of the starting cord, I notice a small chip in the black paint of the engine casing and fasten my eyes to it. I tear the cord out. The engine chuckles briefly.

The sound is infuriating. I pull the cord again, breathing hard, not with exertion but with excitement. The engine doesn't even chuckle. I pull again. By the tenth pull, I have given up. There is no point in pulling anymore, but I know I will go on until I am flattened by exhaustion. I pull once more, and the engine slowly catches, starts, then roars.

For a moment I look at it, and then I dash forward and cut the choke before the damn thing floods itself and dies. The sound evens out, and I move the control lever into the forward position. In a state of shock, I turn the wheel as I would a car wheel, and the boat veers sharply toward the shore while I wildly spin it the other way. After several mad arcs, the boat gets straightened out and moves through the bay toward the open lake. I gun the engine until it is running flat out, and rest my hand on the controls. I've done it at last. A victory of a kind. I am still uneasy, though. Still feeling at the mercy of the waves. Does this boat go to independence, lady? No, ma'am. This boat don't go anywhere near. Fact is, you can't get there from here.

All alone on the great big lake. I set my course straight for the dock, and get there as fast as I can.

->->->)(<-<-<-

This morning, I stand at the wheel again, looking down the lake. The wheel vibrates beneath my palm; my thumbs hooked securely around the finger grip keep my hands from being shaken off. The engine sound trails lengthily behind me, like a huge mosquito determined to keep up with its movable feast. The lake is dull grey beside the boat, and I imagine I can see small fish bubbling and bursting in a spray of white. A plane passes overhead, heading north. Culchunoe is just visible in the distance now. I wonder if Wally and Joyce will be there, as we hope, or if we've come too late to catch them.

Bob shouts in my ear, "You're doing great! How do you feel?"

"O.K.," I yell. "Ask me again when we get there." The engine seems to change pitch. It grows deeper and slower and then higher and faster once again. I wonder uneasily if something is wrong, then concentrate on steering down the center of the passage between the American Islands, expecting at any moment the crunch of propeller on rock. Being in charge of the boat is not relaxing. We move smoothly through the channel and out into the open lake once more.

At Culchunoe I cut the engine to a tiny purr and pull in alongside the wharf on the near side of the island. The maneuver is awkward; we float four feet off the landing, and Bob grabs desperately for the wharf with a paddle. He manages to pull us in far enough to jump for it.

I climb out too, and we tie up. I am glad to have done this trip all by myself, from start to finish, but glad also that I won't have to get back onto the water right away. At the end of the wharf's steps a man waits with a small briefcase. He is large and heavily buttoned up in a sort of safari jacket and pants with little straps at the ankles.

"Hey, did you take the garbage over already?" he calls out to me.

"What?" I say.

"The garbage. I was supposed to grab a ride with you to the shore. I have to go to town for the day."

"I don't work here," I say.

"Oh. Well, isn't that the garbage scow? That boat you came in?" he says.

"No," I say. "It's our boat." Can there be another one like it? I wonder.

He laughs. "Sorry, it looks just like the garbage scow they use here."

"Ha, ha," I say politely.

"Oh well," he adds grandly, "that's all right. Guess I'll go check at the main office and find out what's going on." He departs, briefcase in hand.

At the caretaker's cabin, Wally's dog Loki greets us with an elephantine leap into the air. Wally and Joyce must still be here. I knock on the door and Joyce opens it.

"Hello!" she says. "We're just leaving today. We didn't think we'd see you again before we left. Come in."

In the cabin, Wally moves about in a flurry of activity, packing and dusting, moving furniture and taking things off the walls. Without stopping, he greets us energetically and moves two chairs for us to sit in.

"I hope you don't mind if I keep packing," he says. "We are leaving soon—as soon as they get organized enough to take us over to the shore." He laughs. "We were supposed to leave a week ago—a whole week—but their cook didn't show up on time, so I have been cooking for them for a week now. They wanted to hire me for the summer!" He laughs again, his face glowing with the complete amusement of superior knowledge. "No, thank you! We've been here long enough. We have to get up to our own lake and plant all the little plants so they will grow in time, and put things in order at the cabin and fix the boat. It is time to get home now." Vigorously, he sweeps the hallway and the kitchen, raising a little cloud of dust around the broom.

"What kind of a boat do you have?" I ask, the question popping out of my mouth with very little bypass through the brain first. It is almost an obsession now, thinking about boats and what to do with them and where you can go with them and why you would want to.

"Oh, just a little boat. A funny little tub with an engine," says Wally, sweeping the dust into a dustpan. "I didn't build it—although I am a boatbuilder, you know—but I didn't build this one. I found it up the lake one day—deserted and with a hole in it—and I liked it. It was such a silly thing, but built well, with good wood, so I took it home and fixed it up, and now it is my boat. We get along somehow. We are the same shape." I can see the boat clearly, squat and broad and cheerful, bustling about McLeod Lake. Charlie the crow pokes his head through the open window as Wally finishes speaking, and I shrink back, trying to look unobtrusive. At the sight of me and Bob, though, he hops in and struts up and down the windowsill, turning his head from time to time in stern reproof, and fixing one black eye in my direction.

"Liz can run our boat now," Bob says.

"You can?" asks Wally in delight. "That is excellent. Excellent!"

he repeats with emphasis. Thinking of my precarious new ability, I hurry to interrupt him.

"Well, sort of," I say. "I mean I can start the engine and run the controls and so on. Somehow, though, I feel even less secure than I did before."

"Well," says Wally, stopping in midstream. "It may be that you should get a different boat. You have to find the boat that is right for you, and then it will work out. It is important because there are as many different kinds of boats as there are people, really—just because it floats doesn't mean that it will be what you need. A lake is a wonderful place, though, when you can get a feeling for it—all that water beneath you, it sets your mind free, to think and wonder. You should not think of it as a battle; that is not what it should be on a lake. You have to be friends with the lake, not enemies, or you'll never get anywhere. Especially if you live on an island," he adds, nodding his head up and down. "Yes, maybe you should have a different boat," he says in a doubtful tone. "But anyway, try and relax! What can happen, after all? Well, it is dangerous, of course, but try to relax." He nods again, taking relaxation very seriously.

Joyce picks up a homemade cage of wood and rattan and sets it on the couch near the window. "Come on, Charlie, come on, boy," she says in a soft tone. Charlie ignores her spitefully, clearly out of sorts with our intrusion into his domain.

"Well, I will," I say, smiling. "I'd better. Having a house here is a little different from coming up for a week or so to a lodge like this one."

"Oh, yes," says Wally, opening the cupboards beneath the sink. The top half of his body disappears for a moment as he bends in to remove several cans of milk. "The people who come here, they are all quite insane. They go out for a day's fishing, out onto the lake to fish, and the boat is all ready and gassed up in the morning, and the tackle is set, and they have a guide, and a lunch made. Everything done! But they still take forever to get going. Putting on their special shirt and special vest and special boots. That is essential, you know, to catch fish, special boots! Quite insane. Not only that, but they pay one hundred dollars a day here. Can you imagine? One hundred dollars a day!"

We murmur disbelief.

"No, it's true, it's true!" says Wally. "They are quite insane. They come back with their fish, a dead fish, and they want you to take a picture of them holding it. Holding this dead fish! I wonder if they have pictures of them holding their chickens and what they eat for supper at home, too. Scrambled eggs and so on." He thumps the canned goods into a box. Bob and I are convulsed with laughter.

After a while, everything is packed, and the man with the ankle straps comes to the door.

"They asked me to tell you that the garbage scow is ready anytime. We're all going over in it." He looks at Wally curiously and then says, "Aren't you the cook?"

"The cook?" says Wally. "No, no, no, I am not the cook. Whatever gave you that idea?"

"Oh," says the man. "Well, I'll see you down at the wharf."

"See what I mean?" says Wally happily. "Crazy, quite crazy."

We help Wally and Joyce with their luggage. Joyce carries Charlie's little cage, with Charlie baleful inside it. After the scow is loaded— and it really does look all too much like our boat—it putters off in the direction of the shore. I let Bob drive us back to the island, content this time to ride. After we get moving, I lean over the side of the boat and stare into the darkness of the water, wondering what we are passing over. Every once in a while the spray splashes lightly onto my face.

I picture Wally puttering around his garden, hauling water from the lake, fixing his chimney and his funny little boat. I picture the lake over the course of the long, hot summer, slowly drying and drying and just as wet as ever. I lean far over the edge of the boat, until my stomach is crushed against the wooden railing and I can dangle my fingers in the wetness around me and feel the unbroken satin of the cold. Maybe in the fall we'll buy a canoe, and drift with it upon the tide. Crazy, quite crazy. All that water beneath you. It sets your mind free.

→≫ (5) ≪←

Last night I dreamt of faces. Like bubbles bursting from the bottom of my mind they came shooting up and past my eyes. Faces of people that I've known and people that I've never known, of people that I've seen and people that I've never seen. Thousands of faces, each one different and each one real.

The smell of summer blew in the window as I lay in bed. Catching the grassy, needled breeze, I leaned on my elbows and watched summers tumble before me. I was packing for camp, with my trunk open on the floor and twelve pairs of white socks inside it, neatly folded, never to be worn. I was running down the meadow to the flagpole, barefoot, with the morning dew cold and wet like spray around my moving feet, and the stubble from last year's hay pricking up through the soft grass. Later summers too. I was climbing Halston Peak with Bob and felt the cold rock scraping my knuckles as I jammed them in. I was crossing Indian Pass on a cloudless glacier day, and glissading through the snow until I fell in a pile of sunburned coolness. I was arriving at the factory, punching the time clock, before the bell rang, feeling the warm breeze follow me through the double doors. I am glad that we are leaving soon, leaving our island behind and moving out into the world again.

Right now I am about to bathe, in celebration of the day. The wind is blowing in huge, brief gusts, and the sun drenches the new dock. I take off all my clothes, piece by piece. First my sweater. Then my shirt. Button, button, button, button, button. The cuffs last. Button, button. I slip it off and toss it to the shore. My socks next. I struggle to keep my balance, standing on one foot at a time. A gust of wind slaps the water dark, and hits me next. I have no time to run. I shiver, watching the goosebumps appear on my arms and chest like ripples on the surface of a pond. I unzip my jeans and shove them down around my ankles, then step out of them and fling them away. I am naked, and the wind hits me again. I drop to my knees on the edge of the dock and wrap my arms around me.

I can hardly bear to think of the next step. I extend the tips of my fingers beneath the surface of the water. Quickly I withdraw them again. The dock is warm and sweet smelling under the sun. Lying flat upon it, I can feel a neat pattern of nails beneath my thighs. I breathe the fresh pine and remember building the dock. The two of us at work, quickly and together fitting logs and boards and nails. Splicing wood in place until it protruded from the shore like the island's tongue, tasting the smooth, wet lake. I extend my arms as far above my head as I can reach and point my toes tightly behind. Now, ladies and gentlemen, the human cannon ball. Will be shot from the island into the lake beyond. Drum rolls. But no, I must do it myself. No fuse.

I jump to my feet and fill the bucket in the lake, spilling some water on my toes as I pull it from the water, and whipping them back in great alarm. Ha. Am I a person or a worm? Quickly again, I lift and pour. Right above my head the bucket tips. AAAAAAAAAHHHHHHHH!!!! I scream until the hills behind me echo. Then in quick motion I scrub all over with soap. Face, chest, arms, crotch, thighs, knees—knees? A gust of wind attacks me and I cringe. Nothing to do now but jump. I skid into the water, catching my foot on a nail. I am already climbing out, onto the dock and into the wind. Where's the towel? There. There.

I feel clean, to the roots of my mind. I lie back in the sun on our dock, and I'm glad to be here, and glad to be leaving. Glad to be alive, glad to have a lake to dive into. I shout again. HELLO!! and listen to the echoes come rolling back. Hello! Hello . . . hello . . . loo . . . lo. The echoes fade. HELLO!! I shout again. The echoes return in waves of sound, continuous moving threads of sound. Hello! Hello . . . hello . . . loo . . . lo. I dangle one foot in the water again, and try to catch the sound waves as they hurtle by, coupling my hands above my head. Like the wind itself, they touch me, but they blow right by. There's no stopping them now.

→≫ (6) ≪←

We're leaving tomorrow, and Bob has been in a state of high energy all morning, cleaning and packing, greasing his boots and sewing up the holes in his clothes. He is looking forward to being in the mountains again, teaching mountaineering in places which are, at best, improbable building sites. He hums to himself, varying the tunes with words from time to time.

"And the last thing General Custer said / When he turned around and saw all the Sioux / Was 'I don't know where I'm going / But I'm going nowhere in a hurry, too' / He got the I don't know where I'm going / But I'm going nowhere in a hurry blues."

Suddenly, while cleaning out the cupboards, I interrupt him.

"You know what?"

"What?"

"I don't see how we're ever going to be able to make a living out here."

"Oh, ah?" says Bob intelligently, more interested at the moment in Snowseal on his boots.

"Well, yeah. Really. The Indians can't do it, and they've got a whole village. All we've got is an island. We'll always be leaving it."

"I thought we were going to try trapping," Bob says, and hums some more, still hopeful.

"Yeah, but what about leases and licenses? Not to mention cruelty to animals."

"We'll just see how it goes. Besides, I thought you had plans for becoming a writer, rich and famous?"

"Ha," I say. "Fat chance."

"Look, what do you want? You want to live here or not?"

"I do, that's the whole problem. I do, but—oh, never mind."

Bob hums, relieved, engaged in Snowseal.

"I do! But it just seems everybody goes to the wilderness—the new land—counting on self-sufficiency somehow. And look what happens. The very people who can't be satisfied with civilization drag it with them to the ends of the earth. So they can stay there. You trap furs for idiots so you never have to meet them—or else start a city or two to supply you. Railroads. Roads. Et cetera." I am getting overwrought. I gesture with my hands.

"Et cetera," Bob agrees, but will not be drawn in. He wipes the Snowseal off his hands and comes over to me, linking his arms gently behind my back.

"You feeling grungy? We know what to do about that." He kisses the tip of my nose.

"You kiss the tip of my nose?" I ask. "This is the great panacea for island disease?"

"You got it. Then we kiss the tip of your chin." He demonstrates that as well. "Why don't we go lie down for a while, and read?"

"Sure," I say. "I'll be glad to go lie down, as long as we *don't* read."

"Ah, as long as we *don't* read, is it?" says Bob. "Shall we take a nap, then?"

"I wouldn't mind taking a nap in a while," I say. "If I had any good reason to."

"Well, let's go."

In the bedroom, we burrow under the quilts, dragging them over our heads and making a tent, dark and warm, to giggle in. Outside, Bundy scratches at the side of the bed. Emerging, we see her, looking earnest and eager, ready to get in on the fun.

"Ah," says Bob. "Here's Miss Four Paws, our recreational director."

"Come on up," I say. As she lands with a delicate thud, I say, "Bundy knows better than to worry about her relationship to the world. Animals just accept themselves as they are."

"Not this one," Bob says. "She thinks she's a person."

Bundy crawls under the quilt, and we pull it over all three of us. After a time Boots appears too. For a while we lie together, a warm tangle of bodies with fur and clothing intermingled, everyone breathing audibly, and moist tongues reaching out from time to time. Then Bundy and Boots are unceremoniously dumped onto the floor again.

"I like it here, don't you?" I say.

"Umm," says Bob. "To which *here* do you refer? The world, the island, or the bed?"

"All three. The bed."

"I like you," he says. "Here, there, wherever. How about—there?"

→>>> (7) <<<←

It's fall again, and we're home, up from the south with a new/old truck, a new/old river boat, and some money in the bank. The new boat was waiting for us in the Fort when we got back, selected before we left and paid for on our return. It's older than the first one, much older, but better built and leakless. It is long and thin and has a lovely water-shearing prow. It rides high in the water and sometimes even planes above the surface.

The house was fine when we returned, undisturbed save by the swallows, who have built elegant nests in all the eaves. They swoop around our heads on deep-purple wings and sit on the eaves side by side staring at us and chattering sternly, like so many lawyers explaining our position. A precarious one, it seems. They have given us thirty days' notice. But I think that, then, it will be they who vacate.

It's so good to be back, and to know that this winter there will be no need to leave. To know that this winter we can keep the island with us. I am busy getting re-acquainted with everything, and planning walks, and jobs, and lazy days in the boat. I want to explore the whole lakeshore, and find the old logging roads, and the tall dead trees rising like church spires in the woods. I want to gather bits of driftwood, and berries, and water-smooth pieces of glass, and strange rocks. I want to find old bottles, and put pebbles into a jar, and see the late summer flowers, still blooming; to fill my pockets with twine, and light fires on the beach like signals. I want to watch the eagles fishing, and hunt for moose, and build a railing for the porch. I want to paint the ceilings, and paint the floors, and paint the window ledges. I want to take my clothes off, and lower myself into the lake, slowly, with the crown of my head going in last. I want to watch the storms blow in and out, and learn to like the breaking of the waves. I want to be here.

The September days are warm this year—Indian summer. The water itself is still warm, and the sun is always shining. I pack a picnic lunch of oranges and cookies, tie it into a bundle, and put it on a stick. Bob fills the tanks and changes the spark plugs, and we boat.

I climb onto the roof of the boat and dangle my legs down the windshield. I lie back, my hair spreading in the sun. Bob sets the controls on low and climbs up beside me. We peel an orange apiece and eat them. The juice drips and gathers on the shiny blue roof.

The day passes. I turn over and roast my back. We cruise into the North Arm, all the way down to the end, and pull up on the shore. I run through the sand, squiggling it between my toes. Bob swims.

We explore an old grassy road for a mile or two, surprising the tiny toads which leap between the grasses. We lie in the grass and watch the wind push the light-flecked leaves overhead. We hold hands. Bundy pursues all smells.

Dusk comes earlier now than it did in June. On the return trip, the roof of the boat is chilly. The loons are loud tonight, interrupting the stillness with laughs and shrieks, barks and gurgles.

The dock looms and the engine is silent. I dip an oar over the side of the boat into the water, and it makes a little closing sound, muted but decisive. When the boat hits the dock, the dull thump sets the night to vibrating.

Coming back to the island is the finest thing of all. We wander up the path, yards apart, and tie up gently when the day is done.

$$\rightarrow\!\!\gg (8) \lll\!\!\leftarrow$$

Maurice Joseph stopped by yesterday with his wife, Doreen, and some of his children. We were piling wood on the beach when a large grey boat pulled alongside the dock. Only when they had tied up and started to climb out did I recognize them—they looked different outside the walls of their home. Doreen was wearing a kerchief around her hair and shoulders.

We invited them to the house, and they climbed slowly, silently up the steps, and settled themselves into the living-room chairs—four children and their parents. While I made coffee and got out some cookies from the storeroom, they sat in silence. After we all had mugs, Maurice explained their arrival.

"You know the Walkers?" he asked, his large hands resting on the arms of the captain's chair like lynx paws. "They asked us to stop by and get your car keys, so they can move your car. It is in the wrong place."

"Really?" I said. "I thought it was out of the way."

"It is that it is parked on the wrong land. The land belonging to the lodge." Maurice nodded his head up and down once, and smiled almost imperceptibly. "The man who runs it, he is over and he says that if the car is not moved, he will push it into the lake. He is not a very friendly man," Maurice concluded, his arms still motionless upon the chair.

"Well, we really appreciate your stopping. I'll go get the keys now."

No one spoke until Bob returned. Maurice lifted both arms off the chair and tucked the keys carefully into his jacket pocket, folding the flap of the pocket down again and snapping it shut. I was afraid our conversation might end there, but he made no move to leave.

"So how is everything in Tachie?" said Bob with an effort. "Whatever happened about that rail blockade, anyway?"

"It is down now," said Maurice. "It is down for a month. There are trains passing again."

"Did you get anything for the land?" I asked.

"Not yet." Maurice smiled sadly. "They are talking now. Still talking." He looked toward his wife as if for confirmation of this statement, and she tightened her eyes and lips for an instant in a stylized nod.

"So nothing at all got done?" I asked, not entirely surprised.

"Nothing. Except that now they are talking," said Maurice. "Talking." He smiled again.

Trying to find a happier topic, I asked, "How is August this fall? Still talking?"

"August? Oh, he is not so good. No, he is not so good."

"What's wrong?" I asked, thinking of his eyes.

"It is not his eyes," said Maurice, reading my mind. "They are the same. It is his grandson."

"Joseph?"

"Yes." Maurice paused, thinking. "You know, he was living with them. He took the boat out to go fishing many times this summer. Sometimes he took Louis Prince along. Last week they go out and head up the river. It is getting low again, and there are many rocks. Many rocks. Louis was running the engine, and he likes to run it very fast. He hit a rock, and the boat smashed. The propeller was bent; the boat stove in. They were near shore. But the boat was ruined. Then Joseph moved out."

"He went back to his parents' house?"

"No. He and Louis moved to Prince George."

"Oh," I said.

"Yes, they live with some other young men there until they can find a job. August knows there is nothing he can do." Maurice finished his coffee and looked at his wife, who had sat patiently and silently the whole time. The children had disappeared outside after finishing up the cookies.

"There is nothing you can do," Doreen said. "No." She shook her heavy face sadly, listening to the children jumping on the back porch. A boat passed by in the distance, and she looked at Maurice with inquiry.

"We will go, then, before the lake blows up," said Maurice, rising to his feet. We saw them down to the dock and off, and went back to splitting and piling wood, while the lake blew up and filled the air with sound and moisture. Under the clear autumn sky it was rich and deep blue in color, with twists of white. We decided to stop our wood runs for the day, instead of struggling through the waves.

There is nothing you can do? No. The waves blow up, and they get higher and higher, and there is nothing you can do. Set off in them, and they will shove at you. Wait them out, and they will take their time in calming. You have one choice only, and that is to accept them. I am only slowly learning what that means, but the Indians have always known. It seems to be the secret both of their strength and of their weakness. Their strength because it brings them peace and community together. Their weakness because it brings down the rail blockade at last. They do not really want to live on an island. They want to live in a world. When that means self-destruction, that, too, they can accept.

What else must you accept? That a storm blows over the lake; that the railroad kills the moose and leaves them wasted on the tracks; that Joseph has gone to Prince George. Hope, perhaps, that Joseph will return, and go fishing on the lake again, and mend the boat or build a new one. Accept that you may go blind. Run your fingers through the water and let the smell of the lake suck you away on the wind.

I cannot seem to do that. Not enough. Not yet. I am not even sure I want to. Damn Louis Prince and the rocks in the Tachie River and the trashing of the world. Damn the fact that islands are only to be found in lakes. I listen to the roaring of the sky, and I tense, unwilling to be spun away, fingers floating on the breeze. I turn, and climb the steps to my island, carrying wood.

->>)(<<-

We've been here almost a year and a half now. A year and a half on the island. I have helped to build a house, explored the island in many weathers, and shared my days with Bob. I am still, however, frightened of the lake. I am wary of it, and its moods. I am alarmed by its capacity for absorption. Rock, air, rain, sky, boats, cans, and human lives, it seizes them all, or hides them. Those who have been drowned in Stuart Lake have for the most part been recovered from it; they leave their deaths here only in part. All other things which are sucked down stay down, and the paths of their descent are unmarked by any signs save in the imagination.

We sank our old boat last week. I was tired of seeing it on the beach, rotting and shredding, ugly and tired. A summer on the beach had not added to its charm or usefulness. The blunt snout had been pulled up high enough so that the whole front half rested on dry ground; but the rear section was not only in the water, after two months of repose it was entirely under water. It sagged mightily, into the deeper part of the lake where the shelf falls away. The section that sat right on the edge of the shelf had been worked and shoved by the water over a small boulder, and a hole as big as my head had splintered and widened in the bottom.

The blue paint at the water line was shredding. Bits of garbage, bailing cans, and paint flakes floated in the boat, and the windshield had been cracked by a falling branch. The thing no longer even looked like a boat.

Although we wanted to get rid of it, we could not at first figure out how to do so. Chopping it up and burning it seemed like a potentially infinite amount of work. In addition, it would take days, if not weeks, for the wood to dry out sufficiently to burn. And how do you chop up something that is half under water? So, we decided to sink it.

Once conceived, I could hardly wait to effect the plan. We filled the working boat with rocks, which would help to insure that the wreck would go down where we wanted it to. Hauling it out proved to be no trouble, and we dragged it to a point five hundred yards off the island, and started to toss rocks into the bottom. Nothing happened for a remarkably long time. Then suddenly the boat upended, the bow shooting down into the water and the stern jumping out of it. The water that filled the bow seemed grey and oily, although it was actually clear. Already I could see the unseen fish exploring it, swimming through it and scoffing, or devouring.

There was a long moment when nothing whatever seemed to happen. We were frozen into position, watching the rocks and the occasional small air bubbles which rose from the water. Then, in the space of thirty seconds, the boat sank. It started to slip forward, gathered speed, and took off on a long diagonal trajectory for the bottom. It pushed aside the water, which churned on the surface with great noisy bubbles of air. After it passed from sight, the bubbles continued to rise.

There was a sickness at the sight. The boat seemed tied to me by invisible strings, seeking to drag me down with it. All that had ever known the boat's favor were expected to accompany it into oblivion. Or not oblivion—into a secret life carried on away from the sight of the sun. Into a slower time, a darker place, where rot and warp rock forever.

The sight continues to follow me. The memory comes to me when I travel in the new boat, long and sleek and graceful as it is. Every time you journey by boat, making untraceable trails on the water, you leave a little of your aura imprinted on it. Like a series of double exposures, I see myself here and there on the water, always riding on my boat.

When you enter a boat, you bring with you boat expectations. A boat is like an island, only smaller. You can cram fewer dreams into it, but it is as clearly defined a limit, as restrictive an environment. Where the boat ends is where you end and where the rest of the world begins. If the boat you have ridden in sinks, it becomes one with the wide and unrestricted world outside. All the essence of containment that you have left in it goes down with it, and merges with the water and the fish, and loses its limits, and becomes as amorphous as the water itself. I see myself on the bottom of the lake, dark as mud and drifting gently. When the boat went down, it took with it part of my precarious belief that it is possible to accept the lake, to work with it or to risk its touch. The waves are too dangerous. They can absorb too much.

→≫ (9) ≪←

Our new boat sank last week. We had just returned from a major winter shopping expedition to Prince George; the truck was full of food for six months, and tools and oil and gas. Weighted down, we swerved and bounced along the Tachie road—as always, the tension grew as we approached the Walkers'. Both of us craned for a glimpse of the lake through the trees, tight with anticipation that it would be twinkling with whitecaps and rushing east or west in heavy rolls. Would we have to wait again, trapped away from home until the lake calmed down? It seemed likely.

The lake was blazing through the trees, and I could see the bursting spray, the rolls and glitters of the water. Strangely, the wind was blowing from the south.

We rounded into the Walkers' yard, and saw Flay down on the dock, heaving to get his boat secured. Over the roar of the wind, he shouted to us, slicking his hair back with one hand, but whatever he said was shipped away unheard. The new river boat was half full of water. My rage at the stupidity which had allowed us to leave it tied up with its transom facing the lake sent a rush of blood to my head. The south wind is rare on Stuart Lake, but when it blows, the Walkers' dock is unprotected. Water was breaking over the transom of the boat. We started to run.

At the dock, Flay had finished securing his boat. He was soaking wet.

"The lake blew up in two minutes," he shouted. "I've never seen anything like it. I didn't even have time to get your boat turned around."

Bob and I started tugging at the river boat. It was as heavy as only a swamped boat can be.

"Leave it!" Flay called. "We can pull it up and pump it out when the storm blows over. It doesn't matter if it sinks now."

Carried away, wrestling with the wind, we managed to get the boat exactly perpendicular to the dock. A wave rammed it sideways against a pier, stove a hole in the side as big as a watermelon, and then helped to push it under. Six feet down it rested on the bottom.

Nadine waited for us at the kitchen door. We pulled off wet boots and hats and coats, and went inside with her. She brought out her usual delicious cakes and cookies, served us huge mugs of coffee, invited us to dinner, and told us we could spend the night in the extra cabin. Flay would pull the boat out tomorrow with his tractor, and we could pump it out and fix it on the beach.

We gripped our coffee mugs, trying to respond. I felt that it was the last time, the absolutely last time, I was going to see water pour into my boat. If it could be called a boat, with a three-foot-long hole in the side. If it could be called a boat, after a night on the bottom. The fact that this time the disaster was due to nothing but our own stupidity helped to clarify my feelings. I simply didn't want to try any longer to become the boatsman I will never be. I would rather canoe out to the island than ever ride in a river boat again. At least we could pull a canoe out of the water every time we left it, and we could easily paddle it if the engine gave out. At least a canoe would respond to my directions.

The next day we watched Flay pull the boat out onto the beach, water sluicing over the transom in the latter stages of the haul. When it had been pumped out and bailed dry, there was two inches of sand in the bottom, sand in the seams, sand in the engine casing. We took the engine off and dumped it in the back of the truck. We asked Flay if we could leave the boat on his beach for the winter. Then we drove back to the Fort, put the engine up for sale at New Cal, arranged for Doug to bring our winter food out by barge, and bought a canoe. Eighteen feet long. Orange. Three seats. Four paddles. And a tiny engine. It is tied to the dock now, bobbing in the water, simple and full of promises.

The clouds move swiftly overhead in a quick exchange of dark and light, dark and light. We sit on the Walkers' beach looking west, waiting to get back home. The whole lake seems to be involved in a secret rite, and the small orange canoe, pulled well up on the beach with its engine lifted, is the only spot of color in a canvas of warm and sultry greys. The wind blows warm for October, and we are here in the north, alone on the shores of the lake, compelled by its ecstasy to wait. I do not mind. I am no longer as frightened of the waves, and so I have more patience with them. Our canoe will get us home at last. Meanwhile, wherever we sit is home.

The trees here on this windy point have almost lost their leaves, but the bare branches skitter and fling themselves about. We gather dry wood and build a fire on the beach. The flames of the fire join in the celebration, rushing one way, pausing, then rushing back to the limits of their wooden tether. The fierce orange glow throws a benevolent reflection on my hands as I write. There is no one around, and there are no lights anywhere. The temptation to load the canoe and push off into the churning mass of water is great. The bitter spray would burst over the bows. The waves on the lake would sustain us.

The evening sky is stretched tight above my head. As I fall asleep, wrapped in my sleeping bag, the sky begins to clear. From time to time I wake to hear the roaring of the lake—and the creaking of the branches overhead. I watch the last coals of the fire flaring up and dying down. I am asleep, but open to the sounds of wind and water; the stilling of sound brings me awake. There are some whitecaps, but it is possible to travel. We load the boat, wrap a tarp tightly about the clothes and supplies, and tighten the wing nuts on the pontoons. It is 1:00 A.M. The sky is clear but moonless. The lake is lit with the reflections of the northern lights. I sit in the bow, Bundy at my feet, and Bob pushes us off, past the first wild breaking shore wave, into the moving stream of water.

The air is cold, colder than the water. The wind mixes it with spray, and the stinging shafts cover my face and hands with tiny points of pain. The pontoons hit the waves with slow determination. The water shoots in an arc above them and lands with a light slap upon the plastic of the tarp behind me.

From the northern horizon, but reaching up into the very center of the night sky, the lights move. Some are like searchlights, elongated triangles of luminescence which sweep the arena and disappear. Some are huge, glowing blocks which move in stately progress, covering first one mass of the sky and then another. One light starts all compressed together in a brilliant ball and then expands, moving in a gyroscopic rotation and flinging out ever more energy, until it becomes a slowly whirling spiral which reaches its outermost limits and vanishes. Banks of red and green light, like rectangular clouds, simply pulse; white lines as thin as fingernails move across the night illuminating nothing but themselves.

No reefs or shoals are hidden in this part of the lake, but Bob has to keep his hand upon the steering column of the engine. I lean my body back against the tarp, bent at the knees and flat upon my back, while the lake continues to break around my feet.

Tonight I am both part of the storm, and its center. Stiff with cold, I'm surrounded by movement, waves of darkness underneath, waves of light overhead. The expanding spirals open steadily and are gone.

The lake is getting calmer. Quick, short waves change slowly into long rolls of water which swell toward the west. Bob turns the engine off and we drift. I sit up and look around, lifting the wet and shivering dog into my lap, and see that the moon is rising, huge on the eastern horizon. Tonight, I can absorb that too, and not be full; at peace with the lake and the things it breaks upon, I am at the center of the world.

The island is in sight: a dark lump against the hills beyond. We come to the dock, and I catch at it with my paddle, and hop ashore taking the towrope with me. I tie up in silence, and we walk up the path in silence. The path softens in greeting, the trees rustle. Our house stands large and hopeful, waiting for our return. We stop a moment below it, hands clasped together, and then climb the steps and open the door. Boots, a cat as black as the center of a wave, comes charging out to greet us, and I take him up; we go to the bedroom together. After piling every sleeping bag, quilt, and blanket in the house onto the bed, I strip off my clothes and, cuddling Boots, who purrs against my stomach, climb in beneath the cold and heavy weight.

→≫(10)≪←

Perfect October weather today. The desire to get off the island and see the changing world is strong as arrows flying with the wind. The tiny engine would push us too fast, past things we want to see and hear, obscuring the smells of fall. So I take it off the canoe, lifting it from the transom while the water pours neatly around the propeller and back into the lake. Bob empties the canoe, washing it with clean water. The canoe settles back into the lake with a thud. I toss in the orange life jackets, lay three paddles across the thwarts, and tell Bundy to hop in. I climb into the bow while Bob shoves the stern off the dock and leaps after it. We sway briefly in the water, balance again, and paddle away along the island's north shore.

The water is low again; the rocks are bare against the mossy growth of the hillside behind them. Some lurk just beneath the surface and I avoid the touch of their sharp edges by the merest flick of a paddle in the still water. There is little wind, and what wind there is blows with us.

Although we paddle on the water, today it is not the water which captures my attention as we move. That is simply the vehicle for smooth motion, for rolling the world past me like a show. Today I have the feeling that no matter how fine a place may be, it is all the finer for leaving it behind, looking at it out of the corner of my eye, touching it only fleetingly, moving on at once to somewhere else. So we paddle both fast and slow, not to get to any particular point of land but to get past all points of land, with the images of them adding up into a scroll of memory.

The ability to move freely around the world brings to me now the gift of perspective. As I paddle from place to place, the whole world changes, and my thoughts change with it. Hills are smaller and larger. A mushroom is the size of a pebble or the size of a fist. Bark is grey in the distance, but brown and red close up. Shore lines progress calmly away and behind at the movement of a wrist; sand and pebbles on the beach glint like silver in the sunlight, then fade into white. Aspens dip their heads, making perches for the larger birds, then straighten again as they fall behind.

Paddling gives me the material with which to remember this time. I can rewind today if I wish, and run over it with an eye for the finest images. Or I can leave it rolled, the scroll of a lake flowing east, to be saved for a later unwinding, when I want to see the pebbles again, and the winds in the grasses, and the leaves quivering. Today, I am a memory collector, and the lake is carrying my net. An eagle sits in his tree, first ahead, then beside, then behind us.

We find ourselves at the far end of the third bay, four miles from home. We have followed every curve and wrinkle of the shore, while the wind has picked up slowly, idling along and pushing us forward.

When we arrive at the bay's far shore and turn around, the wind confronts us with all of its contrary and unpredictable force.

Every turn of the canoe now brings the same result: the wind shoves us back. Bob suggests stopping, building a fire and waiting until the wind dies down, but I want to paddle against it and prove the power of the canoe.

The water splashes and breaks through the sparkling air. The lake is ocean blue, throwing back the face of the sky and then catching it again. Everywhere it is sprinkled with white. We move forward. As I paddle, I can feel the whole canoe beneath me coming alive, our power driving the craft forward through the wind.

Each journey over a wave brings me face to face with the lake; the water swells upward in a satin bulge, puffing inward and enveloping the sides of the bow almost to the thwarts. The canoe gives me confidence. It is one with the shapes of waves; it belongs in troughs and riding curls.

When we reach the open lake, still over a mile from the island, I see a bright-red river boat moving in the direction of Portage. It throws up quite a wake, brilliant silver, around its invisible outboard. Two men are in it. As they cross our path, they spot us and veer toward us. Twenty yards away they stop and cut their engine to a murmur. The bow man shouts a question, lost in the wind.

"We're fine!" I shout back, and both Bob and I make vigorous waving gestures to show that nothing is wrong. The bow man nods and waves, and the stern man guns the engine until the boat all but disappears behind its own wake. Bob and I share a smile of contentment as the Indians move away, and we drive our paddles into the water again, driving the canoe forward as we drive the lake back. The wake from the river boat hits us, and we roll sideways over it, as if rolling, exhausted, over the body of a lover and down the other side. Thus the first canoeists must have embraced the waves.

Indians travelled these lakes and rivers in canoes long before motorboats were brought here, and I can't help but feel of our red-boated friends that they of all people should understand the security which simplicity can bring to life. At the same time, it fills me with joy that they should have stopped to care about us. It is as if our new receptivity to the water has spilled over and spread like an oil slick until it touches other people who ride upon it too. At last we have found the right boat for us, and I can trust the lake to carry me and set my mind free. My face is wet, and I dig the paddle into the water with such vigor that Bob is covered with the spray.

When we get to the island, we paddle straight into the lee of the western cliff. The sudden shock of windless water never lessens. In the breathless cessation of air my attention springs forward, as if falling forward at the sudden release of backward tension, and it focuses on the tumbling slide of rock and shale which plummets to the water from the promontory far above. Each rock is sharp and jagged, distinct, leaning toward the water. This part of the island is one which we rarely see, and the novelty of each separate rock holds my attention now. They seem to be the essence of the island, these western rocks, the root of it exposed to the air and tumbling down. Bare and hard and grey and strong. Simple. As simple as the canoe we ride in; the rock we live on.

The red river boat purrs in the distance. I smile at the sound, remembering the concern for us which prompted the Indians to stop. Strangers to us, but not unknown. I appreciate people, other people, more now than I ever have before. Just as the canoe has set me free to collect the visions of the shore, the island has given to me people, people who fill the world like leaves, each one distinct, making together a delicate variety. Wherever you go, you can find them, but here I can see the best in them; my perspective has changed. Their understanding and concern travel across the waves; they form at times an inseparable unity— a human race.

After floating for a while in the sanctuary of the rock, we pull the canoe out again and round the south shore of the island to the beach. The waves here are the most powerful that we've met; one carries us near to the big boulder, and I see it for an instant close up. Each little grain of rock shines, and pits in the grey surface are huge. Then the wave carries us away again, and the rock is a boulder, its shoulders outlined against the trees, which rustle in the wind. Changing perspectives.

At last the dock is beside us. A single wave breaks over it, nudging us toward the shore. I jump out, not onto the dock but onto the beach, wading through the satin water until I feel the shore rocks jagged beneath my feet and wet with spray. Even these rocks look different now, seen so many times but new again, wet with waves. Things fall into place. Our paddle today has transformed them for me, or clarified a change which already had occurred. It's suddenly clear to me that although we found this island, we were also carried here. We have always used the motion of the waves to define our own. Not just paddling today; even more so when we first beached on this shore. If it weren't for the world beyond the island, we wouldn't be here now. The artistry of other men has given us the means to live here; the love of other men has given us the strength to stay. No one forms his own life, edges and all; islands can only be found in lakes. That's just the way it is.

Waves are not only unescapable, dangerous, liberating; they are essential, the root of life itself. Sound and light move in waves; wind and water flow in waves; blood and love stream in waves. Ragged, cohesive, sparkling, breaking, no bits and pieces but all connected. Waves which are everyplace. Anyplace. Here.

At the dock, we pull the canoe from the water and set it on the platform, upside down. It bobs, secured and stable, a flash of color in the wind.

⇥≫(11)≪⇤

Winter is almost here again. The first snow fell last week, and we ran outside to watch it come down, and stuck our tongues up to the sky to try to catch the snowflakes, each one supposedly unique, though who has ever studied them all to see? The lake absorbed the flakes as soon as they touched it, but the ground was less resilient—some of the snow remains there still. I hardly needed that first white reminder that winter is coming, however, with eighteen cords of wood under the house and on the beach, a moose quartered in the woods, and almost six months' worth of food in the house. Doug Hoy delivered it two weeks ago, in all its frightening bulk, and it is now installed in the storeroom, the cupboards, and along the kitchen walls. The quantity of food which is to pass through our bodies in the course of the winter almost overwhelms me. Sugar, flour, sweets, vegetables, coffee, tea, chocolate; all in bulk amounts. The half a ton of food is strangely admonitory. One wants to be worthy of all that profusion, and live to see it consumed.

There were no eggs in the delivery, and we decided yesterday that that was a good enough excuse to make one last trip to town before freeze-up, although we really just wanted to see our friends once again before the ice made it more difficult. In the early morning yesterday, the lake was tumultuous, and the wind roared—a last fling before the long winter peace. The weather had grown so cutting cold that the next calm night must bring the penciled shafts of crystal to still the surface of the water, tying it with webs of glass. That the water was rough in the morning was all to the good; we hoped the lake would not start to freeze while we were gone.

After a quick breakfast of coffee and toast, we shrugged into our parkas and ran for the beach. In the canoe, I settled into the front seat, pulling on my mittens and hat and scarf, knowing that the enforced stillness of two hours in the canoe would make me cold no matter what I wore, but blithe about the prospect anyway. If the lake and the wind absorbed my heat, in return they would give me my life.

The slow motion of the canoe was the right speed for watching the world. We moved out past The Fishing Cabins Island and past the tiny island, maybe ten feet by fifteen, which is in shape an exact replica of our own. I imagined that it contained a small duplicate of our house, with a long set of stairs leading to the beach, a tiny dock like a lizard's tongue upon the water, and a miniature canoe with two people in it just setting off for town as we went by. The woman was small enough to fit into my palm.

We passed the sea-gull rock, sprinkled with white from the summer gulls. We passed the new clearing on the north shore where the ugly, boxlike summer cabins have recently been thrown, but they were empty; no smoke drifted from the chimneys. In the winter, they will be buried deep in snow, untouchable and forgotten.

By the time we got to the Walkers', I was stiff with cold, and the glory of the day surfaced only in the numb travesty of a smile for Nadine and Flay. In their kitchen, I thawed slowly, listening to my bones and muscles creaking in the heat. For a time, neither Bob nor I could speak. We drank hot coffee; Nadine put on a fresh pot. When we recovered the use of our facial muscles, we talked about winter on the lake and hibernation. Nadine likes winter here almost more than summer. Flay— probably because he does so much work outside—seemed to have mixed feelings. He told us a story about a bear cub which a Prince George man had raised in his back yard. When winter began, the cub got restless and ornery. The man brought him a load of hay and several mattresses. The bear knew just what to do with his supplies. He grabbed them and hauled them off and built himself a little cave next to the fence. Then he crawled right in and went to sleep. Flay got a mischievous pleasure out of this tale; he implied that he wouldn't say no to a little cave himself; winters up here can be mighty cold.

-»»«<-

When we got back from town at nine o'clock, the lake was almost calm, and the water was decorated with long slivers of randomly floating ice. They seemed to draw strength from their proximity to each other; imperceptibly the crystals grew longer and broader, and joined together in a mesh. As we pushed off, the surface of the water rippled, and the small sheets slid gently down the rises without breaking apart. The freeze was beginning.

Normally, it takes almost two hours to get home from Caesar's Point in the canoe with the engine going flat out. I wasn't worried that the lake would freeze fast enough to give us trouble in that length of time, and the first half hour went well enough. But four hundred yards offshore from the Tachie dock, the engine choked and died.

In cold weather the 3.5-hp has difficulty coping with the dampness in the air. The carburetor gets moisture in it which freezes and stops the engine. It had happened three or four times during the trip that morning, and I thought now that Bob would just take off the engine cover, remove the ice from the carburetor bowl, and restart the engine. He did—but almost immediately the engine died again.

"Have you checked the air-intake valve?" I asked.

"Yes, of course."

It was a moonless night. We did not have a flashlight, or even a candle. I had a pocketful of matches in a plastic bag, but they proved inadequate to the task of lighting the engine sufficiently to discover what was wrong with it. Bob took the carburetor off largely by feel, to see if there was still a lump of ice which he had missed the first time. In the process he dropped an engine part. It made no noise striking the bottom of the canoe—it was no bigger than a pin. Without it the engine would not start.

I crawled over the bales and boxes of clothes, fresh eggs, and one last bag of cement, until I was perched just in front of the middle thwart. Bob was feeling with his hands through the engine casing, through the invisible knobs and screws and levers, to see if any of them had caught the engine part. I reached down, balancing on my knees, to try and feel for it on the bottom of the canoe. Typically, the bottom was puddled with water, and bits of wood left over from the transporting of our winter wood supply. Every once in a while I felt a sliver I was sure was the missing part, then broke it between my fingers to the pungent smell of pine.

Finally, we decided to paddle. A layer of ice was forming on the sides and bow, however, and a few powerful strokes convinced us it would be useless to try and get back to the island before the ice closed in, if we had to paddle. We turned and headed for the lights of Tachie, glad that they were so near.

Still, it took us the better part of half an hour to reach the Tachie dock. I climbed onto the wharf by way of the slats nailed to its side, and walked to August's house, where a light was still showing in the bedroom window. There was no sign of his boat, normally tied to the front of the wharf, but a broken propeller lay beside the wall of the shed. The outside light caught it, twisted and dented; there was a huge chunk torn out of one of the blades. I knocked on the door, and August came out in his underwear, seeming glad to see me.

"Come in, come in! Don't stand out in cold!"

"Hi. Actually . . ."

"Oh, come in. Whew! Cold night. Where is your man?"

"He's out in the boat. Our engine seems to have stopped working, and I was wondering if we could borrow a flashlight to try and find out what's wrong with it."

"Yes, I have a flashlight. Come on." August gestured me to follow him into the kitchen, where his wife sat in the chair, glancing toward us and then away. There was no sign of anyone else living in the house. No Joseph. No boat out front. Nothing much seemed to have changed since the first time I entered August's house. Maybe his eyes were a little worse, that was all. He rummaged around in a drawer next to the sink and finally emerged with a black plastic flashlight.

"There!" he said proudly. "Now we see if it works." He pushed the button, and the feeblest of rays emerged. "Oh, well, let me think. We got some new batteries in town; they should be in the shed. Just let me put my pants on, and we find them." He disappeared into the bedroom, and from the prodigious banging that emerged, I assumed he was putting on his pants, and thought about the ice.

Back from the shed, the new batteries were installed and the light shone bright.

"Here, no hurry to give it back. I see the lake is freezing. You better hurry up, or you won't get home this winter!"

"Yes, I know. Well, thanks a lot. I'll bring this back right away."

"No hurry," said August with a wave of his hand. He stood at the door and bit his lower lip as he peered after me into the cold darkness.

I crawled down the ladder to the wharf and handed the flashlight to Bob. He found the part immediately. It was lying at his feet. It looked more like a bobby pin than a straight pin, but was smaller than either.

While Bob put the engine casing back on, and the engine itself back onto the boat, I returned the flashlight to August. He smiled a very toothy smile, and said, "Always very good to have a flashlight. Even if you are a millionaire!"

By now the route home is so familiar that there is little need for light, but since the water is at its lowest in November there may be unexpected rocks near the surface, so I was glad to see the moon rising in the east. Although the engine was working again, it kept icing up, and the trip was interrupted by longer and longer sessions of engine coaxing. I felt myself passing into the now-familiar first stages of hypothermia. I grew stiffer and stiffer, more and more calmly observant and placidly still. The sheets of ice on the lake shone in the moonlight like footlights, but they moved, twinkling to the left, and then the right, with the caprice of surfacing whales. Two miles from home, I felt the silence behind grow compact, and I turned to discover that Bob had taken the engine off and put it on the floor of the canoe.

"I can't get it going anymore. We'll have to paddle." His face was clear in the moonlight, with the ridges of his nose and chin deeply shadowed against the white of his cheeks and forehead.

"Right," I said, not moving.

Paddle, I thought. Paddle. I'm so glad that I can paddle home. It's a human thing, paddling. A bear can always hibernate—a person has to paddle. You've got to be glad of that in the end. It's depending on engines that saps your strength. It's looking for parts. Not paddling. Never paddling. Not that it always gets you home. Sometimes you do it just to keep warm, just to keep from moving backwards. Like August, paddling all the time, and still seeming to be in the same place. Never moving forward to a final vision. That's not so bad, either. What did you expect? At least you're here, all of you, passing the flashlights around.

At least you're here, keeping warm. Not quite drifting on the tide. Just using it to support you while you paddle.

My mind was numb. Even my face was getting numb. I sat for a minute in peace, wondering why I didn't reach for the paddle. At the conscious command, my arms reached down, picked it up, and dipped it into the water. I shoved the water backward, lifted the blade out and moved it forward, then shoved the water back again. Little ripples rolled behind me. The canoe moved through the water, heavy, heavy with ice. From time to time the paddle tip caught and sprayed my face with ice water. I licked my lips, tasting the ice, touching a wall of silence. Watching my hands move up and down, back and forth, I saw that those stiff hands, those icy toes were my perimeter. There was no more—no plans or hopes, no pride or anger, no love or fear, no deep thoughts, no recognition of stars. Just fingers and toes and paddling. Just me distilled. No more powerful than the canoe I rode in—but floating. No stronger than a candle in the wind—but burning.

The movement that I made pushed me forward and spun me backwards; it tossed me toward the sky and sucked me down. A tiny dot upon the lake. A coal of fire in the heart of ice. Vulnerable. All-powerful. There is no arguing with that which knows its limits. There is no fear where I can taste my insignificance. I dip a tiny wooden paddle into the great wet lake—and it moves me. Slowly, compared to the stars. Weakly, compared to the waves. But it's the same motion, the very same motion—I scoop it from the lake, and it sets me on my way. Forever rocked by lakes and men. Forever paddling and alone.

We pulled up to the dock at midnight, with plenty of time to spare, and hoisted the tremendous weight of the ice-encrusted canoe onto the dock. We stood for a while and watched the mist rising from the water, the last heat in the surface being pushed into the air and swirling there in macabre patterns. The now fog-bound lake would break and close, the ice and air sliding together and sliding apart again, existing only to form their patterns—moonlight reflecting on the ice, water wrinkling beneath the fog, mist drifting like a magician's cloak, enwrapping and unwrapping all the changes. Mysterious as an underwater plant, the process of freezing was occurring before my eyes, and yet invisibly, camouflaged by the slightest motion of the water and the slightest motion in the air. I could not be sure where any piece of ice originated—and since I could not trace its history, there was no way to prove that it had not always been ice.

5

UPON THE ROCK

⟫ (1) ⟪

It seems as if the lake will never freeze. When we stood on the dock the other night and watched the long particles of ice becoming cohesive and the little sheets drifting lightly under the touch of the cold moonlight, I was sure the lake would have a solid, heavy coat by morning. I went to sleep with the certainty that at last winter was here, at last we would be safely surrounded by the winter substance of solidity. And indeed, when I turned over and looked at the lake in the morning, there was ice to the south and west as far as I could see.

But there was a roaring in the east and a pounding. Out on the front porch, it was clear why. The water was still open to the east, six or seven miles away. Perhaps the main portion of the lake had never frozen at all; perhaps it had frozen but been ripped open again. The east wind was blowing, and the east wind is both strong and persistent. It was pushing the ice back toward the west.

Despite all the hope I could summon, I knew that the wind would push the ice back until it was just a mound of broken shards piled on the beach. With a grim fascination, I sat on the porch and watched. As with the progress of a volcano or a forest fire, there was nothing that could be done about the inexorable movement, but equally, no way to quell the insane hope that somehow, suddenly, it would reverse itself, or stop in its tracks. As the leading edge of water came closer, I could hear the sounds of the ice as it was crushed, like gravel being bulldozed—a grinding, pushing, thumping sound which never ceased. The ice piled up on itself, layer after layer, under the force of the wind's passage, so that the front of open water was preceded by a high mound of ice.

149

When the front reached the island, it became apparent that there was yet another force at work. The waves which pushed against the ice-line broke over the mound of ice, spraying liquid far back onto the solid water, a liquid which froze as soon as it hit. The water must have been less than thirty-two degrees to freeze so quickly. The waves were always increasing the thickness of the very ice they attacked so furiously. The ice which the wind piled on itself was the thickest ice on the lake. It was a battle between two properties.

By midafternoon, the lake was open again, and the wind has blown from the east ever since. The waves dominate my sleep and waking both, with their unceasing, pregnant noise. The dock is underwater half the time—the spray even reaches the bottommost of our sea steps. The beach rocks glisten with moisture and the air is full of it. We are both silent, and wait for winter to come.

->>><<<-

I wake. The sound has ceased. The air is still, so silent that I can almost hear the earth freezing. The lake is lovely as it has never been before. In the early-morning sunlight, the trees and hills see their faces in it. It reflects the sun as well, sparkling and tossing light outward. It is ice.

There is nothing to do but lie and listen to the silence. When Bob wakes, we lie and listen to it together. I hook my left leg over his right one, and the silence allows us to feel the warm and tingling flesh of our thighs. In a way, I can hardly wait to get dressed and go down to the beach and throw pebbles on the lake to watch them skitter and slide across it, coming to rest in the sunlight, instead of sinking at once into the depths. But in a way, I want to lie and welcome winter by showing it that I am in no rush either; I am slow too, and still, and I too can toss the sun back to the sky, with the whole surface of my being. I want to show winter that, much as I need the rhythm of the waves, there comes a time when I too appreciate the need for smoothing them out and closing them in. I want to lie flat as a board, breathing so softly it cannot be heard. My heart beats, though; I can hear its pulse making quite a racket in the silence.

We get dressed after a while and go down to the dock. It is frozen above the frozen surface that surrounds it. We toss pebbles onto the ice, watching them skitter and slide across it and come to rest in the sunlight.

By the next morning the ice is more than an inch thick. We jump on the lake, slide on it, sit on it, staring through its crystal-clear lid. I am amazed that the rocks and the bottom below us retain their positions with all the dignity of solid matter. When viewed through the water, they shimmer and sway, not insubstantial, but uncertain of their locations. Through the ice they sit in stolid constancy. There is the cap from the old Mercury gas tank, a length of rubber hose, the crushed and rusted remains of the galvanized bucket, the remaining stub of a stick of ski wax (purple), a piece of paper, a piece of tinfoil. My god, what a lot of garbage we have managed to slip into the lake, despite all our efforts to be clean. There are rocks too, of all shapes and sizes, and all of them jagged, not round. At the end of the dock the rock crib holds up quite well, though tilted now at an angle.

Bob wants to go for a walk on the shore. I am not sure I dare, not sure the ice is thick enough yet. He offers to push me across in the canoe—then if the ice cracks, he can jump in with me. I climb into the middle of the canoe. Everything is very still. Without much noise, the human engine behind me starts, and the canoe moves forward across the glass-clear lake. It is a ghost ship, silent, moving faster and faster, the wind rising around it. Bob lets go of the canoe and slides up beside me, skating on his rubber West Pac boots, his arms stretched out to either side of him, his blue cap pulled around his face. The smoke from the house rises behind his head. I jump out and we slide together, leaving the canoe behind, a large and uncertain object stranded in the air as we skate away, across the crystalline waves. It's all winter, everywhere. In the middle of winter sits the island; in the middle of the island sits the house, and the sky is tossed above it all. It's all land again! It's all island, as far as the eye can see; meshed and twinkling, banded and smooth, tree and rock covered. I run as fast as I can go and let my legs stop again and slide. I trip, and fall, and hold the ice to my cheek like a lover—velvet-cloaked.

$$\text{⇢⟫ (2) ⟪⇠}$$

Yesterday morning we tried to ski to Tarnezell Lake, while the ice is still glassy and before too much of the winter's snow falls to block the way. We left early in the morning, glad to be able to ski again, with picnics and thermoses and wax. We didn't make it to the lake, however. It still does not exist for us, a dab on the map, Tarnezell

Lake, with beaver and bear on the other side of the hill. On the return trip it started to snow—wet, heavy snow which stuck to the skis like clots of the sky. The last few miles were hard, and it was almost dusk when we got back.

Coming back to the island after an absence of even a day brings to me a sense of surrender. No matter what difficulties have preceded our arrival, and no matter what tasks lie before us, when I see the island come into sight, the lumpiest blot of trees against the sky, I am tense with the excitement which precedes serenity. The island has absorbed part of me, and when I step off the lake onto the rocks or icy snow of the beach, I am reunited with that part. There is the island's distinctive smell—sometimes of pines and dead wood, sometimes of humus and roses and aspens, sometimes of snow, and always of the freshness of split wood. The smell means parting and joining.

Most times when we get back, I go tearing up to the house right away, and, completely out of breath, dash in the front door to make sure everything is all right. And it is. The wood is neatly stacked by the fireplace, the brass scale hangs over the half-wall, holding a hand-painted wooden horse, red with gold braid, and weighing, always, five-eighths of a pound. The two oriental rugs from my grandmother's house lie, slightly askew, on the floor, but motionless, unchanged, since I saw them last. The dining-room table gleams, two red mats set permanently in place on either side of it, an Aladdin lamp resting on a blue straw hot pad at the end by the window. The curtains are just as bright, just as synchronized and colorful—reds and blues and yellow, rich and independent but blending together, tying the spaces of the room together. The framed drawing of two children playing leapfrog hangs above the fireplace, and there is an odd assortment of books and magazines lying on the living-room table, promising to be there forever. The elk hide draped over one chair conceals it well, but the other three are plain as ever—blue and white captain's chairs.

Usually I dash quickly into the bedroom too. I am relieved to find everything in order, our big bed like a huge box, covered with the blue Indian-print bedspread, still holds the mound of down at its foot; the white curtains are still pinned back to reveal the outhouse in the woods behind—the door usually standing open because the hinges have gotten out of kilter for the umpteenth time, or because someone (me) took a last-minute pee and then dashed quickly down to the beach where some-one (Bob) was waiting.

Everything is all right.

If we have been away awhile, my serenity lasts for days. When I wake in the morning, I am faced only with the warm and contented pleasure of deciding what I should do that day. Even though we have not been away very long, I feel like that today. It's like musing through the pages of a catalogue, deciding what is most appealing—choosing one thing at last, but knowing that many others would have been just as satisfying. Only here, once I do select, I can just proceed to do, not set the catalogue aside with a thoughtful grunt.

If it were summer, maybe I would finally get around to making a smooth path to the outhouse, straightening and leveling the ground, shoveling the lumps away and filling in the holes. Now the ground is frozen, and there is no chance of that till spring. I could wash and wax the kitchen floor, but I feel too clean for that. I could paint the kitchen ceiling where it has gotten smoke blackened from the Aladdin lamps, or I could curl up in the easy chair with a book. I certainly plan to watch Bob chop some wood, and take a few swings myself, standing way back from the block with my legs spread apart. There is always a sensation of surprise as I suddenly hit it right, and the ax slices through a log as easily as splitting air.

There are some jobs which will probably never get done. The black bootprint which decorates the topmost board on the bedroom wall will stay unsanded for a long while yet, and the kitchen cupboards remain ignorant of molding. But I like to wash windows until the few sticky spots which are too troublesome to remove stand out with utmost clarity.

One of the biggest delights is the question of what to have for supper. I play with ideas from time to time during the day, taking hours to complete the menu, picking up one item and discarding another until the concept is perfectly formed. This is all the more remarkable because there is a static number of variations available, and a constantly increasing limiting factor, as the stored goods diminish. Today, while I think about it, I've decided to bake bread. I like the sweet bubbling of the sponge as it rises for the first time, the strange cohesiveness of the dough as I add more and more flour to it. There is a physical satisfaction in kneading; my muscles ache rhythmically, glad to be of such use. I feel toward bread the way I feel toward my hiking boots. Both require a certain care. Both are sweet-smelling and familiar, and both take me places.

With enough materials under the house and in the storeroom, a toolbox full of tools and kitchen cabinets full of foods, there is an almost infinite choice of occupations. With a bookshelf of books, and a desk holding plain white paper, there is almost endless opportunity for mental exercise. With the sun shining on the snow and the water freezing below it, all the silence of the world is calling. The animals and the passages of men provide me with entertainment, Bob with friendship, and the wind with perspective. That is how I feel today. Tomorrow, though, will always be different.

→≫(3)≪←

On any afternoon there are two walks you can take. One is toward something and the other is away. There is also a journey which combines the two, and it is the journey we took when we came to the island. Sometimes, though, it seems more like sitting still. Especially in winter. I sit a lot now, and watch, and read, and think. With the house finished, and the lake frozen, the sources of power have been muted. They are there, still, but the island is now our domain, and we have less chance to move with the rhythms of change.

Tonight the fire is lit, and is reflected in the front window. It looks as if it is burning in midair, somewhere over the porch, like the spirit of the south wind. The air still smells toasty: this afternoon I made English muffins. Bob picks one up from the kitchen counter and splits it in half. He walks up behind my chair and places one over each of my ears. They are soft and warm, just like earmuffs, and they muffle sound.

"This is mission control; come in please," he says. "Have you seen my wife anywhere? Unable to locate. Over."

"Mission control? This is the Island. Wife has been located, sitting in a chair in front of your nose, over and out."

Bob takes away the muffins, and butters them, and eats them. I wonder what he is thinking.

→≫≪←

I am reading about islands. Apparently the words "isle" and "isolation" derive from the same root. Well, we are in for it both ways. The fact that we live on an island is a metaphor for the fact that we live set apart. Of course, it is the forty miles of water and woods between us and Fort St. James and the fact that we have no neighbors closer than six miles away that give our life most of its special quality. But the island helps too.

The island fantasy is almost universal. Most people imagine an island when they think about an earthly paradise. Even Aldous Huxley, that professional pessimist, constructed a utopia when he wrote about an island society. The idea seems to be that if we were each allowed to build our own world from scratch, we would do a fine job of it. And aside from that, everyone would like to have the space around him which his uniqueness deserves.

Funny. An island is a perfect shape to build a dream in. Whether it is long or wide, high or low, it is round in one's thoughts; surrounded by water, it must be circular. A circular space is an efficient space to fill with dreams, and it is likely that the water which surrounds it will keep them from wandering away. A circular space is also one which is easily defended, and from which you can see in all directions.

The self-containment which an island seems to promise is the most important aspect of the fantasy. It is so clearly defined where you end, and everything else begins. Stick your toe in the water. You're off! Pull it back. You're on! The idea behind the island fantasy is control. Control of input and output. Having your fingers on all the strings.

I don't like the fantasy anymore. I like the island. Right under the house there is a cool, slightly damp space, protected from the sun and snow. Right in front of it a smell builds up in the sun, as strong a one as there is anywhere on the island. It cannot get beneath the foundations—the house defeats it—but it lies in wait just beyond. It is the smell of the island itself—pine and earth and sun and grass and snow. A real place, here before we landed, here after we go. The smell reminds me of the first time we came, in spring, when we lay in the long, rose-choked grass under the great fir, and the island dominated us. It makes its statement whenever I walk by, and my senses reel with the force of that time we will never recover, but which the island has never lost, the time when the island was island alone. Now, for a time, we are islands together.

We both watch the world go by. Living on an island, with an island, in an island, you learn that far from being able to control the strings, the best you can do is watch them dance. Living here, I learn to watch, and observe the tiny changes that surround us. It's one of the nicest things about living on an island—there's always a chance that something will happen by.

Sometimes, I just sit and watch the ruffled surface of the lake, listening to the swallows chattering excitedly in and out of the eaves. Behind that sound I hear the light pops and hisses of wood in the stove. Even farther away I hear the silence. Almost imperceptibly there develops a distant buzzing noise which grows louder and louder. I stand up and look out the picture window, wondering which way the boat will be moving, and whether it will be a river boat or a cruiser. The sound is a low buzz rather than a high-pitched one, so I guess a river boat, and catch sight of a long, low craft moving across the Portage-Tachie route, an Indian boat. The bow is pointed and slightly raised in silhouette—most of the weight is toward the back, and the boat is planing well. I can see two people, one running the outboard, the other sitting in the midsection. As they move away and the sound grows dimmer, the swallows are for a moment quiet, and I hear the wood noises again. The cycle of fading and growing sounds is constant. Once in a while a fly buzzes.

You never know what may come next into the picture window. Usually it's just an ordinary fishing boat, but one day last summer an amazing apparition floated into view. It was a three-decker houseboat, about forty-five feet long, painted white with blue gingerbread decorations around the windows and deck rails. It was full of people. The boat looked like a Mississippi River pleasure palace, and against the stark outline of a rocky point of land set firmly with spruces, it had a surrealistic quality. Since it floated on the water, it had the final dreamlike touch it needed, and we abandoned all chores to sit and watch it. The boat moved forward with surprising speed, and then stopped abruptly. A shorter forward move was followed by a longer pause until eventually the boat came to a complete halt half a mile off the island.

Even more people surfaced from the interior. We thought they might be preparing to throw out their fishing lines, and gleefully speculated on the incredible tangle which would result. As far as we were concerned, the pompous boat had been placed on the lake for our enjoyment. We could see John Wayne standing in the bow, throwing out his line, while all the other movie stars followed in quick succession.

After a motionless half-hour it occurred to me that the boat probably had engine trouble; a fishing boat will move slowly forward. The day

was calm, which was lucky, because the craft looked absolutely unlakewor-
thy. We went back to building while the boat drifted, a little closer, a
little farther away. After it had been there for about two hours, a float
plane came into view, and, after circling around it, made an exquisite
landing right beside the pleasure palace. A small boat was lowered from
the big one, people climbed after it, and the plane took off again. It
returned twice during the next two hours, and at last all the pleasure
seekers were flown away. The boat bobbed emptily until evening; then
a small and powerful cruiser came by and towed it away. It dragged
slowly off, disgraced and unhappy, all its blue trimming wilted.

Float planes are among my favorite shows. It is rare that they will
land on the lake, but they pass overhead fairly often, and pursue some
peculiar behavior in the course of their passage. Whenever I hear that
distinctive high-pitched buzzing in the distance, I rush to the nearest
window and crane my head around, trying to spot the plane. Bob does
the same, and eventually one of us locates it. We watch its movements
with fascination, always expecting the best, which is that it will land
nearby. Sometimes it flies very low, so that the bright orange or yellow
or blue colors are plainly visible, and the big awkward floats or skis,
hanging distinctly at the bottom. Twice we have had planes fly right
overhead, directly over the roof, as if they were studying our island.
Once a plane flew by just at the level of the picture window, and we
waved madly, but the pilot didn't see us. Most days they stay very
high, flying, I suppose, to the logging operation on Takla Lake.

Early this summer some fishermen flew up to The Fishing Cabins
Island. They landed on a Friday afternoon when the lake was fairly
calm; after a beautiful dipping curve of a landing they taxied to the
dock. The plane was quite small, but it unloaded four men and a lot
of gear, then bobbed at the dock for two days. When Sunday afternoon
arrived and the fishermen thought it was time to be gone, a storm
blew up from the east and north. Their northeastern mooring was rocked
with powerful and erratic waves. It was clear to us that the men would
be fools to try and take off into the storm, but it was not clear to the
men. They all piled into the plane and started to ferry around the western
edge of the island, so that they could take off into the wind.

We went down to our dock, wrapped against the rain, and watched.
The plane hung crazily in the water, swaying from side to side, nose
down, then up again. It moved into the open lake and gathered speed.
At the last minute before takeoff, it jerked to a halt, turned back, and

repositioned itself in the lee of the island. The pilot had decided, apparently, that the only way to take off with enough shelter from the changeable winds was to hang in the lee of the island and gather speed straight for the cliff at the western end. Which he did. He barrelled straight at the rock wall, lifted into the air, and cleared the cliff with at least five feet to spare. A good pilot with an important engagement.

-->>)<<--

With the coming of winter, there is less chance of such visiting shows outside the windows. Since we still need the relaxation they provide, I turn inside, and find eccentricity creeping up on me.

The dog and cat provide most of my movable entertainment these days, the rest being provided by my own preoccupation with them. All the stories of crazy ladies with fourteen cats come back to me with force. Why not fourteen cats? That would make the chances so much better that something worth watching would always be going on.

The cat and dog lie asleep now, respectably distant from one another. Bundy lies right in the middle of her spine, the white ruff beneath her neck curving back into a smooth ridge. Her front paws flop over at the joint, heavy and ungraceful, but utterly relaxed. Her back legs are spread in perfect contentment, and they curve only slightly downward. She looks absurd, unprotected and trusting to the absolute limit of trust. If I go over and put my foot on her stomach, she will wag her tail against the floor in anticipation of being rubbed.

Boots is asleep also, but his stomach is on the floor, back legs hidden beneath it. His body makes a graceful curve when it nears the shoulders, and the neck is exposed, resting elegantly on the floor. His two front paws are loosely curled into soft balls of fur, limp and aristocratic. All of his curves are sensuous, all of Bundy's are abrupt. If Boots wakes up when I am not watching, I will never know that he has moved. Bundy will hoist herself to her feet only with well-expressed effort.

The animals' behavior never loses its fascination. Watching them must be a kind of meditation, like the calm induced from staring at a candle and letting your mind slip back to it again and again. I am living in a different time now, and I might as well rest with it. It is good practice for growing old. This is a splendid place for magnifying small events into their true dimensions.

The other night I woke to the thunder of Boots's paws. Half in a daze, I watched the moonlight on the icy snow, my head turned on the pillow.

Boots came padding at high speed—not galloping, but moving at a fast trot into the bedroom until he stood right at the bed. There he stopped for a moment, then turned and trotted back into the living room. I heard the most amazing ruckus of galloping paws and crashing in the bookshelf area, and then several slow pounces. Then Boots trotted into the bedroom again, stood by the bed for a time, and returned to the living room. Again the crashing, the galloping, the pouncing. When he came back for the third time, I was starting to get annoyed. It wasn't going to be easy to get to sleep with all this commotion. But how do you tell a cat to stop doing what he wants to do? So I lay and listened to his movements, and took to counting his trips into the bedroom. He returned sixteen times. Sixteen trips into the bedroom—to do nothing as far as I could see—then sixteen trips back to the living room to carry on his mysterious activities. After trip number sixteen, I could stand it no longer, so I swung my legs over the edge of the high bed, slid to the floor as lightly as I could, and trotted behind Boots on his return trip.

In the living room he stopped and looked around warily. Then he dashed to a dark corner beside the big easy chair, and flung his paws around a mouse. When he opened his paws again and waited for the attempted escape, the mouse took only one shaky step toward the chair. Deciding apparently that that would have to be good enough, Boots picked the animal up in his teeth and flung it around in the air with relish. Then he put it down, turned around, and trotted into the bedroom again.

The cat was playing hide and seek. His idea of midnight entertainment was to dash into the bedroom, cover his eyes with his paws and give the mouse a chance to lose itself in the shadows of the living room.

This time while Boots was out of the room, I picked the mouse up. One of its ears was torn and bloody, and it had a superficial scratch in its side, but it did not have any other external wounds. It was in the last stages of exhaustion and shock, however. Its small heart beat furiously and weakly. Boots came back into the room, and, instantly spotting the mouse in my hands, glared at me balefully. I knocked the tiny head against the wall of the fireplace and returned it to Boots, dead. His disgust was apparent. He flipped the small body around a few times, catching it as it fell through the air, then settled down to eat it, starting with the head. It took about a minute, and then all that was left was a little skinny tail hanging from his mouth. I put some more wood on the stove, thinking that at least this would mean tomorrow we could wake up to a warm house.

Boots is a good mouser. I am ambivalent about mice. I'd just as soon have them as pets. Ours are not really mice at all, they are voles, so they don't have those charming round ears that true mice do, but they have all their other charms, predominantly a silly look of wide-eyed innocence and an attitude toward life that makes me think they run around in the walls scratching their heads and muttering "dashed puzzling . . . dashed puzzling."

Routine is their strong point. We used to have one mouse who came out every evening at 8:30 from the same hole in the wall, just above the bookshelf. He would leap nimbly down the outside of the books shelf by shelf to the floor, then run all the way around the perimeter of the room and so finally into the kitchen. He had first discovered the food by way of this circuitous route, and he saw no reason to change his approach pattern. One evening my suede shoe lay across his usual path, and he was so startled by it that he took a running jump and leapt straight into the air from its toe, disappearing into the wall and never venturing that route again.

Bundy is also ambivalent about mice. She considers the chasing of squirrels to be her main mission in life, but mice are both too small and too silent to bother with. One night I happened to be sitting at the dining-room table when a mouse came out from behind the stove, twelve inches from where Bundy was tucking into her food. Bundy glanced up, saw the mouse in slight surprise, and returned to her food while the mouse sped across the kitchen floor in the direction of the flour sacks.

→≫≪←

These are sometime matters though. The moments come and capture my attention fully, and then they are gone. Other moments open before me, many moments in which we will sit or walk, and watch the weather, and hunt. In the next six months of winter we will be here, sometimes snowbound, sometimes bound only by space or darkness. After much preparation, and many dreams made real, we will be living the island life. Winter storms will come, and days will pass. It's all island, as far as the eye can see, meshed and twinkling, tree and rock covered, banded and smooth. The island has spread, and crystallized around us, and left us this time, the gumdrops in the cake, waiting to discover what living on an island's all about.

$\Rightarrow\!\!\gg (4) \lll\!\!\Leftarrow$

Only January now, and I am finding out. About the island and what living here can mean. I cannot decide when it is harder to get off this rock, in winter or in summer. In the summer the storms rise, as the water swells and bursts into the air. In the winter the storms fall, as the snow falls and buries all progress.

For ten days now a storm has continued unbroken. It has not raged; rage is a quick emotion. This storm seems to be rambling along, flurried at times, in doubt as to where it is going, but in any case in no hurry to get there. Each morning we wake, and the same foglike cloud drifts over the lake. Each night we go to bed, and the darkness only adds a sulkier denseness to the air. The porch is loaded with white mounds, and the lake is buried beneath a weighty mass of snow. It is still cold. I haven't noticed that there is any cold too cold for it to snow in. At night, and sometimes not at night, the lake booms its protest, as the ice continues to freeze and break in expanding ruptures of fault line which stretch for miles. It is an exercise in resignation to stand on or move across the lake when it is booming. The cracks open with the sound of a bullet released from a gun, and it seems the world must open beneath my feet. If I am on the lake when it booms, I freeze, my heart starts beating fast, and I wait in silence for the final plunge.

But now it is almost a relief when the cracking shoots into the air. Any sound is a relief, a release of the unbearable tension of silence which is more than silence—the silence of being becalmed in the heart of a winter so muffled and swathed that no sound can escape. No sound of birds or animals. No sound of wind or restless trees.

Today we try to ski. The slush is impossibly bad, and it is cold. We get as far as the Portage-Tachie trail, which is no longer any trail at all. We return. My nose and cheeks are whitening, Bob's toes are numb. We wait out another day, muffled. I open the window and shout aloud.

Hello . . . Helloo . . . the sound fades before it is formed. There are no echoes.

—➤➤➤≪≪≪—

I move around the house carefully this morning, certain that someone is watching. Seven weeks without a new face, but someone is watching me now. As I walk into the front bedroom to my desk, I can feel the eyes, and I try to stand tall and walk with grace, leg muscles rippling in a steady rhythm, arms hanging loosely at my hips. When I pull out the desk chair, I try not to scrape it on the floor, silently smoothing the curved back under my hands. Placing my hands at the sides of a pile of papers, I tap it lightly on the surface of the desk until all the edges are lined up, and then lay it carefully beside the window. I sit, gazing thoughtfully into the woods, knowing that no thoughts lie behind the mask, but arranging my face for the benefit of the unseen watcher.

After a time, I get up again, and go into the other bedroom to look into the mirror. My skin seems very dry, and I have lines in my forehead which were not there a year ago. Exposure to the weather does not smooth the skin. Pouring a little oil into my palm, I neatly massage it into my face, hoping to wipe away the lines.

Someone should be arriving today. I dread someone arriving today. When a snowmobile goes by, I walk to the window to see if it will turn off the trail to the house, relieved when it goes by. A visitor would mar the communication I have established with the watcher. The porch creaks. Someone has come. I go to the door and open it, but there is no one there. Aimlessly I straighten things up, walking from the bedroom to the kitchen garbage can to throw out a tiny scrap of paper. I wipe the countertop for its entire length, brushing a few crumbs into my hand.

Finally I take a book, and put on my parka, and walk to the west end of the island, below the eagle's nest, into the rocks. It does not seem far enough away. I search the island, looking for a place to go. The crevice, the steep, snow-covered chasm hung with lichen, rusting in its roots, the place that has always been yonder. I slide down into its open hand and sit in the snow with my back against a rock. I try to read. After a time, the eyes find me there. I start up, suddenly. Someone has gotten to the beach, silently and swiftly. I move to a more sheltered spot, behind the great felled tree, charcoal burned and damp. But if there is anyone who wants to see me, he can find me even here. There is no such place as yonder, after all.

>>><<<

These moments come and go. When the weather breaks, and a warm spring wind blows in from the south, I tramp through the wet snow and watch the bubbling melting of the surface crystals of ice. There are no eyes on me now, and sounds release themselves freely into the air. But a residue of tension lingers. No external motions catch my eye, and I do not find the sight of a snowmobile moving across the horizon entertaining. I am still, inside.

Heading for the house, I pick up an armload of split wood from the beach. One piece of stovewood falls out of my arms halfway up the hill, but it is too awkward to pick it up again without dropping the rest, so I leave it there. I dump the load on the porch, and shake the snow off my boots before going inside. Just inside the front door the grey paint is stained with many dried puddles of melted snow. I peel off my heavy clothes. I want to jump and whoop. Inside me there is a kind of white pressure which can release itself in either wild activity or rage. This time I play.

We play a lot these days together. I grab Bob from behind, and he turns and we hug. He never smells of sweat, always of clean air. I kiss the little indentation between the halves of his chest and giggle.

"How many hairs do you have now? Last time I counted you had twelve, if you want to count the little one."

"I've got more than you do anyway, young lady."

I touch a piece of hair that stands straight up on his head.

"You have a cowlick, you know."

"Like this?" He sticks out his tongue and, before I can duck back, licks my face from chin to forehead. It feels strange, at perfect body temperature.

"No, not like that!"

"You let Bundy lick you; why shouldn't I?"

"Bundy is a dog, and gives me dog-licks. You are not a cow, and besides you have other ways to communicate."

"Nice of you to say so." He grins demonically.

"You turkey."

"Ah, you want to see a turkey lick?"

"No!" I bolt for the kitchen, pursued from behind. The dog barks, the cat withdraws, aghast. Bob drops to the floor and grabs my ankle.

"Wait, stop, I want to see what the temperature is." I check the thermometer at the back door. It is thirty-five degrees Fahrenheit. I can hardly believe it, in January. Bob dips the one-gallon plastic jug into the water barrel and sets it on the countertop. He puts in the dipper and takes a drink of water, raising the handle of the dipper high in the air above his head in order to get the cup of it to his mouth. He drinks it to the bottom, then dips and drinks again.

While I start to cook dinner, Bob lights the lamps. The play has ended, and we are quiet and private again. I cook moose, onions, potatoes. The air grows quite thick with heat and cooking smells and Aladdin-lamp smoke. When the lamp starts to smoke, it sends a great funnel of black into the room. I turn it way down for a moment and sprinkle salt down the chimney, watching the carbon spark and spread white on the mantle and vanish into light again.

→≫ (5) ≪←

A good way to cope with time is to read. Living in the bush, I read about the bush. We have a shelf full of books about the wilderness. Sitting here, I read them.

The wilderness literature which is most popular almost invariably communicates the idea that the wilderness is a place of sunshine and wonder. Rain and snow always freshen the air. Everyone gets along. Campfires burn brightly and dawns are red.

A lyrical censor must be at work in the memory of the writers of such books and manuals. When you read the straightforward accounts of expeditions mounted by people who never heard of Thoreau, a very different pattern emerges. The difficulties of survival in the arctic, the bush, or the barrens have often led to real disasters. But the difficulties of human intercourse under such conditions have led to many others. Charles Hall died in the arctic in 1871. He did not freeze to death, nor was he killed by a polar bear. He was slowly poisoned with arsenic. Thomas Simpson died of a gunshot wound on the barrens. His death was long held to be suicide, but Vilhjalmur Stefansson maintains convincingly that he was murdered by his men.

More relevant to our own life on the island is the story I recently came across of a northern trapper who shared a winter cabin with his partner, and eventually murdered him for whistling the same tune all day long, for months on end. The murderer was acquitted by a jury of his peers. Twelve sourdoughs declared it justifiable homicide.

Perhaps even more interesting than the clearcut murder of wilderness companions (which is after all, you may think, not so different from murder anywhere) is the kind of situation which is described by Pierre Berton in his history of the Klondike. He tells the story of two partners, friends from boyhood, who split their outfit in half at the end of the Chilkoot Trail. They sawed in half everything they owned, down to the bags of flour, in order to deprive each other of any chance of getting out alive. They succeeded, each at the cost of his own life.

These stories fascinate me now. A madness which leads to murder, or a madness which leads to suicide, or a madness which comes close to both.

→≫≪←

I am having a recurring dream. I lie in a room, in a bed, alone. There is nothing in the room except the bed. The rest is formless and empty. There is one wall, and in that wall there is a window. The window has a set of curtains hanging in it, blue curtains, blue as the sky. The wind blows the curtains inward, and their motion, their billowing, their satin ripple, is the only motion in the room.

I lie in bed and stare directly at the window. I am in terror. The wind blowing the curtains into the room is the wind of sheer darkness, of all the unforgotten, deeply hidden horrors of the mind. I wake, gasping and crying. With some relief. But knowing the wind still blows and another night I will feel its touch again.

→≫≪←

There is silence in the house today. We talk little, and that is too much. The wind blows again, and the snow falls. I sit and walk and stand. I pick up wood and burn it. Nothing has happened. Nothing is wrong. But just getting through the day is like fighting my way through dense brush, thin branches whipping at my face. I feel a growing rage which slowly chokes and consumes. My former interest in the animals seems like sickness; the house is crooked and dark, ill-made. Bob's responses are tiny irritants, pricking at the thick air. The island has become a hollow drum, and I am its booming. Action leads to nothing but blankness, and the wind blows, trying to strip away everything it touches. I cling to the few essentials now. Lighting the lamps. Sleep. Coffee in the morning. But it all seems like a charade upon a stage, with the wind the producer and only audience, and the heavy booms swelling from inside me in an attempt to equalize the pressure.

The natives call it going bushed.

-->>)<<--

I read again, to try and gain perspective. Just as when you learn a new word, you see it everywhere, so when you feel something new, you seek it out in others. I read about going bushed.

Mostly it is not fatal. But sometimes it is, various ways. On a lake not too far north of us a trapper built a cabin in the fifties. In December the trapping was good, as good as he had ever seen it. Silver foxes moved slowly across the glass-clear lake. But deep winter brought the heavy snows and cold, and the driven lynx visited his walls, screaming like a woman in mortal fear.

The trapper did not return in the spring to the friends who waited for him. He lay on his bed, having died of starvation, with the shelves full of food and the door barred on the inside. When his friends broke down the door, there were no skins to be found in the cabin, save the one which covered him.

Bushed. A prosaic word for madness. Like "the bush" from which the word derives—the phrase which encompasses all the dark and snow-laden forest around us. It implies not that the person in question has been visited by the forest, but that he has sunk into it, gone into it, and not found his way out. It has the connotations of a journey—and that is right, because there are many steps along the road, from being stir-crazy to being dead.

Of course it is different here. We live on a high hill, a fortress rock upon the lake, and the view is open for miles to the south and west. I do not intend to murder, or go mad, or kill myself. But winter is long, and the snow keeps falling, and new days bring no relief.

The wilderness outside becomes the wilderness inside. The bush, the world which the animals perceive, the world which is not distinguished by names, but rather by spaces, by shadows and forms and smells, becomes the world which is most real. When the objects that surround me inside the house seem to lose their identification with the words which describe them, when I look at my typewriter and cannot feel, though I may know, what it is for, then I have taken the first step.

We came here to escape from a world which believes that danger can be permanently contained, and that everything has a name. So we take our chances with the rest that we'll go too far along this road to escape ourselves. In my moments of clarity, I am glad of it. I came to the island thinking that if I built my own roof, it would obey my commands. I suppose I also thought that if I built my own door, I could tell it what to be closed against. And now?

Now it is almost dark again, and Bob moves in the next room. My silence is white, and the sound pricks. I wonder what he will do next. A log crackles. He sits. My silence is ready to turn to rage.

→》》(6)《《←

The question of how much hate our love can absorb and still survive seems to be answered by how much it has to. Two years ago, and far away from this island, we were still close enough to illusions of ultimate freedom to believe in the absolute finality of some fights, and the complete unforgivability of some actions. "Why does she put up with it?" or "How can he stand it?" We had no idea then that people do put up with it and stand it, trying to kill each other first and loving again afterwards. Our life upon this rock has been a flow of years condensed into months. Our proximity to one another has allowed no other choice. We have spent more time together in two years than many couples do in ten. And in this winter we have attained a degree of mutual awareness which hovers always on the edge of painful intensity. If my awareness of myself is crystal sharp, how much stronger is it when added to my awareness of Bob.

The island itself is a magnifying glass for our emotions. We are stranded here, cast away onto a small platform beneath the sky. When we had built no more than the floor and it was a level expanse of pine around us, we stood on it and shouted as people might on a modern stage, and the water made it theatre-in-the-round. The water picked up and magnified our shouts, and the hills behind reflected them back again. There was a structured inescapability to the law. When Bundy barked, a dog barked back. Water is wet, and the land is dry, and the hills echo sound, and the water magnifies it, and the earth pushes it upward. Islands contain far more than dreams.

Many nights when the fire burns and the lamps are lit, I read aloud to Bob. We have read *The Once and Future King, The Lost World,* and *The Complete Sherlock Holmes.* We are now in the third volume of *The Lord of the Rings.* Although the experience of being together is softened by the imaginary worlds we enter together, some nights even reading aloud is too much contact. Some nights nothing will do but complete retreat, and even that is not enough, and the struggle against mutual awareness is like the twentieth time you scratch an irresistible itch—it becomes agony, but the itch remains. Animals who have an itch caused by some serious disorder will scratch themselves until they tear away their flesh, and the disease becomes at least in part a wound, raw and bleeding, and still they do not stop scratching. They know they are destroying their own flesh, but are helpless to resist.

Flesh of my flesh. In the itch of the brain, too, no one is safe from himself. A person with sensitive skin will know several days before an outbreak of hives that one is coming. The skin tightens and tingles all over, and to touch any rough material is unpleasant; to touch anything with one's body is repulsive after a time, the skin becomes so sensitized. The idea of lovemaking is a nightmare—the nipples are tuned to a razor's-edge sensitivity. A breakdown is on the way. So for some days here the breakdown approached, and I knew it, and there was no cortisone to cure the condition, and once the outbreak reached the surface, we scratched and scratched until the brain was bleeding, and still there was no respite from awareness.

Beyond us there are only the walls, the rock, and the ice. I and thou and nothing else. No distraction. No one else to talk with. No movies. No libraries. No stereo sets with headphones. No products to buy, NEW SUPER IMPROVED! No SENSATIONAL developments! No cowboys and Indians, no scenes of rampage and destruction. No motors to stick between our legs until the highway fades beneath us. There is no garbage can into which to toss our togetherness.

We came to the island at least in part to get away from the disposables of modern life, to get away from the packages which remain after their contents have been used by us, from the packages which obscure the essence they have contained. Somehow I knew that the wastebasket into which I tossed the remains of each year could not contain the waste for long. Always the wind rises and blows it into a new random pattern. It does so here too. We cannot figure out what to do with yesterday's feelings.

So we scratch at our awareness until it bleeds.

→>> (7) <<←

The weather had been ghastly for days, grey with wet snow, and when a break came, the clouds would hang so low that they became mist. My skin was tingling. We had not been to town for nine weeks, and no visitors came by. The radio batteries were so weak that it was impossible to get any clear stations. It got to be early afternoon somehow, the sweeping and the washing, the water and wood took us there, and Bob started to get ready to go for a ski. When I saw him get out his summit pack, I felt a sense of relief, mingled with irritation that he hadn't bothered to mention his intention first. Maybe I would have liked to go too. The relief I felt was at getting him out of the house; but I had a right to go too, didn't I? As he put on his boots, Bob said, "Well, I'm going skiing."

"Well, the weather's certainly shitty, but I'm going to come too."

"You seem very ambivalent," Bob said.

Of course he was right, which increased my desire to go along at all costs.

"I can dislike the weather, but still want to go skiing, can't I?" The itch.

"I just hope I don't have to wait for you every ten steps in the wet powder."

"You don't have to wait for me anyway, you know." And won't.

I got on my boots and went down to the lake. I quickly lost sight of Bob in the snow. Amazingly, the wind blew right through me. The crystal flakes were delicate and wet, and touched my face with messages from distant places. The air was cool in my lungs, but warm enough to fill them to the bottom. I skied along in a cocoon. After two or three miles, I felt cleaned and weary, and turned around and skied for the island again, kick glide, kick glide, arms swinging, pole in, pole out, stretch it forward, grab it from behind. There was a muffled sound of wind behind when I stopped. On the beach, I carefully released the pin bindings, brushed every bit of snow from the skis, and set them neatly upright in a drift. I shook the poles and did the same with them, two blue poles with black leather straps dangling from the top.

I was standing at the stove putting on a pot of rice when Bob got back. He walked in the door still covered with snow, and said as he unlaced his ski boots, "Well, it's going to be a lousy evening, isn't it?"

"Why?" I said. My skin had been blown clean, but now he had the itch.

"You're mad because I didn't wait for you."

"No, I'm not."

Walking into the kitchen, still dripping snow, Bob asked what was in the pressure cooker.

"Rice, there's enough for you."

While I was washing up some dishes, he went out and sawed some meat off the frozen moose, brought it back, and fried it up.

"Smells good," I said.

"Oh, you want some?" A mad attempt to gain privacy. My meat, my meal, my stomach.

Tingling now, I said, "Sure, I cook for you; I assume you cook for me too."

"O.K." He got out two dishes and distributed the meat—three quarters of the meat on one plate, one quarter on the other.

"You didn't exactly load it on me."

"Well, if that's all you can say, I'll take it all." He picked up my plate and dumped the meat onto his.

White fury. I took the meat back, reaching across the table and picking it up in my hands. He threw it all over the room, then went and sat down in the living room with his book. I picked the meat off the floor and put it back on a plate. I had no desire to eat it, but no desire to clean up the hardened grease later. Bob leapt to his feet, rushed over, grabbed the plate, and flung the meat, plate and all, out the door into the night.

Much later, we went to bed, sleeping in two different rooms.

In the morning, Bob saw a fox wandering across the lake and went rushing after it with his gun, before breakfast, before coffee, practically before dressing. I made some coffee and some toast, enjoying the solitude. I left the coffee pot warming on the back of the stove, and put his toast into the oven.

Since I had been in no mood to clean up the night before, there were dirty dishes lying around, and a film of memory over everything. Wanting to wash it away and throw the water onto the ground, I heated a kettle of water, and fifteen minutes later was starting on the last and blackest pot when Bob came back. He ate his toast and drank a cup of coffee, and then returned to the stove to shake the coffee pot. There was about a half cup left. He opened the water barrel, which was empty, as I had used the last of the water washing the dishes. In a rush of energy, Bob dumped the last of the coffee into his cup, then, pot in hand, tore down to the lake. Returning, he put more coffee on, and said, "Oh, by the way, I'm not getting any more water today. And don't try and drink any of this coffee."

I didn't say anything. There is often a last-minute illusion that you can avert a disaster by ignoring its approach. Apparently, like all women, I have to wash the dishes with the last cup of water even if someone lies nearby dying of thirst; it is a fetish, a mania, a man cannot get any peace.

The morning passed. The sweeping and the washing, the water and the wood got us through it once again. Bob went out onto the porch, and practiced shooting pine cones with the .22. The air was beginning to lighten.

Ping. Ping. Two pine cones down. Ping, ping, two more. The rhythm of shooting was soothing, the satisfaction of hitting was dependable. He collected hits like bricks, barricading himself with successes. Twenty bullets made twenty bands of self-respect, and twenty changes in the landscape made twenty passages of escape. He laid the gun against the wall, took up the bright-red jugs, and went down to the lake for water. It was certainly getting lighter. It looked as if it might clear.

The water hole had frozen overnight, and although he had been able to get the coffee pot into the hole, to get a jug into the lake a larger hole was required. The ax sliced smoothly through the air, and small chips of ice flew in neat sprays onto the lake. After filling the two jugs, neatly twisting on their plastic caps, he put them on the bottom step and sorted out some wood from the snow, shaking each log free of powder and tossing it aside into a separate pile. He chose the birch logs, the hardest wood, and split them into smaller and smaller pieces, strength and polished metal combining to fragment the wood. He carried the water up, and then the wood, and went for more water, and then more wood. The sky had cleared; the chance of snow was gone.

I had not left the house. When Bob brought in the last load of wood, I was washing the kitchen floor, my forehead sticky with sweat and the filthy water greasy on my arms. I heard Bob light a fire in the fireplace, and on my way to get a towel from the closet, I saw that he had put on it the biggest chunk of wood we had on the island, a remaining quarter of the bottom section of the big fir. He was feeling in control again. Wind, blow the clouds away. Fire, burn this log. But I had been planning on skiing. Irritated, sticky, I told him he'd better think again about that log, because it would be unsafe to leave a fire burning if we both went out.

He took the fire apart, piece by piece, carrying each piece to the door, and throwing it out into the snow. The house was full of smoke. I asked him why he couldn't just drench it in the fireplace, where the smoke could leave by way of the chimney. Without answering, he stirred all the remaining embers to the front of the box so that the smoke would pour into the house.

I tried to get the poker out of his hands. He pushed me away, at the same time holding me against the floor so that it put a lightning sharp pressure on my spine. All that I could see was his hair, dark and curly, smoky-looking, loose and free. I pictured it drenched with blood, sticky as my arms, covered with fire. I reached for it, and wrapped my hands around it, and tried to tear it out. In anguished reflex, he released me, and I stood up, the world condensed now even from island to my own black shell. Before I could lunge toward him again, he jumped to his feet and drove his fist into my solar plexus.

I fell, trying very hard to breathe: rolling, shifting my position, doubling over, in an attempt to find a passage for the air to enter my lungs. It felt as if an internal suction machine had been turned on. When I did at last get a gasp of air, the first thing I thought was, "My god, so that's what it feels like; why on earth do men decide to become prize fighters?"

Bob walked away. I could not bear to see the way he moved, and the way he walked was repulsive to me, but the release was fantastic. I was free to hate him now, no doubts and no regrets. We could hate each other for having at last released the things we hated most in ourselves.

Bob and I did not talk for a day and a half. The calm was the calm of rocks in the summer sun, static, peaceful in appearance, but unpleasantly hot to touch. I wondered why we could not have done it that way first; complete withdrawal for a time was what we really needed. But we were not trained in the ways of silence.

Scientists who investigate the phenomena of space perception have pinpointed a mystery which they call mirror-ego perception. If you stand before a mirror and look at your face, and someone draws his hand in front of you and touches your cheek, which cheek is it that he touched? Do you experience the touch as if it were the inverse of that which appears in the mirror, or do you perceive it to be in contact with your body as it actually appears in the mirror? How can you know, and how can you describe it? There is no answer to this question. Try it and see.

If you think of the two people in a marriage as the two cheeks of a face and imagine that the walls of the island on which they live are the mirrors which reflect their perceptions, it is obvious that it is impossible to describe who is being touched or even who is doing the touching. Killing someone else can be a fancy way of committing suicide, even if your being does not depend on his life. But when we fill the air with destruction here, of course all that either of us can breathe is destruction. My hair is drenched with blood, sticky as my arms, covered with fire. Bob rolls on the floor, gagging.

The island never moves. It is not interested in these questions. It simply contains them. If we had been two trappers, travelling a fur route, deep in the woods and far from any shelter, we would perhaps have cut everything we owned in half—the sled, the bags of flour, possibly even the odd dog. We might have split up in the night and, before we had a chance to regain our senses, lost each other in the snow. If we had been unlucky then, we might have died.

It is said that a man will do anything to survive. I have not noticed that this is true. If anything, the modern search for comfort and convenience has developed side by side with a desperate need for risk. The worth of an enterprise is often measured by the unpredictability of its outcome. Whether the danger is real or purely imaginary, it is partly stress and risk which make for the appeal of mountaineering, hang gliding, fighting forest fires—living in the wilderness. Even many people who never venture out of the comfortable and convenient routines want to read about danger, to know about survival. They think it is a game you play. "How to Survive in the Woods: The Complete Manual from A to Z." (A = Astronomical Sightings; Z = Zebra Attacks) People think they want to know. Show me, tell me, I want to do it too. Well, little lady, we may lose our lives on this big, tough planet, but I have here my handy dandy little magnifying glass, so at least we have a fighting chance.

But survival is not a process you can attempt. It is an end result which you can sometimes find or, rather, a central place you can sometimes get to. It is a rock you can sit on. Survival is neither a game, nor an aspect of life. It is the essence of being at the center of yourself. It is not victory in any way. It is understanding. In surviving you become well lit; there is a bright moon shining into all your corners. No matter the size or shape of those corners. They are at last seen.

So we did recover from the blackness and the loss, and the recovery has made us a little more immune to destruction. We are becoming survivors in the only way which counts. The game of wilderness-seeking has become the reality.

It is strange to remember how it happened that we passed through madness into balance again. So simple, as all things are once they have happened.

I spent the day painting the kitchen ceiling. It had become black in spots from the many accidents with the Aladdin lamps. When they get too hot, they pour out black smoke, and the smoke spreads out in a smooth circle when it hits the ceiling. The ceiling joists apparently create some kind of static electric charge, because when the smoke settles, it does so in long, thin lines along the joists which lie above the Sheetrock. The steadily darkening ceiling made it depressing to work in the kitchen. I decided to roll out a new one over my head.

In the morning I went to the storeroom to get a gallon of white paint. A mouse has been making his nest in an empty box there. It grows larger in the darkness, all tiny pieces of toilet paper and felt boot liner and cotton bundled together to make a bed. I got the paint—after feeling the bed to see if the mouse was there—and a roll of masking tape. Under the house I picked up the paint tray and roller and turpentine and the stepladder. Some plastic was recovered from behind the outhouse, and I spread it all around the kitchen and set the stepladder in one corner.

A small chisel pried the paint-can lid off. I stirred it with a smooth stick, then lifted the gallon can and tilted it over the paint tray, watching the smooth flow of the liquid which is not quite liquid, but heavy, like quicksilver. I set the tray on the little shelf at the top of the stepladder, and climbed up, wearing only my long red cotton underwear, which already has holes and could not be much damaged by paint. In the first few rolls, when the roller was heavy with new paint which had not been fully absorbed by the soft cloth, my red underwear and face and hair got covered with a fine mist of tiny white dots.

I painted slowly, building the patch of clean white outward in all directions, smoothing on the lightness in circles of celebration. Every ten minutes I got down for more paint, and to move the ladder and put masking tape on the corners of the walls. The day spread like the whiteness of the ceiling, until it was late, and all was white, smoothed to newness under my hand. I cleaned the roller and the tray and put it all away. By the time I finished, the ceiling was dry. I lay on the floor and looked at it, imagining the summer days when the light of early morning and late evening alike would shine on the new white paint.

Bob had taken off in the morning on skis, with a day's supplies and his high-powered rifle. It was a partly cloudy day, but the sun broke through quite often as he skied toward the mainland. He headed for the logging road which joins a system leading deep into the woods and circles back perhaps six miles east along the shore. The roads are heavily obscured with deadfall and go through some of the darkest and wildest parts of the pine forest. They are not roads which are good for an evening walk, but they are perfect for a time in which to sink into the woods. They grab the heart and twist it to their own dark and sweetly damp contours; they force the body over logs and under until you feel that you are deeply intertwined with the woods life, away from time and the sun. There is no easy route into them, or out of them, especially in snow.

I watched Bob head up the logging road in the steady and directed rhythm that had evolved from many trips into the mountains. The rhythm of meditation, the movement of forgetting and remembering. It is a motion that culls thought, like the dance on the threshing-room floor, like the spin of centrifugal force.

When it was getting toward late afternoon, he told me later, he came out of the woods in the big meadow which leads down to the water again. As he stopped for a minute to look toward the lake, seeing the wide stretch of beach which would make for an easier return home, he heard a crackling sound in the crusty snow of the meadow, clearly the passage of some large animal. Immediately sitting down, his rifle cradled on his knees, he waited.

There was only stillness for a time, and then a moose stepped from the brush. He was huge. His antlers spread out in all directions like the heavy crown of some ancient king. His body, brown and muscled, was half again as large as any normal bull's. The bell that hung from his lower jaw swung heavily as he turned his head from side to side.

Bob felt that he was in the presence of the prototype of all moose— the great moose with whom it had begun. He was sure that if he moved, the moose would either disappear, or run him into the ground. He didn't move. He watched as the animal made its way through the field, turning his head from side to side, stopping and looking around with an intelligence that was unusual in a moose, and even more surprising because it seemed absurd to think that such an animal could fear any danger. Then he turned and walked directly toward the logging road on which Bob was sitting. Bob knew that he must do something, but sat dead still instead, watching the great legs move up and down.

At last he raised the rifle to fire a warning shot. As quickly as the thought entered his head, the moose was gone. It turned to the side, and in a dead run it pounded into the trees, ten yards away. The spread of its antlers was at least seven feet. And the trees in those woods lie so close together that it is sometimes hard for even a man to walk between them.

->>><<<-

So I changed my container, and Bob was visited by a vision of power. We did not talk that night, but we sat in peace. The itch had been completely washed away. The wonder of altering the structures of the inanimate world, and receiving messages from the world of power, had filled us, and left no room for darkness. It is possible to survive night without incandescent lights. There are changes all around, made by us, or revealed to us. We must give them time to come in, and silence to speak in. If nothing can be done about the past, there is everything to be expected from the future. There is motion, movement forward and backwards both. When we woke in the morning, the dawn was red, and the sun could be seen on the horizon. We embraced in the hall, watching the dawn. The smell of Bob's skin was the smell of home, and what we had known together was the most important knowledge of all. We can probe deep and still survive. We can be isolated together and still survive. We can sit like prisoners upon a rock and still survive. And we can love the rock which has given us the strength to see with.

6

TRACKS

➤➤➤ (1) ⫷⫷⫷

We try to go to town every two weeks now, to get the mail and visit friends and get in the truck and move. Sometimes the trips are tiring and hard, but they are necessary. In the absence of imaginative changes, making tracks keeps us sane. Bundy loves the trips away from the island; she runs here and there, marking up the snow with enough prints for a hundred dogs. Though we trudge along, heavy and often slushbound, we always return more contented. When we travel away from it, the house is a home to come back to. Fires and storms bring recognition, and play is play.

An early spring has come—at last. The air has opened up; the wind almost supports the smell of distant buds and flowers, birds fly by again, and moose cross the lake on their long, gawky legs. Feelings surface that have been dormant. Plans and questions. Histories and patterns. Destinations. My mind is on people and places far away.

Our last trip took us to Culchunoe. We sat in the drafty game hall, close to the fire in big easy chairs, drinking hot chocolate by the light of the flames. Joyce was wearing a big blue sweater of Wally's and a pair of handmade bright-red socks.

"I'm glad you came," she said. "We were about to go off the deep end."

"Which is the deep end?" Bob asked, happy, setting his cup down on the hearth.

"There's nothing like going nuts on an island," I said, and set my cup down too. The hearthstones were a dull red, polished and clean.

"At least you can leave yours," said Joyce. She took a drag from her

179

cigarette and smiled, her head tilted back. "We're getting paid to stay." She turned her eyes to me across the firelight; she looked strangely beautiful, her face drawn, her pupils large and black. We held each other's eyes for a long moment, and then I looked away. Why had I never before seen past Wally to her silence? I wondered what she might have done had she not met him and moved up north.

"Yes," I said.

Wally sniffed and suddenly leapt up to lift the pot off the fire. Dragging it to the hearth, he took the top off and peered inside, then sighed with relief.

"It isn't burned. Yes," he said, "Joyce and I have decided not to come back here for another winter—it is just too boring! We like symphonies, you know, and plays, and to have a good library nearby."

"People, too," said Joyce. "Never seeing other people. We can't get used to that."

"I know," I said. "Where will you go?"

"We'll move to our cabin on McLeod Lake. It isn't far from the road to Alaska, you know. People will stop in. You will come see us there, too, won't you?"

"Of course," I said.

"I'd have thought you'd like it here, though," said Bob. "After what you told us about working in the bush in the thirties."

"Oh!" said Wally deprecatingly, pouring hot chocolate into our cups. "I was trapping then, and trading; that is different. The Indians all live out in the bush too, and they always stop in, all of them related; everybody is at least a cousin to the last one; they all know the news. I still have my trader's license. If I could trap near here, it would be different. But how can I trap near here?" he asked, turning to look at me so questioningly that I lurched into awareness to try and find an answer.

"Yes," said Bob. "All the trap-line leases are certainly long gone."

"Yes, yes." Wally nodded, thoughtful.

"The Indians are lucky," I said. "It'd be nice to make a living in the bush. It'd make living out here less of a game, in a way. Though I hate the thought of trapping." I sipped my hot chocolate, sweet and hot and slimy, and slumped down in my chair.

Bob questioned Wally intently, about traps and bait, concealment and scent, full of plans to trap next winter, lease or no, for money and to stay more sane. On the hearthstone Wally sketched plans for stretchers to preserve small skins. Bob leaned forward, his arms propped on his knees, watching Wally's finger. The hair on Bob's forearm glinted in the firelight. Joyce and I sat, contented, talking from time to time about Indians, and self-reliance, and the benefits of cooperation. Later Joyce went out onto the deck, returning with an armload of wood, placing each piece carefully on the fire. Her legs were tucked beneath her as she knelt; I felt tenderness for the shiny bottoms of her feet.

When we went to bed in the caretaker's cabin, I grabbed Bob around the waist; he looped his arm around my head, letting his hand curl in my hair. His skin smelled warm from the fire.

"Why do women always have to cuddle?" he asked.

"Why not?" I kissed his arm. "I'm sorry they're leaving."

"Yes." He paused, scratching my scalp. "Did you know that wolf skins are selling for fifty dollars now?"

"No. Did you know that islands are selling for fifty thousand?"

Bob squeezed my shoulder, kissed my hair.

"I know," he said.

"It's not just making a living, Bob. It's making a life. If even *they* can't do it?"

"I know," he said.

→>>⟪⟪⟪-

The other day two crows appeared, goodness knows from where. They sat on a branch outside my study window. They sat close together, looking cold, while the wind ruffled their head feathers and they shifted the grip of their feet. Suddenly, the crow who was lower down on the branch raised his left foot to his back and scratched it so fast and furiously that the motion was only a blur to my eyes. Then he relaxed and hopped sideways until he pressed against his companion.

The other turned at the touch and plunged his beak vigorously into the exact spot that had been so thoroughly scratched. With his beak sunk deep in the feathers he poked and probed for nearly thirty seconds. Exhausted, he hopped away. The first followed him, persistent, and once settled firmly on the branch, proceeded to scratch himself again. His companion, now precariously near to the end of the branch, turned and rooted once more in the other's feathers. He stopped. They both stared ahead while the wind lifted their feathers in small swaths. Then they flew away, their toes curled beneath them.

Everybody's moving on. And we?

$\rightarrow\!\!>\!\!> (2) \ll\!\!\ll$

It's fall again, and we're home.

Yes.

Home again from teaching, with memories of new people and new mountains.

Mornings we wake early, restless and cool. We throw the window open behind us, breathing deep, planning each day with care. No trace lingers now of last spring's blackness. We look ahead of and around us, holding this autumn precious. In the rich September mornings the winds blow the leaves from the tops of the aspen trees; as they somersault through the air, they rustle and lose their colors to the earth. Bob and I live quietly, not dwelling aloud on what we both feel—that this will be our last island fall. Without any way to earn a living on the island and without a group of people nearby, how can we stay? With a whole world around us full of energy and transformation, why should we?

We don't discuss it though. We talk of trapping instead, and hunting, and tracks in the woods. We see the signs of movement on land and in the air. Birds fly south now, full of a strange urgency. Moose seek mates in the woods, and bears claw dens out of the still-soft earth. While we are here, I want to hunt down and meet every creature who lives here with us. In the absence of friends, I'll settle for quarry. And, though my bond with humanity is clearly too strong to break, I'd like to see how the other animals live. Lately, I dream of pursuing the fox and the beaver, the moose and the wolf. I've already missed a bear.

Last week, shortly after we returned, we spent a day trying to walk to Tarnezell Lake. It has become a challenge—trying to find the lake and make it real. But though all roads may merge at last, the road to Tarnezell Lake must take a very long detour before it arrives at last at the waterside. A detour around the last twenty years of growth, the paths of animals over the land, and the quiver of the compass on a cloudless day.

It was a dry day, so dry the grasses crackled and the meadows shimmered with heat—we felt as if August had been specially held over for us to hike in. North of the booming ground on the north shore we searched the edge of a grassy meadow for the logging road which led (on the map) from Stuart to Tarnezell Lake. Only when we were almost upon it could we see the road running ahead and out of sight—a road as perfectly flat and grassy and flower-dotted as any country lane. None of the usual evidence existed that heavy machinery had once passed the same way we intended to travel. Indeed, from the evidence, nothing had passed that way since the road was made but the wind off the lake and the air-blown seeds of columbine and paintbrush.

As we went on, however, the road got worse. The shaded path started to open up to the sun as it climbed to higher ground; aspen trees were spreading furiously into the open spaces there. Many trails, evidence of the partiality of moose for aspen groves, led through the shrubs for two or three more miles. But when we reached the top of a major hill, the trails and aspens both disappeared, replaced by berry bushes in all directions. There was no clear sign of where the road had once been.

There was, however, a lot of clear sign of another kind. Mounds of fresh bear scat decorated the area. If there had been only one bear in the berry patch, he had certainly had a vast intestinal tract. When bears have been eating saskatoons and raspberries, their scat is very moist and red, clearly full of undigested berries. The moister the scat is, the easier it is to tell how old it is. This scat was very recent.

To see bear sign on our walks is not unusual. Normally, though, when I see such recent sign, I clutch Bob's arm and lobby for a quick departure from the immediate area. In fact, when we bought the island, one factor which weighed heavily in its favor (as far as I was concerned) was the consideration that if we lived on an island, we would have no bears sneaking up from behind.

Most of the bears I have seen in the flesh have been quite disarming. They have headed for the nearest tree when they saw me coming, climbing it frantically until they could go no higher, and then hanging there, the little pink soles of their feet dangling down while they waited earnestly for me to go away. They have loped hurriedly down the road in the opposite direction from the one I seemed to be interested in, looking back over their shoulders from time to time. They have simply gone on eating berries, hoping I would disappear.

But I have never yet seen a bear around Stuart Lake, although there are supposed to be grizzlies in the area, as well as the black bears whose footprints we see so often. You might think the more times I see sign here without running into the bear that left it, the less of a threat they would seem to be. Not at all.

Bears lie in wait for me in the woods. They attack me, and, ripping me to shreds, they eat me thoughtfully. They glare at me with little beady eyes, and they lurch purposefully in my direction with cruel strength, huge muscles rippling as they move. They smile before they slash.

So when we got to the berry patch, I suggested we go home. We were almost exactly halfway between the two lakes—as far as we could tell from the map—and the road had disappeared. It would be pretty hard to bushwhack another three or four miles to Tarnezell Lake and back. It would be sensible to go home. But Bob didn't want to. He isn't afraid of bears. So we went on.

Actually, the road reappeared and got better for a time. One could at least follow it, although with a good deal of climbing over deadfall and skirting enormous bushes. After another mile, though, it petered out right in the middle of the most forsaken-looking patch of land around. It was not simply a marsh; it was a wood which had once been lightning struck, and the stumps of dead and blackened trees marched around it in grim rhythm. The deadfall was dense, and yet there were patches of green aspens growing up which screened all view of the general land-scape. It took ten minutes to walk thirty feet, hauling myself up onto logs, lowering myself into sloughs and holes. Bob and I each took our own circuitous trail, and within ten minutes were well separated, each sitting on a stump and wondering how to get out of the mess.

As I sat on the stump, a sound came out of the woods behind me, the sound of a large animal changing its location. It was followed by a snorting grunt, and then a crash. Considering the country we were in, it would have been sensible to suspect moose, but I thought that it must be a bear. I called out to Bob, who was out of sight behind a screen of aspens, and he, intent on listening for the sound, did not answer. The sound came again, and then once more, while I sat on the stump trying to look like new growth. Finally Bob came clambering into sight.

"Did you hear that?" he asked. "Must have been a moose."

"A moose." I nodded seriously. I almost believed it, for half a second or less.

We decided it would be madness to keep going, and we started laboriously working our way out of the fire-blackened marsh. About three hundred yards out of it, we came to a branch in the road which had not been obvious on the way in; it seemed likely to be a more direct route back to the shore, and we turned off onto it. Wetter than the other road, it was interrupted by large stretches of muddy ground. Before long, we saw a set of the finest, freshest bear tracks I ever want to see. Big ones. They were heading the same way we were. Suddenly, there seemed a lot of ground between the lakeshore and my feet.

I started to walk more slowly; every ten or twenty feet Bob paused to let me catch up. The road branched several times; each time we picked a route, it turned out to be the same route the bear had picked. Had we been trying to track him, we could not have done a better job. I dragged behind Bob, whistling. I hoped we wouldn't unexpectedly round the corner just ahead to find a berry patch. At last Bob, now well out in front, vanished from sight. He called me to come quick and see the bear.

The measure of my previous reluctance to see the bear was suddenly the measure of my eagerness to see him. I broke into a run and rounded the bend in the road—to see some bushes moving. Nothing more. I scanned them for a glimpse of brown, but the bear was gone. I picked a blade of grass and set it between my lips, disappointed and hurt. He had not been sneaking up behind me; he had not wanted to tear me to shreds and eat me slowly. No, it was I who had been pursuing him and I who had not quite caught him. He'd made his four-pawed track through the woods unconscious of his pursuers, not thinking of sudden meetings. Yet he had reason to fear the animals behind. I had no reason to fear the one ahead.

The bear tracks stopped; we went on. On a grassy patch of road overlooking the lake we ate our lunch, talking about bears. I was compelled to admit that I had no reason to dread them—four-legged, long-snouted creatures with fur. I made a little horse of bread crumbs and set it riding on my knee. Bob spoke of goblins and things that go bump in the night. I scoffed at that and argued fiercely for the difference between goblins and bears, knowing that there is none. He is right. It isn't the bear I fear, but the sudden meeting—and the abrupt ending which may come of it. Reversals lie in wait in the woods, ready to pounce; I try to tiptoe by them. Yet I desire them too. I ran to see the bear, scanning the bushes where he had gone, following the source of my fear with longing, hoping to change my life.

➤➤➤(3)◀◀◀

A long time ago, in the mountains, I caught my first trout, a nineteen-inch rainbow. I was standing in a milky lake, aqua blue with glacial silt. I did not want to catch the fish. He needn't have taken my casting seriously. The day was, I thought, far too rarefied for action; too many years lay calmly on the shore. Suddenly, he was on my line; he wanted to come in. We had a bit of a tussle, but I dragged him to the shore and flipped him onto a rock. There he lay, and his eyes grew clouded, troubled. I wanted to throw him back, but quite suddenly, I couldn't move. I felt in the presence of a catastrophic power, his eye like a window of the earth, calmly staring up at me, slowly misting over. Somewhere deep within the eye there was a leer which said, "You call yourself a creature? Ha. Kill me if you wish to be anything at all. Kill me before you melt at my feet."

I picked him up and smashed his head in. The colors of his skin glinted as he jerked, convulsed like the eruption of a volcano. The air around me crystallized; the trees rustled in kind applause. Later I cooked the fish.

He's still a part of me.

➤➤➤(4)◀◀◀

This afternoon we went to check on the beaver traps which we set in the pond behind Mud Bay. We took the engine off the canoe, and paddled through the calm and mist-pressed day; the wooden paddles made the only sound until two mergansers took off in the mist with a great rushing and flapping of wings. At this time of year Mud Bay lives up to its name. No boat with more draft than a canoe could easily enter the wide shallows, through which you can see the soft and muddy bottom sprouting long green fronds of water sedges. The beaver pond can be reached by water, and we decided to paddle into it. I am always amazed when I see the massive dam rising before us, strong and neat.

Most animals are content with the wilderness as it is presented to them, and they fill it cleverly. Almost every location in the woods is home to some animal or insect—the branches of trees, the clusters of bushes, the grasses, the space beneath the roots of fallen trees, bark and stone and overhanging banks. Beavers, however, are not content with these choices. Like men, they construct their own environment. Since a beaver wants a large pond in which to live, he dams up flowing water until it forms one. Since he enjoys the leaves at the tops of aspen trees, he chews through trunks until the trees fall.

The beaver pond stores up water in which otters, fish, and frogs live happily. Migrating ducks stop by in it. Muskrat, mink, and moose all like to live in the area of a beaver pond. A beaver pond is a good place to go to see wildlife. It is also a good place to set traps. The beavers make their canals and they build their dams, and thus they are easy prey to men, who understand the desire to make paths and to put water in its proper place.

Bob and I had set a trap just underwater in the mud of the bank where the beavers climb out to forage. We had also made a little hole in the dam, and set a trap beneath it, knowing that a beaver would come to repair the damage with sticks and mud. In both cases the trap was attached by a sliding ring to a wire anchored to the bottom with a rock. If a beaver's foot had been caught in a trap, he would have wrenched the trap loose from its mud emplacement and dived for the bottom, obeying the survival instinct of water animals. The weight of the trap would have made it impossible for him to rise to the surface again when he needed air. After a time he would have drowned.

The hole in the dam had been neatly repaired. I looked away when Bob reached for the trap, but we had caught no beaver. We pulled the canoe up beside the dam, lovely in the grey light, simple and well cared for. I climbed out and walked across the dam—it bounced, but it was solid, and never threatened to come apart beneath my weight. Bob pulled the traps in one by one and dropped them to the floor of the canoe. We won't be setting them again. Some forms of hunting are justified by the gifts they give the hunter; man can give meaning to an animal's death or let it die alone. But traps foster power without sacrifice; the killer is not present at the death. One should always try to be there in moments which have great power.

The mist was lifting on the lake, and we paddled softly along the shore of Mud Bay, looking for life. The wind picked up. Small rollers began to form as we neared the point which led into the main lake. A beaver was swimming along the shore, his small chinless head held nose forward, sniffing the wind. His little eyes peered ahead nearsightedly. The fur which is so thick and soft when dry was slicked to his head like a bathing cap. He paddled furiously along, and we paddled after him, ten feet behind. He looked over his shoulder and executed a neat surface dive, slapping the water soundly with his flat tail as he disappeared. A minute later he came up again off the starboard bow, and we paddled after him, giggling at his chagrin. He moved suddenly sideways, and we moved after him, close on his tail. He dived again, but this time in such haste and confusion that he almost forgot to slap the water to warn his absent family of the danger. At the last possible instant a section of his tail jerked and hit the water with the feeblest smack. We paddled away. The next time the beaver surfaced he was heading in the direction of home, his small head a ball which skimmed the surface of the rollers.

Bundy was in a state of high excitement during the beaver's appearances. She is now convinced that every mud-trapped log and isolated rock is a beaver, and she quivers with tension as we approach a piece of the landscape, sniffing the air in anticipation. We teased her by pretending that we were concerned over the identification of a particular log which jutted from the mud of the bottom and bobbed above the surface with the water's motion. We circled it cautiously, getting slowly closer, and evidently more astonished. Bundy was almost out of the canoe as we finally came to rest beside the log end. She started to sniff it, but just as she lowered her head, the log sank beneath the weight of the canoe. Uncomprehending and outraged, Bundy looked for a moment after the lost log and then thrust her snout beneath the surface of the water, inhaling as she did so.

She came up choking and snorting. She still thinks the log was a beaver, and her natural prey—also a tricky little animal, to hide where she could not sniff it.

→>>‹‹‹←

There are two kinds of animals in the world, the killers and the runners. They can be distinguished by the shape of their jaws and teeth and the position of their eyesockets. Deer and elk, moose and rabbit and beaver, have their eyes set closer to the sides of their head, where they will be most useful. They do not need to look to the front so much as all around, to the side and rear. The lynx, the bear, the weasel, and the dog have eyes set closer to the front of the skull, where they will best serve in the pursuit. But even their eyes are not truly binocular. Only one animal around here has binocular vision, eyes set together in such a way that it can see its prey with total clarity. That animal is man.

I am glad we caught no beaver, and we won't be setting traps again. But it is hard to understand the life of an animal without thinking about hunting it. I cannot count the times that I have tripped over wolf tracks, stamped out bear tracks, or stepped over moose tracks; and all without knowing that something had been that way before me. Something always has. I wonder why it takes the equivalent of a gun to show me that? Perhaps because I need to use the power of my eyes— binocular, and trained to look carefully through open sights.

⇶ (5) ⇷

We are hunting moose. The afternoon is foggy and damp, unusually warm for this season of contraction. The day is very still, and I walk in stupid absorption, looking for fresh moose tracks. Most of the tracks on the road are old. Some, made during last spring's mud season, are so deep that I have to walk around them. I see a calf track, only two inches long, isolated on a mound of mud. There seems no life around. Many bushes and trees are still leafed; the grass retains glints of summer green.

An hour of silent walking passes. Twigs crack. Rustles stir the woods. We turn at last and head for the canoe once more. Bob takes great strides toward it while I meander over the logs and leaves. A brown leaf has curled together like a tiny fist.

When we get to the long stretch of straight road leading into the bay, Bob is a hundred yards ahead of me. He stops, still save for the gesture of his hand. I am transformed in an instant. My heart starts to throb and my mouth is full of choking. The animal Bob is watching might be anything from a nuthatch to a fox, but I know it is a bear. Silently I walk forward to where Bob is crouched. Saying nothing, he hands me the rifle.

Two cow moose are drinking water at the edge of the bay. The lake lurks beyond them, and the white gasps of mist separate and come together with no apparent cause. The air is so still I can hardly believe that the moose have not heard us, but there is no wind to carry our smell. In all the landscape, the only shapes that have real substance are the two moose, brown and bent, standing in the mud and drinking.

They listen carelessly if at all, not hearing the short, wild gulps I make for air. I want them to hear me and run. I want to run myself.

I sit down and balance the gun upon my knees and slowly raise it to my shoulder. The gun is in my hands, but I do not want to shoot the moose. I do not want to shoot so much that I am overcome with panic. So this is buck fever. Not blood lust at all. I cannot see straight, I cannot see through the sights of the gun at all; all I can see before I even aim is the panic of the moose and then its death. While I shoot the bolt, I pray for it to hear me.

I aim the rifle and fire. I know that I have closed my eyes the moment I pulled the trigger, and I am throbbing now with fury. I quickly shoot again, hardly aiming, my eyes wide but filled with water, blurred. One moose looks about in some puzzlement, but the other continues to drink placidly. I aim at the one who is drinking, level the sights at her heart, hold the gun till it is steady, and squeeze the trigger. I know this shot will kill her, and that I have gained control—late, but still in time.

The moose lifts one leg and moves backward. Holding her leg in the air as if in wonder, she tries to walk, and moves forward into the water. For a moment I am sure she will swim off and die in the lake. But it is only one step and one long second before she hurries the only way which is left to her, down into the mud of the bay.

The other cow takes off at last, whipping along, her awkward-looking leg joints allowing her great speed. I find that I am running forward, rubbing my shoulder. Not until I look at my hand do I feel the pain the three recoils have caused. I move toward the water to finish the cow off. She is certainly hit in the lungs or heart, and it will not be long before she dies; but I run. Bob catches up with me on the way, running at what seems like great speed, and he grabs the gun and passes on. I shout for him to stop, but cannot hear my own voice. The moose lies motionless as Bob approaches her. When the bullet goes through her forehead, the body moves heavily in the water, and is still.

I get to the shore and look at my moose. She floats in about two feet of water, the mud stirred and mixed with blood, so that the lake around her is a filthy, oily color. Her tongue protrudes from her mouth, and I think that I have never seen such a perfect tongue. Her large ears are soft to the touch, and lined with fine white hairs. She is probably only a two-year-old—her body is not much larger than a pony's, and barrel shaped as she rolls in the water. The delicate hoofs are quite uncracked, and her fur is a warm, rippling flow which feels the way grass looks in a summer meadow. We roll her over onto her back, and her legs fall to the sides.

The fur on the belly is a lighter color than that on her back—a soft and even brown untouched by black. Between her hind legs the fur is lighter still. I run my hand over it, and touch a nipple, small and pink, no bigger than a dog's, but softer. It has never been used, it is a baby's nipple. I find them all, six of them, hidden and protected by the fur. She is still so warm.

We struggle with the body, up to our thighs in mud and water, grasping at the huge dead weight, the bulk of rapidly cooling flesh. The lake is strewn with floating entrails, like the water lilies of a storm-beaten pond. Her head has floated away, and I am covered with the blood of my sacrifice. She is lovely still, and will be warm forever under my palms. There is a chain of power which is nourished by the water of the bay, the water of her veins, and the water of my eyes. I am drenched in it. She has died through my will and purified that will with her perfection. It is a clean and decisive love I feel: I did my crying before I knew the object of my tears.

⇶ (6) ⇷

The lamps are lit, and a smell of roasting moose fills the house. I am scrubbing potatoes at the sink. Over by the stove Bob has spread plastic on the floor and is standing the canoe paddle, which has split down the middle of the blade, preparing it for glue. I set each potato on the counter to my left, until five potatoes form a concentric flower pattern of lumps.

Bob pauses for an instant to sniff the air.

"Best moose we've ever had, isn't it?" I say proudly.

"It's great," he agrees, tearing off a new piece of sandpaper and tilting his head back to look at me quizzically.

"Don't you think it tastes different from most moose? Less gamey, tenderer, kind of?"

"Now that you mention it," he says judiciously, "I think you're right." Bob's attempts to act always fill me with mirth. Unappreciatively I giggle.

"Oh well. Maybe I'm just getting to like game meat more," I say.

Bob sands the paddle furiously, not entirely conscious of the dust which flies around him. He seems to have stopped considering the subject of meat, but then he says:

"You should be. We eat enough to feed an army. Moose. It's like subtraction stew—the more you eat the hungrier you get."

"That sounds significant. Maybe we should vary the diet."

"With what? Twigs?"

"We could hunt a caribou."

"What do you mean 'we,' white woman?"

"Oh, well, two then."

"We don't need *two*. But I'm up for it if you're serious. Are you serious?" he asks. At my nod he goes on. "Not knowing the country makes it harder to hunt, you know. Are you in the mood for track soup?"

"Track soup! Did you make that up?" I ask, scrubbing the last potato and setting it aside.

"Arthur," Bob says. "Your ignorance continues to astound me. I got 'track soup' out of the same pot in which cream rises to the top."

"What pot?" I ask. "Cream?"

Bob calls on an unresponsive heaven for assistance.

"Figure it out," he says callously. "I'll never understand how you grew up without a basic knowledge of the epigram and the axiom."

"I know what they are! I just haven't heard every little one. So we're going hunting?" I ask.

"Sure, all the wood's in. Let's go."

I inhale deeply, pleased. I open the oven door to look at the bubbling pan of meat inside. The blood, dripping down, has coagulated into small puddles of soft brown jelly, which mix with the fat and water to make brown juice. I close the oven door and stick four more pieces of wood into the firebox, cramming the last one tightly against the roof. One of the thick cast-iron plates is jarred and slides into the fire with a thump.

"God, what a bloodthirsty woman you're becoming," says Bob, stirring the dust up with a whisk broom. "What would the Sierra Club say? And Greenpeace?"

"Oh, don't be ridiculous. They're not anti-hunting in general. You're so paranoid. I certainly don't intend to run riot."

"Bloodthirsty," Bob mutters.

"Hah," I say.

For a time, I work on the soup in silence. Moving the potatoes onto the cutting board, I start to slice them and transfer them by handfuls to the pressure cooker. Working deliberately with my hands makes me thoughtful. Bloodthirsty? True enough. Thirsty for—blood.

"If you look at it right," I say, "being bloodthirsty is being thirsty for life. After all, blood isn't even blood anymore after it stops pumping."

Bob looks at me. I have a vague impression that blood coagulates almost instantly after death, but hesitate to air it. Instead I say:

"Well, you know, it's only blood while the heart's beating. Isn't that true?"

"No," says Bob. "But I know what you mean."

"Yes."

"We were born into the wrong age," he adds.

"Shall I bring on the violins?" I ask. "It's amazing, though, how fond you can get of animals you're trying to kill. Remember that beaver we saw? After we pulled in the traps?"

"Silly beaver," Bob says. "You're sure you want to hunt a caribou?"

"Of course. That's different. We'll eat him."

->>> (7) <<<-

The truck bounces gaily north, leaving Caesar's Point in a gurgle of wheels. Flay and Nadine have friends staying with them—Rick and Mary Donovan from Washington—so we didn't pause long at their house. We aim for the North Road, and once on it look for intersections. We plan to go as far as McLeod Lake tonight, stopping there to see Wally and Joyce. According to the map there is a little-used road to McLeod Lake running east through the hills. It's hard to tell just where the road should start, so when we reach a crossroads, unmarked by signs but heavily rutted, we debate for a time. Finally, with a fatalistic shrug, Bob wheels onto the dirt, heading east.

As we pass over it, the road deteriorates steadily, becoming more and more rutted, less and less navigable. Ten miles bounce by. Suddenly, the woods open onto a small clearing, jammed with trailers. Ten large metal trailers stand neatly side by side in two rows. Bob stops the truck, and I climb out to see if there is anyone in residence who can tell us about the route.

Before I am two steps from the truck, a door in the nearest trailer opens, and a man hurries out, walking toward me and nodding his head, grinning from ear to ear.

"Hello, hello, hello," he says, nervously and shyly. "Come right in, I'll put the coffee on. Or perhaps you would prefer tea? Come in, come in." He doesn't actually touch me, but I feel as if I am being herded toward the trailer. The man is in his sixties. He wears a pair of wheat-colored work pants with cuffs, and a stained white shirt designed for use with stud links, and lacking them. Bob gets out of the truck and follows us, running one hand through his hair. A mitten drops out of his back pocket onto the ground, and he stoops to pick it up while I go into the trailer.

The trailer has only one window, in the end wall. The barest necessities line the walls—a bunk with grey woolen blankets, chipped white china, a two-burner Coleman stove. The latter the man lights, hurriedly, pumping away as if he fears we will leave before he gets the water on. I sit on the edge of the bunk and ask him about himself.

He says he is caretaking the trailers for the winter for a logging company. He had worked most of his life as a grader in a sawmill, but had eventually lost his job because his eyesight started to fail. He'd been out of work for over a year, and had finally gotten this job. It's the first time he's ever lived alone in the bush, and he's only been here three weeks so far; we are the first people to stop.

He says that he needs the money or he wouldn't be here.

"It's kinda godforsaken here. I play the radio a lot, and all that, but it's kinda godforsaken. I guess I'm just too old for this sort of thing— sixty-two come December."

The water boils, and he gets quickly to his feet and lays three chipped white cups neatly on the counter.

"You said tea, didn't you?"

I hadn't, but I agree.

I watch him take a small brown teapot from the shelf, lift the lid, and spoon in two teaspoons of tea from an open can. His hands tremble as they move, and the veins stand out in purple relief.

We learn from him the best way to McLeod Lake, and drink our tea to the bottom. When we leave, he comes with us to the truck, and stands there searching for words, while we get Bundy back in and brush off the seat.

"I'm sure glad you came by. Thanks for coming in like that."

"Thank you for the tea and the directions. I don't know what we'd have done if you hadn't been here." I smile and look quickly away, and we drive off. He stands by the road till we are out of sight.

Shortly after, we turn onto a one-lane road, if it can be called that. It is deeply rutted and gets smaller and smaller as we drive. Just when it seems impossible to continue (the trees inches from the sides of the truck, and the wheels dropping down great steps of mud with every forward motion), the road turns into a normal dirt track. Fifteen more miles bring us higher and higher, into the beginning of the snow.

I had not anticipated snow. It covers the road, and the stripped tires of the truck spin regularly. Twenty feet below the top of the highest pass, first gear fails. We back down, and a new fast run gets us to the top, and there we park, looking down into a valley which holds winter in its bowl, although the rest of the world is still in autumn. The snowy road runs down into the valley and disappears beneath the trees.

We hesitate. Is this the right way? We don't really know. Behind us there is a lonely man in a tin trailer by a rutted road, and somewhere on the other side of the snow, our friends. We drive into the deep white powder, down and down, through a muffling welcoming quilt of winter. The roads lead us by the right ways, and we arrive at Wally's cabin just as darkness closes in. The fires are burning inside, and the lamps are lit. Loki runs barking to greet us, and someone peers out the door.

"Liz and Bob? Is that you? Joyce, guess who's here to visit us. It's Liz and Bob!" We kick off our muddy boots, and the door closes behind us on the night.

→>>≪←

In the back of the truck are fresh vegetables, parting gifts from Wally and Joyce. No caribou, but something just as good. A box of little white potatoes, and a box of carrots, crinkled and dark orange. Turnips in a sack and three cabbages, close and warm with dirt. The sun is shining and the air is sweet with drying leaves.

Rick Donovan is in the yard when we pull into the Walkers'. He is riding Flay's tractor, slowly pulling the big boat out of the water. I can hardly believe it—the tractor is Flay's favorite tool, and his boat should stay in the water for another week at least. Bob calls out a greeting to Rick, and says, "So Flay let you use his tractor, did he?"

Slowly and carefully Rick sets the brake and gets onto the running board of the tractor and jumps to the ground. The pebbles crunch under his boots.

"Flay had a heart attack yesterday. He died very quickly."

Uncalled, the silence comes. Bob stands beside me; I can feel him thinking, "How to help? What to do?" My eyes start to water, but inside I am numb. I dig one fingernail as hard as I can into my palm; I pinch my thigh until it aches.

When we get to the house, Nadine is at the door as always, and I start to cry, helplessly, hugging her tightly, knowing I am increasing her pain—knowing that nothing can increase her pain, knowing that she is still in shock as she pats my shoulder, and I tear at my palm, trying to stop the tears.

We sit at the table, Nadine and Bob and I and Mary Donovan. We drink coffee, and I pour too much milk in mine until it almost overflows. Outside the tractor starts to move again, put-put, slowly at first, then fast—put-put-put. Nadine looks up, quickly, and then she looks down again.

"That was Flay's toy," she says. "The tractor. No one else ever used it. The sound of it just means Flay to me. I thought it might be him." She feels she has to explain, to put us at ease.

Mary, a large woman with heavy cheeks and arms, starts to tell the story. Nadine interrupts her sometimes to add details she forgets. The day before yesterday, in the morning, Flay had told Nadine he had a surprise for her. He had handed her a hundred dollars and told her to take Mary and go to Prince George and enjoy herself. Get a motel room, go to a movie, eat three meals out. Shop. Take a little vacation, get away from baking and serving people. It was a birthday present.

So they went. They took the pickup truck, warning the men not to mess the house up too much. After a night in Prince George, and after a leisurely breakfast out, they started back yesterday.

The men had decided to spend yesterday widening and improving the road. The last curve into the Walkers' place is very abrupt and quite narrow. They had always hated knowing that visitors might get stuck there anytime. But it was a job Flay had never wanted to tackle by himself.

They worked at it all morning. Flay was happy—he thought of surprising Nadine with the new road, as he always thought to please her with all the work he did. The big tracks on the tractor rolled over the new smoothed earth, not only taking the curve out of the road, but tamping the earth into interesting patterns. Flay got off the tractor to make an adjustment in the tread. He fell on the new-turned soil, clutching his chest. He died within the minute, without speaking.

"At least he died quickly," says Nadine. "Flay was such a strong, healthy man, so proud of his strength. If he had one fault, it was that pride. But I never could stand the thought of him sick, dying slowly in bed. He wouldn't have been able to stand it himself. He always said, 'When the Lord takes me, I pray he does it quickly.' " She smiles, taking comfort in the thought.

"Just last week we were talking of what we should do to celebrate our thirty-fifth wedding anniversary. I never thought I would lose him so soon."

After a while, the others go out, and Nadine turns to me.

"You know, I married Flay when I was eighteen. We've done everything together, for thirty-five years. I just don't know how I'm going to get along without him. We've lived in remote places, and he's been everything to me. I don't remember what life was like before I met him. I don't know what I was like, without him. It's too long ago."

Mary brings in a cake and makes some more coffee. Bob offers to help with closing up the house, but Nadine says they will not do much except lock the door.

I ask Nadine where she will go, and she smiles again, gently.

"A few years ago, Flay decided we should buy a house trailer in our home town in Washington, a place to live when we got too old to be of use up here. The payments were one hundred dollars a month, but we paid ten dollars extra—that was insurance so that if Flay died, the rest of the cost would be paid by the bank. I said that was silly—we could use the ten dollars, and there was no need to worry about dying, but he insisted. He said he didn't think he was going to die either, but if he did, he didn't want me to have to worry about how to live."

"You'll have all your friends there, too, Nadine," puts in Mary. Nadine smiles, but doesn't answer.

We try to talk of other things for a while. The boat. The mission. Who will shovel the cabin roof this winter. Some Indians arrive to extend their sympathy.

Finally, Bob says that we should go. The lake may blow up anytime in the afternoon. Already there is a damp smell to the breeze. Nadine talks once more of Flay's death.

"You know, Rick was waiting by the road into the Fort, to catch us when we drove by. I didn't suspect anything was wrong when I saw him there. But we stopped, and he said, 'Nadine, I'm afraid you're going to have to be very brave.' And I knew.

"We went to see Flay's body in the hospital. He looked so young and strong and beautiful. I couldn't help but feel that he must be happy now. Then we drove back to the house, and I went into the bedroom. The bed hadn't been made—men never do like to make beds, do they?—and I could still see the covers all messed up where he had slept, and the imprint of where his head had lain on the pillow. After all our lives together, we spent the last night apart. And when I saw where his head had lain, I started to cry."

Finally, she starts to cry again, and I hold her hand, helpless.

She raises her head and smiles through her tears.

"He always used to sleep naked, you know; he was so warm even in the winter that he wouldn't wear pajamas. But his head used to get cold, sticking out of the blankets. We kept a crack of window open. So in the winter he had a nightcap that I made him, bright orange with a long drooping peak and a tassel. You know what he used to say before he went to bed? 'Well, I guess it's about time for me to put on my nightgown.' Naked, all except for that silly orange nightcap. He called it his nightgown."

At last we hug Nadine tightly, load the canoe, and start for home. Now they are gone as well.

⇻≫ (8) ≪⇺

It is the kind of late fall day when it seems that winter will never come. Fall is not a progress toward a later season, but a state of permanent adornment. The trees are bare and withered through a dark day of rain. They seem glad that the birds have gone away and they are unencumbered by wings. No messages remain from the summer past, no bite of winter is in the wind. It is the pureness of November everywhere— the colors are all different shades of grey, the sounds are all variations on a muted crackle or a sodden pressure. Somehow it seems that this season will not support animal life. The moose and geese have vanished, too large and colorful in the echoing woods, too easy to glimpse through the spare design of dying things. The water is leaden and calm, and the sky pearl behind the black patterns of the clouds.

We walk along the south bay where the marshy willow land gives way to deeper woods. In them the leaves are dry underfoot despite the recent rain. The rain has stopped and the air is freshening; there may be changes in store after all. We are looking for moose again, and Bob shushes me repeatedly as I follow behind him cracking twigs in half, scrunching leaves, and whipping aside the branches of trees. The woods seem so ignorant of life that I want to scrunch and crackle and shout to hear the clear, distinct sounds in the still air, to fill up the emptiness with the opening of packages. Bob says, "Shush!" again, and whispers fiercely, "Can't you walk more quietly?," rifle at the ready, while I dwindle behind, hoping for the sharp reward of another unmuffled sound.

There is no recent moose sign to be seen. I walk along looking at the ground, covered with a carpet of leaves, and I think about Flay's death. A vibrantly healthy man, and young. If Bob should die like that? He walks ahead, looking for a way through the woods, the seat patch on his pants torn at the bottom right-hand corner, looking as if it is sagging toward the ground. He carries the rifle carefully in both hands. The woods direct us into an old road, old and useless, leading simply from one bay to the next one over, across the point of land between. I wonder why it was built. Its purpose was surely not transporting logs— could it simply have been the easiest way to get some machine from one bay to the next, bulldozing all that lay in its path? It is now used by moose, and saves us a long bushwhack. Soon, however, the road stops dead and circles round, a hundred yards from the water, and a dense screen of young aspen and willow confronts us. We push through the brush, trying to keep low and motionless while moving. A perfect roar of crackling sound pursues me.

It is getting darker. I step out onto the beach, crouched low. A startling white blur decorates the water directly in front of us. I cannot see clearly what it is until I come up next to Bob, who has sunk down into a patch of long marsh grass twenty feet from the water. The blur solidifies. Two trumpeter swans are floating in the bay, white as paper, with bills printed black. Their long necks display the curve of fishhooks. I sink into the grass and watch.

Almost as if they are showing off their lines, the swans float nearer, turning their heads to give the profile view, turning their backs to display the truncated tails, coming straight at us until their black bills fill the picture and the white bodies sprout back, spill back, like white ribbons from a black head.

The two swans are the only swans in sight. Since swans mate for life, no doubt the two are travelling together, male and female, looking for a place to spend the winter. They will find a river somewhere which has open water all through the cold months, and there they will wait for spring and nesting time again. In the meanwhile they seem to be in no more of a hurry than we are, or the day, or the season itself. They float lightly, dipping their necks into the water from time to time, nibbling at their feathers or the feathers of their mate. One of them cranes its head around to examine its tail.

They aren't fearful of us, though they must have seen the motion of our arrival in the grass. We aren't moving now, though, and they come even closer than before, seeming to propel themselves magically, like carved swan boats—the motion of their paddling legs is invisible beneath the surface of the dark water. Bob and I look at each other and smile. He reaches out and clasps my hand, as the swans float closer still.

Behind them, the heavy dark clouds begin to break, swiftly, until they reveal a patch of the western sky, a little pocket lining the horizon when it flips back its lapel—the color of a robin's egg. Floating on it the white cumulus clouds move, far away. Yonder. It's there if you don't try to reach it. The swans turn toward the breaking light, side by side. The feathers of their wings touch lightly. The male lifts his neck and bends the fishhook out so that it arches gently over the female's head. He lowers his own head until his chin almost touches the top of her feathers, and they float that way for a time, watching the western sky.

At last the rain begins to fall again, obscuring my vision and dripping down my face in warm sheets. Beyond it, though, I can still see the brilliant patch of blue and the two white swans framed in silhouette against it. Watching the light gusts of wind darkening the water, I know that this will be the last day of fall frozen in time. The spring warmth blows away the greys, the blues and whites return with the touch of summer, and winter is almost here.

→≫ (9) ≪←

Winter is here. This morning I said to Bob, "What shall we do for our last Christmas on the lake?" And he answered, "Let's make a bonfire and dance around it," smiling as he spoke, unwilling to take the question seriously because the underlying assumption was clearly the real point. I wish that all decisions came about so naturally.

"You aren't sorry we tried, are you?" I asked.

"Oh, no," he said. "We'll build our next house even better. And besides, we've gotten to see some wolves at last."

Everyone tells us the wolf packs are running close to town this winter, spilling over the edges of their normal grounds. Nobody knows why. On a recent trip to the Fort, an old trapper said to me, "Seems like they just got the itch to see some new country."

But they've been looking us over out here, too. Never close up. They are far too smart and suspicious to get too near. Yesterday morning we woke early to see seven on the lake below the house, a hundred feet from the shore. They walked spread out, neither abreast nor in line but sprinkled about in a random pattern on the snow. We watched them with our faces to the glass, trying to see those things which distance made impossible. Not for the first time, I wished we had a pair of binoculars. Bob went to the front hall to get his Savage, to use the scope for a spyglass.

At the motion of his departure, five of the wolves loped away across the lake, running at a steady trot. The other two stopped dead and stared up at the house. Predators themselves, they knew enough to be wary if they saw a motion, even behind a reflecting pane of glass.

Bob returned with the rifle and slowly raised it to his shoulder. As he brought it up, the wolves turned and took off, moving from a standing position to a dead run in less than five seconds. I watched the larger of the two; his tail streamed flat on the air behind him till he became only a black speck on a field of white.

There is no doubt in my mind that the wolves saw Bob's rifle, knew it for the instrument it is, and ran to save their lives. No chance motion, caught sight of through a window two hundred yards away, would have sent those animals into such a display of grace and power.

The hunting orders set the bag limit for wolf in this area at two a year. Two had seemed to me a generous number, indicative, I believed, both of the number of wolves and the ease of shooting them. Now I think that there could be only two hundred wolves in the entire area, and the bag limit could still be safely set at two per man. The wolves have got what it takes to survive. They learned wariness before it was too late.

People do catch wolves by trapping them; wolf skins are selling for fifty dollars this winter. One of the trappers we know has been having great success with his line, up toward the Salmon River country. He traps only on weekends, and runs a gas station in town for the rest of the week. It's an old-fashioned gas station, surrounded by heaps of ruined cars, which he buys up for parts. If there is something which the Phillips 66 or the Conoco tells you they don't have in stock, and they're not even making them anymore, just go over to Bill Justin's station and find Bill. He is always, it seems, slightly intoxicated, which in no way interferes with his work, but simply gives him an air of always rushing around, with you on his mind, seriously on his mind, but not quite able to deal with your problem for a minute or two. The miracle is, he does get down to it, long before any other gas station would have even put it on its list. Ask him for the universal joint of a '57 Chevy pickup, and after a bit of "Just a minute, let me see," and serving two or three customers gas, and getting their bills messed up twice, he rushes out into his back yard, fusses around under an unrecognizable heap of metal, and emerges with the universal joint of a '57 Chevy.

Bill has an ancient tow truck. On the side, in baby-blue and pink letters, it attests "We may not have the newest trucks, but we sure save the people's bucks." The truck also advertises "Twenty-Four-Hour Service" and means it. Bill sleeps in a small extension of his gas station, and if you knock on his door in the middle of the night, he comes, blinking as usual. "Just a minute, let me see, oh it's you is it?," fumbling with his boots and pulling on his cap.

The gas station is a mess. Worktables are inches deep in tools and parts, the floor has not been washed in years, tires that would not fit any cars made this decade hang from the ceiling gathering dust. Piles of strange iron and rusted chains fill the corners, and the steps leading down to the garage from the waiting room–house are almost rotted away. The waiting room, which contains the cash register and a pop cooler, has two chairs in it—their vinyl seats slashed and peeling—in case you want to come in and get warm while waiting for your tank to fill up or your car to get put back together. On one wall of the waiting room is Bill's prize skin, carefully mounted on felt with fancy crimped edging. A huge grey wolf skin.

I like to stroke the wolf skin. I asked Bill if he had trapped it, a stupid question, the bullet hole neatly trimmed, not in the head but through the heart. He told me the story of the wolf, between rushing in and out and working on the radiator of our truck. No matter how many interruptions we had, he always came back to it—"Well, that wolf now."

He had seen it when he was out on his trap line one winter, years ago, when he still ran it with a dog team. The chances were good that he had caught its mate. He had tracked it through the snow for a day. He had caught it, and shot it through the heart, as it turned at last to face him, cornered in a dense thicket of pine. The story took thirty-five minutes; the wolf skin had hung on his wall for ten years. Fifty dollars if it had been caught in a trap—but filling his life since he tracked it through the winter woods.

–>>><<<–

Tonight is the night of the wolves. It is another pattern of dream or memory fulfilled, so different from my musings on it.

It has been snowing for four days. The front porch is a folded quilt of cold, and there has been no moon. Yesterday morning I heard the wolves. Scarcely awake, I noticed the howling, and the sound was like an echo from another century, a timeless repetition of recordings in the air. Tonight the wolves are serenading us, not distantly, but so close that I can feel the vibrations of their throats and see in my mind's eye the opening of their mouths.

I could see nothing but the snow, and smell nothing but the snow, when the first call sounded—a never-ending howl that faded before it ended. Another voice joined in, but on the other side of the island, and this one was punctuated with short, throaty barks and a murmur like a growl. Then silence. And then the cacophony began, one wolf voice joining another, swiftly adding harmony as variation to the basic moaning howl. In the circle that grew closer, all around the island, the circle of snarls and growls, barks and howls, dying down, getting louder, reaching a crescendo, two voices were suddenly isolated, rising close together—two wolves fighting.

Our dog thinks her friends have come to call, and in an ecstasy of conviction she alternates between straining her eyes into the darkness— forepaws on the window, tail bolt upright in the air—and sitting on her hind legs, beating the floor with her tail and sticking her ears forward as far as she can while she quivers with the anticipation of release. If we let her out to greet her living ancestors, all we would see again of her might be a few tufts of fur. It is hard for the wolves to hunt in this endless snowfall, but there is nothing to keep them from eating.

I cannot fathom why the howling of wolves is generally regarded as something awesome, to strike terror into the hearts of those who hear it. The wolves are not howling in order to impress anyone, not even the prey which they may be seeking tonight. They are howling for their own pleasure and entertainment, for their own self-expression and delight. Should several of the wolves howl for a moment on the same pitch they shift around until they have all found different ones, singing harmonies.

The fight puzzles me though. Perhaps it is as it sounds, and there are two packs, one on either side of the island. It is hard to believe that such a coincidence could occur—but since we are lucky enough to hear the wolves at all, we may well be lucky enough to be listening to a meeting between two different packs. Where did they come from? Where are they going now?

The fight resolves itself into distances. The two opponents gradually move farther from each other, barking all the time, not losing ground but being pushed apart by tension. The barks and moans of anger are slowly subsumed into a solitary howl, as the pack of music splits and flows around the island, heading west and east. After the storm, the silence. But one last howl reaches us from the west, and I think I can hear, faint and far away, that the western wolves have obeyed the call of the first violin, and are starting again upon their symphony.

→≫(10)≪←

Three young Indian men have drowned about five miles from us, at the entrance of the North Arm. It has been icy cold for the last week, a steady fifty below zero. The house is showing its limitations again; it is all we can do, working a six-hour day, to keep the temperature inside at sixty. We have closed off the bedrooms and moved our bed into the living room until the cold spell breaks. Blankets hang over the doors. The other night, very late, I heard some snowmobiles go by on the Portage-Tachie trail. I wondered at the time why anyone would travel in such cold, so late at night, without an emergency to call them.

The snowmobiles belonged to two Joseph boys from Portage and to Louis Prince. He had just returned from Prince George the week before and bought a brand-new TNT in town. With friends, he had spent the evening in Tachie, celebrating by drinking and racing snowmobiles around the village. They did not plan to go on to Portage. At eleven o'clock the idea was suggested and immediately adopted. There was hardly any moon, but the headlights are blindingly bright on those machines, and they left with a roar, snowmobiles gunned to fifty miles an hour. The men were wearing blue jeans, jackets, and gloves. Nothing more.

At one in the morning, a worried friend called Portage by radio phone to ask if they had arrived. They hadn't. Perhaps they had turned back. They hadn't. At daybreak the police were called. Many villagers from both villages joined in the search, and the tracks of the machines were discovered leading right off the edge of the ice into the deepest part of the lake.

We heard the report first on the radio, although it was already clear that something was going on. An R.C.M.P. plane flew over early in the afternoon, and at least fifteen snowmobiles from Tachie went bombing by in the distance. The second day of the search for the bodies, we skied out to the trail and talked to some of the searchers returning from the west. One body and two machines had been recovered, but the others were still missing.

The story has been pieced together from the tracks. The three machines were in line, one behind the other. Somehow their drivers got off the trail, just opposite our house, or decided perhaps to head straight across the entrance to the North Arm rather than pursue the route along the shore. The men we talked to were mystified by that decision.

"They should have known the North Arm wasn't frozen yet. We all knew that, all of us," said Martin Felix. "It is so strange; they opened a trail for almost four miles; they must have known they were not on route." He looked at the other three men who had stopped with him for confirmation of this fact. They all nodded and shook their heads, as they passed around a cup of coffee from the thermos we'd brought out, each one holding it clumsily in two gloved hands.

"The North Arm is always the last to freeze. Always," another man interjected.

"So they just went off the edge of the ice?" Bob asked.

"Well, the machines were moving so fast, we think, that by the time the headlights picked up the water ahead, there was no time left to stop. The first two machines went right in," said Martin.

"Not the third?" I asked.

"No. That is the strangest thing," said Martin. "There was time for him to stop, and he did—the tracks from the third machine go right back to the south shore, to almost twenty feet from the real trail—then they circle and go back across the lake, all the way to the north shore. Only then they go into open water too."

"It sounds like he was suffering from exposure," Bob said.

"Maybe. Maybe," said Martin, drinking the last of the coffee.

We thanked the men for stopping, and they drove away, one machine behind the other. Whump. Whump. As we turned to go back to the house a third machine came out of the west, slowing down as it drew near. The man driving wore a helmet; when he stopped the machine and lifted his face plate, we saw that it was Joseph Matisse. I hardly knew what to say. He looked serious, but glad to see us. His braids were still bound in red, and they hung to either side of his face with heavy grace.

"I guess you've heard about what happened?" he asked.

"Yes. We're so sorry," I said weakly.

"Oh, yes. Louis was always wild, though. It is the Josephs everyone is sorry about. They were very good boys." His voice was slow and steady, almost distant. He kicked at the snow with one booted foot.

"I'm sorry," I said again. "I know that Louis was your friend."

"Yes," he said. "He was my friend."

"You're living with August again, are you?" I asked, compelled to change the subject somehow. "I'm sure he is glad to have you back. Will you stay the winter?"

"I will stay for some time. I don't know yet. And you? You are still here."

"Yes, we'll be leaving in the spring though, after the lake breaks up." A long silence, then Bob said:

"Guess we'll ski back to the house. Stop by if you ever feel like it, O.K.?"

"O.K. Goodbye." Abruptly, he slammed his face plate down, revved his engine, and took off. I backed away out of range of the exhaust, then turned and skied back to the island as fast as I could. I wasn't cold, but I suddenly feared the open space around me. Everything was too empty, too wide.

I picture the scene in my mind, again and again. Three drunk young men raced around the quiet village in the night. Lightly clad, they took off across the open lake, driving against the wind. The liquor they'd been drinking brought a superficial feeling of warmth. They were undoubtedly all in advanced hypothermia when they went into the lake. The last man's erratic behavior is attributed to the complete loss of judgment which accompanies that state. None of them could swim; they died quickly.

I see the last ten seconds of that trip over and over. The sudden sight of the open water; the desperate attempt to stop. A stifling fear of death filling the last moments of their lives. The moment when the water closes above their heads. Riding their machines down through the black lake, until the machines fall away below, dropping faster even than the bodies.

There are a lot of different ways to kill yourself—not all of them called suicide.

→≫≪←

Bill Justin was murdered last month. His gas station is boarded up now, the windows covered with plywood, and all the junk in the yard carted away.

He had been arrested for trading in stolen goods. I am sure he bought radios which didn't work, black and white TVs, electric toasters, and baby carriages, no doubt. "A baby carriage?" I can see him saying to a young thief. "Well, I don't know, now let me see, let me see now," while he checked through his wallet to see if he had the money on him to pay for it. He bought the remains of our old pickup truck, not stolen, nor ever likely to be, with its rusting body and useless engine. Maybe he could use the headlights, though I doubt it. He drove with me to where it ended its last trip, and we discussed its merits, and how good a truck it had been before the engine gave out, and he admired the yellow paint job, and he finally offered me fifty dollars for it, the price of a wolf skin. I looked hopeless (we had no money at the time) and said, "How about sixty-five?" And he said, "Well, sixty-five then, sixty-five," as if I were doing him a favor.

He collected stolen objects the way he collected all objects—he did not scorn them for being stolen, he liked them all the same. I am sure he never got out of them what he put into them. He loved *things*, whether they worked or not; he valued objects for their own sake, and only pretended that he intended to get from them some practical benefit. He couldn't resist helping people, either. He charged us thirty dollars to tow us from Tachie, a two-hour drive for him, and while he was there, he fixed an Indian's truck, refusing money for that—it only took him ten minutes. Last winter we left our truck in his parking lot for six weeks. It wasn't hurting him, just sitting there, he said.

Arrested for being a fence. He was scheduled to appear in court this month and defend himself—"Well, let me see now, let me see"—and he was murdered because of it. They haven't caught the killer. The best guess is that it was a young man who sold him stolen goods. He used to hang around the garage, watching him fix engines, and gabbing, and selling him useless property. When Bill was arrested, the man got scared he would turn him in. In his own waiting room, he slit Bill's throat from ear to ear.

When we drove by, I asked Bob to stop the truck, and I walked over to try and peer between the cracks in the plywood sheathing. I could see the wolf skin, hanging in its place of honor, jaw propped open in an everlasting snarl, honoring Bill with its most powerful emotion. The one thing he would never buy or sell, or give away, on a wall all by itself, lifted free of the objects he spent his life accumulating. "That wolf, now," I can hear him saying, "I tracked it for a long time before I finally caught up with it. Pretty cold it was too. Where I finally got him, there wasn't much room to run. He turned around, snarling, so I shot him through the heart."

The wolves will survive as long as there are men around who care enough to track them. There aren't a whole lot of them left like Bill, though. People who even notice that there are tracks which run ahead of them, much less think them worth the trouble of following.

→≫ (11) ≪←

Some wolves came by again last week. I got to within fifty feet of one great wolf standing off the shore of the island, before he turned and faded into the night. After the wolves had gone, the snow kept falling, and the old itch grew. No birds fly by at this time of year, their toes carefully curled beneath them, and the only moose we have seen in several weeks is the one we feed on daily.

We decided to go to town three days ago, though the powder was drifting everywhere on the lake and blowing up again like spindrift on a mountain. But the wind died in early afternoon and though the sun began to shine at times through the clouds, it was veiled with secret intentions. It wasn't an auspicious day for the trip, nor was it a good time to start, two hours after noon. Worse, there was no one waiting for us at the other end of the day—no Flay and Nadine, no Wally and Joyce. Even Maurice Joseph has moved away.

The trail was drifted over again, so we decided not to ski. There would be no way to avoid having slush freeze on the skis whenever we drifted off the trail, as we surely would. I felt heavy, earth-bound, and dull at the prospect of walking through the snow. But walking, with whatever difficulties, promised to be better than not moving at all, so we left at two o'clock, with matches and a water bottle, and very little else. At the last minute Bob stuffed the sleeping bags into his pack and put it on.

It was clear from the start that the trip would be painfully slow. On a good day, on skis, the trip takes less than three hours. On a good day walking it takes no more than four. This was not a good day. We hit deep slush five feet from the beach. By the time we reached the trail, both of us had wet feet. Bob had his speed control set to flat out, and just below the surface there simmered impatience with me. He is unusually thoughtful just before he explodes, so when he turned to me with a smile and told me to feel free to give him my parka if I got too hot, I knew the day might well turn out even more badly than I was expecting it to. As Bundy ran here and there, she left little round holes which filled with water.

The trail was in better shape than it might have been. Almost pure ice before the snow started, it had been cleared by the blowing wind in many places. The first five miles went by with a rapid thump thump thump. At four thirty it was getting dark, and it started to snow again. With the wind blowing from the east, and the snow falling now in great warm lumps, we were halfway between the house and the village. I wasn't surprised when the snow started; it had been waiting in the sky.

Bob was half a mile ahead of me. The white mist in the air quickly took him from my sight. Bundy was still with me. The wind blew the snow everywhere at once, and the dusky light made it impossible to distinguish the white of the snow from the white of the sky. With no colors or shadows to give any relief, I was glad that the lake was flat. Unexpected holes or mounds would have destroyed all sense of balance.

I was inside a white globe. All planes merged indistinguishably; the vertical, the horizontal, and the diagonals became one shifting plane, freed of gravity. Bundy ran ahead of me in a curvy line. It looked as if she was climbing into the sky. The perspective which artists make use of, but which is so rarely perceived by casual vision, revealed itself in her wavering path. She grew smaller and smaller as she climbed, and the variations in her location took on the appearance of a series of still photographs, revealing the mechanism which lies behind motion pictures. Her small black body in the white landscape made it seem an old film I was watching. Click click click went the camera, catching each motion at the moment of completion. Farther and farther away, smaller and smaller, higher and higher she moved, until she turned and started to descend. Click click click she grew larger, until she was once again on the ground, and at my feet.

The storm continued. The only way of distinguishing the trail was by the process of elimination. I stepped to the left and into slush. I took three steps to the right and found a hard surface beneath my feet once more. I had not seen Bob for over an hour, but I could see his footsteps, already half full of snow, lying at an angle that further distorted the appearance of the level earth. Sometimes I lost the tracks for minutes, and although I knew I was on the trail, there seemed little hope of ending this endless journey if there were no tracks to follow.

I have never felt so alone. I had entered the very center of the winter night, and in utter isolation from the world outside, I felt a momentary desire to leave it outside forever. I felt for the first time that I was truly on an island in the storm. Neither life nor death could gain any hold here; neither arrival nor departure could be distinguished in the white circumference of my world. Just my own warmth and presence, isolated and silent, were real.

In complete peace, I sat for a moment on the snow. I refastened my bootlaces, and looked at the tracks before me. Bundy's lay beside Bob's, disappearing into the white darkness ahead, little irregular pockmarks in the snow. I had not realized that Bundy too had left me, and it made me suddenly uneasy. I could have sworn that I had seen her a moment ago, out of the corner of my eye. I got to my feet again and looked carefully around. I could see nothing for a moment. Then a dark shape became visible, the size of a small dog. It stood, quite still, twenty feet ahead of me, off the trail to the left. It wasn't large enough to be a wolf; not the right shape for a coyote. Why should any animal be on the lake, so near to me and apparently so fearless? I stood motionless, and after another minute the animal came slowly toward me. I knew then, it must be a lynx.

The visibility was not good in the heavy white dusk, but the cat came closer and closer, moving with an absolutely fearless grace, until he stood no more than eight feet away. There he stopped. Standing there, he did something I have never seen another wild animal do. He turned his head slightly sideways, and stared into my eyes. His own did not glint in the dusk, and I could clearly see the large yellow globes, their gaze arrow-straight, untroubled, thrown out like lines to draw me in. He did not run bumbling from me like the bear. He did not flee scornfully like the wolves. The lynx walked out of the night and into my own white world and stared into my eyes. When he had seen all he wanted, he turned his head again, crossed the trail, and faded toward the shore, his great paws touching the snow as gently as moonlight.

An almost painful excitement underlay the wonder I felt that I should have been visited by this cat. Almost, it was as if he thought me worth his gaze. He had chosen converse with me, when he might have chosen another way. I had been all my life in the company of lynx and had never before stared into one's eyes. He opened his eyes upon the world; he stared into the heart of danger and the unknown; then he walked on, fading toward the shore. Could I do less? He took a part of me with him into the darkening woods—I would be safe there with him always. Departure is a way of life, but death comes only once to all things on the earth.

Though he'd walked as light as the moonlight walks upon the clouds, I found his footprints on the snow. Near Bob's and Bundy's there were the finer marks, spaced as snowshoe-hare tracks are spaced, spaced like the marks of the lynx's prey. In the woods he would find the hare he followed, and cover his tracks with a larger paw. I was surrounded, inundated with tracks, some seen and some unseen. All around me in the woods lynx walked—brave enough to dare my eyes, strong enough to chew off their own soft paws and leave them blood-flecked on the snow before they died. Everywhere the tracks ran on ahead. You cannot isolate yourself at last, whether you accept or reject the world around you. In the very center of the winter night, when you feel most isolated, when you feel you are on an island in the storm, the lynx will find you and take you with him into the darkening woods, to pounce on snowshoe hares and step at last into the trap.

I turned and looked behind me at my own tracks, not covered yet, visible for a time. They wandered from side to side, and yet they had direction. I had walked, and had not meant those tracks to be. They simply were. No choice of mine could unmake them. I had not known where I was going, but when I looked ahead, I could see many places to go. I could look at the sky and see a firedrake. I could fall on the earth like a lynx paw.

My eyes felt touched by some lasting contact. Where had those eyes come from, out of the dusk? So knowing and so round. The globe of white spun around me revealing the corners of the world, and all that lay beyond the globe. Northern lights and the moon behind the clouds; darkness and waves beneath the ice; wind from the valley where the winds begin; trappers' cabins aging gently into grey. Journeys, deaths, hunts. A moose head floating on the lake. A lynx passing in a winter storm. What were they all but tracks? Evidence of some great and final power, fleeting, untouchable, unknowable except by the signs it leaves behind, the great soft footprints which cover the earth like braille.

→≫≪←

Such moments last forever, but not in time. I walked on. Eventually Bob came into view. He sat on a boulder which stuck out into the trail. I knew that the sky had cleared when it took almost five minutes after I had seen him to stand at his side. As I approached, he got to his feet in greeting. I looked up and saw the lights of Tachie.

We started off together, steering by the lights toward the village. The nearer we got, the stronger became that old feeling of doubt. There is a realization that builds slowly, a feeling you are hardly aware of until suddenly it crystallizes in your mind, the feeling that you may be on a one-way street, heading in the wrong direction. The lynx had passed me in the night. Almost, I would have turned around right then and headed for home. But Bob was far ahead again, and it was clearly inevitable that we go on. The night was growing cold.

We reached Tachie at nine thirty. The truck would not start. I went into the community hall and, negotiating the smoke and the fluorescent lights and the cigarette butts, I found someone we knew and asked him if he would jump start the truck. It still would not start. I handed five dollars over. It was ten fifteen. There was no one at the Matisses' house, where we might have stayed. We went to the teacher's house and asked her if we could sleep on her basement floor. A great, fat white woman, she was eating a chocolate sundae and drinking tea. She looked at us suspiciously, said no, and closed the door. Too discouraged to go farther, I wrapped myself in my clothes and sleeping bag, and lay down in the snow beside the truck. There was still a smell of gasoline in the air.

Before I fell asleep, I drifted back to the tracks on the lake. I thought again about the deaths of Bill Justin and Louis Prince and Flay—peacefully now. It is not the great things so much as the little pains that are hard in the end to accept. The door shutting in your face. As I drifted away, I dreamed that I was playing with the lynx; I saw him wrapping his front paws around my chest and wrestling me to the ground. I wished that we had fallen together between two shadows on the rippling lake.

→≫(12)≪←

We are naked. The mattress lies before the fire, which burns with a voracious hissing noise. Some of the wood is wet. The quilt is tucked around our feet, and I rest half on Bob's body, half off. There is still a slight smell of kerosene in the air, from blowing out the lamp. Most of what I can smell, though, is Bob's skin. If I lift my head a little, I can smell his smoke-drenched hair as well. My hand is cupped on his right breast, and his right arm rests on the small of my back. I feel a little hot and sticky, delightfully so, and when I shift my body, there is a sucking noise. The sheet is gritty, but I am too lazy to brush the breadcrumbs off onto the floor.

I stare at the pattern of the rug on which the mattress rests. The colors are rich and the patterns complex. There is always something to look at in the rug. I close my eyes again, and say, "Some life."

"Ummm," says Bob.

"You know what's funny?"

"What's funny?" He smiles almost imperceptibly and rubs the small of my back with light and lazy fingers.

"I've liked living here so much ever since we decided to leave. Isn't that sad?"

"Is it?"

"It is. It's so contrary. As if you can't really appreciate something unless you know it's going to end."

"Well, since everything ends eventually, that should leave you with a lot to appreciate." He smiles and rubs my back some more.

"Yeah. If it only worked that way."

"You've got to exercise some discrimination. Choose what you want to do most."

"But that's my point. When you think about it, the whole idea of freedom—of being able to choose where you're going to go and what you're going to do—has in the end no substance."

"What do you mean? We're here, aren't we?"

"Yeah. And leaving."

"So what? The point is, we did it, didn't we? Maybe you can't control your life completely, but you can sure give yourself something to think about."

"Uh-huh. But it seems to me the only choice you can ever really make is the choice of how to respond to your present. Not how to plan your future," I say. "I'm so glad we don't have to leave yet," I add.

"Be pretty hard before the lake breaks up," says Bob. He looks into my eyes and says more gently:

"No, I'm glad too. It'll always be our island, though. It'll always be our house. No matter what happens, once you've made something or known something or been somewhere, no one can ever take it away from you. It's yours. That's why you have to try and put yourself in situations where those things have a chance of happening. So you can have something when you're old. So you can say you've lived."

"I guess so. It's not so much where you live or why you live—or even *when* you live, Gathercole—as how you live. You don't need to live on an island to have a life."

"Hopefully," Bob says more grimly.

"Hopefully!" Suddenly I tickle Bob just below the ribs, and he lunges away and then grabs my wrists.

"Hopefully!" I say. "What kind of a word is that? Don't you speak English, buddy?"

"Hopefully," he says.

He gives me a sticky kiss, then curls up into a ball, wraps the quilt around him, and drags a corner of it over his head.

I am wide awake still, not sticky anymore but hot and somehow eager. The moon is out. I focus my eyes first on one part of it and then on another, so that it grows from a flat disk to a pocked and mountained sphere. A scene from my early childhood pops into my head. I was walking in the winter woods on a moonlit night. I was alone. I felt brave as anything, and wanted to be more daring still. I wanted to see a deer or a rabbit or a squirrel; I wanted to stroke their fur like children do in fairy tales. It occurred to me that the animals probably avoided me because I wore so many clothes, not like them at all—boots and socks and a snowsuit and mittens smelling of wet wool. Maybe if I removed the clothes and crept around naked in the snow, the animals would come out.

I sat down on a tree stump and pulled off my boots and socks. The other clothes were too complex. Barefoot, I jumped down, and tiptoed through the snow for five or ten steps, until my feet were numb and wooden. I rushed back to the stump and struggled furiously to get my boots on again. What a crazy kid I must have been. Yet how much have I really changed?

Inspired, I crawl from the bed and walk across the floor as quietly as I can. It creaks three times before I reach the door. I turn the doorknob and step onto the icy boards of the porch. For a moment I pause, uncertain. Then I run quickly down the steps and into the snow. It melts around my feet. At the largest drift within reach I fling my body into the cold. For a second only. Springing to my feet, I dash back up the steps, across the floor, and into bed, pulling the quilt up to my chin.

I lie and tingle, grinning from ear to ear. Not quite a deer or rabbit, or even a kid in a fairy tale. Just an absurd naked woman lying for an instant in the snow.

→≫(13)≪←

It is the animals we become which teach us most. I am playing woozle today. Like Pooh, I pursue my own tracks around and around the trees, bewildered by all the marks upon the ground.

How can we possibly leave the island behind forever?

If we don't leave the island, then how can we make a living where we live?

Why can't we at least keep it to spend as much time here as possible?

How long will it take then to be able to afford to build another house?

If we sell it, how can we justify ever having come here?

Why do we have to justify it? Isn't it enough that we did it?

Yes, that's why I can't bear to leave it behind.

But it's ridiculous to live in a place that's so far from anywhere, so hard to get to.

If it wasn't hard to get to, it wouldn't be the place it is.

Surely there will be other places to love?

Yes. But never like this one.

No. Never like this one. You can only have a first love once.

EPILOGUE

We are packing the house. Ted Martin will be here at dinner time tonight to pick us and the canoe and the boxes and the furniture up. Even though I know that a house cannot feel, I am doing my best to give it the idea that we care. Rather than taking everything with us, I have decided to leave all sorts of little things here. I am rearranging the cheap posters and the found objects like rock and driftwood to give the fullest possible feeling to the empty space. I have put the large chart of Stuart Lake over the empty bookcase and the old map of Middle Earth on the wall of the dining area. Where the large framed picture used to hang over the fireplace, there is a square of light wood; in the center I have taped the print of VOLCANO, a round spot of color which may in time look natural. I've decided to leave the two small cotton rugs, orange and blue, in the living room where the oriental rugs used to lie. My biggest weakness is to leave the four oak chairs— any house would know it was being deserted if all the chairs were taken away.

I just cannot believe we are leaving for good. I look at the food in the kitchen cabinet—at least twenty pounds of flour remain—and think it would be absurd to pack it; we'll use it next time we are here. Bob has buried a five-gallon can of gasoline behind the house so we won't have to bring as much when we come again. The house is full of stove-wood and fireplace wood; if we arrive late, or in the rain, there will be no problem starting fires. In my notebook I've listed all the food and supplies we are leaving, so we won't have to depend on memory. Another list itemizes the materials which will be useful for making repairs and improvements.

The other night when we got back from a last trip in the canoe, I

219

was so glad to see the house that I shouted to it. "Hello, house! Here we are, we're back! I love you, house!" It seems unfair to leave it empty now. Why did we bring it into existence, if not to keep it warm? Why did we put it on an island?

When Bob and I drove north through British Columbia, we weren't looking for an island; we sought nothing but a refuge on which to put our house. It surprised us when the refuge took this form. The day we arrived I was lost in the unfamiliar spaces here, and I watched the rain fall from the door of the tent and wondered why we had come, sensing already that the island was only a rock. When we dug the foundation for the house, I sniffed the dirt and tossed it over my head and crumbled it in my hand and said, "This dirt is mine." But it didn't feel like mine. Now it does. The island is still just a rock; it is I who have changed, loving what I've invested with my life.

Yet beyond the pain of parting I look forward to renewing our connections with the world from which we fled. I'll go back to school next fall, writing papers far into the night. We'll live closer to my family, and I'll go for a walk before Christmas dinner holding my brother's huge hand. Bob will climb Mount Robson some warm September day. He'll learn to roll a kayak, using his arm for a brace. We'll swim warm in the summer and ski slushless in the winter—and never again live so closely together that we're compelled to tear ourselves apart.

We always have new wants. When we came to the island, we wanted to build our own world, far from the frenzied progress of men, safe from dissolution, located yonder. But living there I discovered you cannot decide what you will find, and the one place you can never reach is the beyond. The sun hurtles through space and I hurtle with it. Waves push at me; fires burn behind my walls; tracks run on ahead, tripping me, beckoning me on. Bears wander too, and ice collapses; even granite wears away.

Being human, I still fear abrupt endings and sudden meetings and the constant threat of change. Some sudden meetings, though, are with friends; some abrupt endings to quarry. Waves carry visions. Fires cleanse. And there are moments, too, when stillness comes and, hammer in hand, I can mold the raw energy of the world. I can put windows into walls and float moose heads on the water. Though the moments pass, and buildings fall to ruin, the power to create remains. We are all lynx paws falling on the earth. We all sojourn and we all can build; the only thing we cannot do is stay.